Science in Environmental Policy

Politics, Science, and the Environment
Peter M. Haas and Sheila Jasanoff, editors

Peter Dauvergne, *Shadows in the Forest: Japan and the Politics of Timber in Southeast Asia*

Peter Cebon, Urs Dahinden, Huw Davies, Dieter M. Imboden, and Carlo C. Jaeger, eds., *Views from the Alps: Regional Perspectives on Climate Change*

Clark C. Gibson, Margaret A. McKean, and Elinor Ostrom, eds., *People and Forests: Communities, Institutions, and Governance*

The Social Learning Group, *Learning to Manage Global Environmental Risks. Volume 1: A Comparative History of Social Responses to Climate Change, Ozone Depletion, and Acid Rain. Volume 2: A Functional Analysis of Social Responses to Climate Change, Ozone Depletion, and Acid Rain*

Clark Miller and Paul N. Edwards, eds., *Changing the Atmosphere: Expert Knowledge and Environmental Governance*

Craig W. Thomas, *Bureaucratic Landscapes: Interagency Cooperation and the Preservation of Biodiversity*

Nives Dolsak and Elinor Ostrom, eds., *The Commons in the New Millennium: Challenges and Adaptation*

Kenneth E. Wilkening, *Acid Rain Science and Politics in Japan: A History of Knowledge and Action Toward Sustainability*

Virginia M. Walsh, *Global Institutions and Social Knowledge: Generating Research at the Scripps Institution and the Inter-American Tropical Tuna Commission, 1900s–1990s*

Sheila Jasanoff and Marybeth Long Martello, eds., *Earthly Politics: Local and Global in Environmental Governance*

Christopher Ansell and David Vogel, eds., *What's the Beef? The Contested Governance of European Food Safety*

Charlotte Epstein, *The Power of Words in International Relations: Birth of an Anti-Whaling Discourse*

Ann Campbell Keller, *Science in Environmental Policy: The Politics of Objective Advice*

Science in Environmental Policy
The Politics of Objective Advice

Ann Campbell Keller

The MIT Press
Cambridge, Massachusetts
London, England

For information on quantity discounts, email special_sales@mitpress.mit.edu.

Set in Sabon by SNP Best-set Typesetter Ltd., Hong Kong. Printed and bound in the United States of America.

Library of Congress Cataloging-in-Publication Data

Keller, Ann Campbell.
Science in environmental policy : the politics of objective advice / Ann Campbell Keller.
    p. cm.—(Politics, science, and the environment)
Includes bibliographical references and index.
ISBN 978-0-262-01312-3 (hardcover : alk. paper)—ISBN 978-0-262-51296-1 (pbk. : alk. paper)
1. Environmental policy. 2. Science and state. 3. Scientists—Political activity. I. Title.
GE170.K453 2009
363.7'0561—dc22
                                                            2008044256

10 9 8 7 6 5 4 3 2 1

for David and Cole

Contents

Acknowledgements   ix

Introduction   1

1 Theories of Science in Policy Making   27

2 Scientists and Agenda Setting   45

3 Scientists and Legislation   85

4 Scientists and Implementation   139

Conclusion   169

Appendix A: A Primer on the Roots of a Constructivist View of
Science in Society   185
Appendix B: Methodology for Analyzing Scientists' Participation in
Legislative Settings   191
Appendix C: Acid Rain Hearings Included in Qualitative
Analysis   195
Appendix D: Climate Change Hearings Included in Qualitative
Analysis   199
Appendix E: Interviews (Dates and Organizations)   205

Notes   207
Bibliography   247
Index   275

Acknowledgements

This book began as my PhD dissertation at the University of California at Berkeley under the guidance of Todd LaPorte, Gene Rochlin, and the late Nelson Polsby. Without their intelligent guidance and mentorship, which continued far past the dissertation stage, I would not have been able to bring the manuscript to successful completion.

A central portion of this book is based on interviews I conducted in Washington from the summer of 1997 through the fall of 1998. I owe particular thanks to all the people I interviewed for taking time away from their busy schedules to talk to me. These interviews opened my eyes to the complexity of drawing science into policy making and demonstrated to me how dedicated civil servants working on environmental issues are to creating good public policy.

As a graduate student at the Institute of Governmental Studies at UC Berkeley, I was surrounded by a number of faculty and graduate students who created a stimulating and supportive intellectual environment. First and foremost were my committee members—Todd, Gene, and Nelson. I also want to thank Jack Citrin for encouraging me to pursue this topic, Bruce Cain for stepping in with a research position when my commitment to graduate school was at its most tenuous, and a number of graduate student colleagues who provided endless encouragement, including Mark Brown, Samantha Luks, Jonathan Marshall, Khalid Medani, Anshu Chatterjee, Adam Stone, Andrew Wiedlea, Nathaniel Persily, Astrid Scholz, and Jennifer Lynn Miller. I am also enormously indebted to Elizabeth Boles, who provided two invaluable gifts: an intellectual home for me while I was in Washington and her friendship.

While at the University of Colorado at Boulder, I relied upon a research grant provided to new faculty to extend my data-collection effort. During this time, my graduate student researcher, Jamie Lennahan, lent her excellent skills to the project. I also want to thank the American Politics Reading Group—John McIver, Vanessa Baird, Amy Gangl, and David Leblang—for their comments on an earlier draft of chapter 3.

The Robert Wood Johnson Foundation, through its Scholars in Health Policy Research Program, encouraged me not only to develop new skills in health policy but also to continue my existing scholarly work. While an RWJ postdoctoral fellow, I benefited not only from the foundation's support of my career path but also from the intellectual community the program created. Specifically, I want to thank Drew Halfmann, Jeb Barnes, Adam Sheingate, Mark Sawyer, Kevin Esterling, Christopher Bonastia, Marissa Golden, and Kate O'Neil, who read chapter drafts and lent their considerable expertise and advice. Thomas Burke, who also weighed in during this period, deserves special mention owing to his guidance in making the manuscript read more like a book than a dissertation. If the introduction is at all readable, it is because Tom pushed me to get the liveliness I felt about the topic onto the page.

The School of Public Health at UC Berkeley provided me a research grant as a new faculty member and awarded me the Martin Sisters' Endowed Chair, enabling me to extend my data-collection efforts and to hire Mark Hunter as a graduate student researcher. Mark's considerable talent and efforts have improved the book, particularly chapter 3. I have also benefited from the encouragement of several members of the faculty at the School of Public Health: Joan Bloom, Will Dow, Jodi Halpern, Helen Halpin, Jamie Robinson, Tom Rundall, and Steve Shortell.

I wish to thank Richard Hiskes, Frank Laird, Louis Schubert, and Vivian Thompson for their comments on early versions of several chapters. I would also like to thank Ned Woodhouse and David Winickoff for their timely and generous help in reading and commenting on an earlier draft of chapter 1.

I want to thank Clay Morgan for his skillful and patient guidance of the manuscript through the review process at the MIT Press. I would also like to thank the series editors, Peter Haas and Shelia Jasanoff, for overseeing the substantive revisions. I would also like to thank Paul Bethge, Laura Callen, and the editorial staff at the MIT Press, who helped to bring the book to completion.

Finally, I want to thank my family for supporting me through this long and sometimes arduous process. In particular, I want to thank my son Cole, whose arrival provided me with one of the most significant and happiest deadlines I have ever faced. And I especially want to thank my husband, David, who has never known me when I was not working on this book but remained engaged, responsive, and supportive each time I tested out a new idea or reworked an old one in his company.

Science in Environmental Policy

Introduction

Roger Revelle concluded the 1957 paper he co-authored with Hans Seuss, which demonstrated the potential for substantial atmospheric increases of carbon dioxide, with an ominous and now routinely quoted observation: "Human beings are now conducting a large-scale geophysical experiment of a kind that could not have happened in the past nor be reproduced in the future." (Revelle and Seuss 1957)[1] Testifying before the US Congress that same year, Revelle characterized Earth as a "spaceship" and argued for federal dollars to be directed toward understanding the climate of that limited system (HCoA 1956: 426). Ten years later, in a similar vein, Svante Odén introduced the public to the phenomenon of acid rain and characterized the issue as a "chemical war" among European nations (Odén 1967). Revelle and Odén were instrumental in placing the respective issues of climate change and acid rain on the policy agendas of industrialized countries. In view of the considerable resources that have since been directed toward their scientific and political resolution, including unprecedented international cooperative efforts, the importance of the agenda status of these two issues cannot be overstated.[2]

Revelle and Odén brought political attention to an issue that had previously been the exclusive concern of a small cadre of scientists. In addition, they used evocative language to support their arguments, rather than describing the issue in the staid technical language typical of scientific publications. These actions fall outside what is typically thought of as "science." Revelle and Odén, in these instances, look more like political advocates than like scientists. This raises questions about the influence that scientists might wield in policy debates. How important were these scientists in bringing about the "translation" of a scientific question—a question that animates scientists but is relatively inert in wider social circles—into a question that captured public attention and quickly led to political action?

In this volume, I consider the role that scientists play in taking an issue from the relatively closed forum of scientific debate to a broader audience so that it begins to resonate in wider social and political circles. Scientists do not act alone in this process and are not insulated from social forces that make some issues more politically and socially salient than others. At the same time, the question of how scientists' interests are transformed into highly visible political issues merits examination. The crux of the issue is how scientific experts and scientific expertise shape public attention and attentiveness and, ultimately, public decision making.

As scientists have become more frequent participants in policy making, social scientists have turned a critical lens on interactions between science and policy.[3] The literature has produced a number of insights into the nature of science-policy interactions, including the folly of attempting to conduct public decision making according to synoptic or rationalist methods (Lindblom 1959), the tendency for political controversies to ignite technical controversies rather than be quelled by technical insights (Collingridge and Reeve 1986; Ezrahi 1980; Nelkin 1979; Mazur 1981), the elusiveness of a stable boundary between questions of science and questions of policy in decision-making settings (Bryner 1987; Gieryn 1983, 1995, 1999; Jasanoff 1990; Shackley and Wynne 1997; Stern and Fineberg 1996), the fact that blurring the boundary between science and policy often produces decisions that are better able to withstand stakeholder efforts at deconstruction (Jasanoff 1990), the emerging organizational structures used to manage difficult negotiations along the science/policy boundary (Guston 1999, 2000), and the role of social, cultural, and political factors in shaping information presented as science in public domains (Jasanoff 2004a; Jasanoff and Wynne 1998; Miller 2000, 2001; Miller and Edwards 2001; Shackley and Wynne 1995).

Remarkably, the expansive literature on the role of scientific knowledge in decision making contains an unresolved debate about the influence that scientists have in shaping policy outcomes, some scholars arguing that scientists have little role in shaping policy and others arguing that scientists are important participants in the policy process. At the most general level, one can see the debate reflected in the starting assumptions of two disciplines that contribute to this literature. In general, political scientists tend to discount the importance of scientists and science in policy making. This translates into a shortage of contemporary studies that specifically consider scientists in policy making.[4] This general disciplinary tendency is countered by scholars in the field of science and technology studies (STS) who argue for the importance of science and technology in shaping contemporary social interaction (Jasanoff 2004a).[5] These distinct disciplinary orientations prevent more productive scholarly exchange across the two disciplines and allow their respective views regarding science in policy making to go unchallenged.

Beneath the disciplinary orientations of scientists in policy making, there is debate at the level of individual studies. For example, some studies of acid rain conclude that scientists had little influence in policy outcomes (Gould 1985; Yanarella 1985) whereas others argue that scientists have played a central role (Zehr 1994a). Likewise, the role of scientists in the success of the Montreal Protocol is viewed as peripheral in some studies (Litfin 1994) and as central in others (Haas 1992; Parson 2003). Collingridge and Reeve, in their 1986 study of three policy issues, conclude that science provides few if any resources for resolving policy debates. Jasanoff (1990), specifically countering Collingridge and Reeve's conclusion, offers evidence that scientists are able, at times, to produce scientific arguments that are accepted as legitimate endpoints for policy debate, and highlights the circumstances that accompany such feats.

One reason the debate about scientists' role in decision making persists is that, by and large, studies that select a specific venue for analysis have not examined how that choice affects the conclusions of those studies. Many studies can be categorized according to policy-making venue. For example, researchers have devoted considerable attention to scientists' roles in the making of regulatory policies (Brickman, Jasanoff, and Ilgen 1986; Bryner 1987; Collingridge and Reeve 1986; Crandall and Lave 1981; Daemmrich 2004; Greenwood 1984, Guston 1999, 2000; Hilgartner 2000; Irwin et al. 1997; Jasanoff 1990; Landy, Roberts, and Thomas 1994; Melnick 1983; Nelkin 1979; Powell 1999; Salter 1988; Wagner 1995; Weinberg 1972). Another venue that has received considerable scholarly attention is science-policy interactions at the international level, where studies focus on treaty negotiations or regime formation. (See, for example, Haas 1990; Litfin 1994; Miller 2001; Miller and Edwards 2001; Parson 2000; VanDeveer 2006; Zehr 1994b.)

Less popular policy domains for research are agenda setting and legislation. Hart (1992), Krimsky (2000), Miller and Edwards (2000), Pielke (2000a), Scheberle (1994), Takacs (1996), Zehr (1994a), and Yearly (1991) specifically consider science-policy interactions in agenda setting. Although Bimber (1996), Weiss (1989), Esterling (2003), and Nakamura (1975) treat the role of expertise in the context of legislative decision making, studies that focus particularly on scientists in legislative policy making are rare (Zehr 2005). Although the above-mentioned studies make important individual contributions to our understanding of the part played by scientists in policy making, the literature has not addressed the question of how choice of venue affects findings or limits the ability to generalize from a specific case. Moreover, the studies cited above do not acknowledge that variation in findings from one study to the next could be a function of the choice of venue.

Those who analyze multiple policy venues tend to leave the span of the policy process undefined. For instance, Collingridge and Reeve (1986) treat issues in distinct policy stages—for example, the creation of new governmental authority in the case of smoking laws versus the specific application of existing governmental authority in the cases of lead pollution and IQ testing. However, Collingridge and Reeve never assess how the shift in domain affects their analysis. Zehr (1994a) analyzes scientists' role in acid rain policy up to the passage of the acid rain control program in the United States in 1990 and stops short of considering scientists' subsequent role in the implementation of that program. Litfin (1994), examining the negotiations that preceded the creation of the Montreal Protocol, downplays the activities of scientists who were instrumental in framing and publicizing the issue when they first discovered the potential of certain chemicals to destroy atmospheric ozone.

The aforementioned studies offer complex and nuanced accounts of how scientific information is incorporated into decision making in various domains of interest. However, the effect of case selection—in particular, at what point in the policy process the role of scientists is considered—is not specified in these studies. Because choice of policy domain is not an explicit part of the research design, how it affects the conclusions of studies is rarely considered.

Cross-national comparisons (e.g., Brickman, Jasanoff, and Ilgen 1985; Vogel 1986; Jasanoff 1993; 2004b; Hajer 1995; Daemmrich 2004; Parthasarathy 2004) offer an improvement over studies that treat science-policy interaction in a single or an undefined institutional setting. When science-policy interactions in different countries are compared, distinctions in what constitutes relevant scientific information are immediately apparent. Such comparisons offer a more complex image of the role of science in decision making than single case studies have produced. They emphasize the importance of context in shaping interactions between scientists and non-scientists, and they point specifically to how national styles of decision making affect the use of scientific claims to justify policy action and policy inaction.

Jasanoff (1998) illustrates national styles of decision making in her analysis of decisions in the United States and in Great Britain to remove lead from gasoline. She argues that advocates of policy change in the United States pointed to evidence of a link between children's exposure to lead and learning disabilities. In Britain, on the other hand, advocates pointed to evidence of the toxicity of low-level exposures to the entire population, without reference to children or cognitive function. Citing additional observations about cross-national differences in how evidence is collected and mobilized to justify policy action or inaction, Jasanoff (2005a) advances the notion of "civic epistemology" to call attention to important differences in how civil society views science and technology in various countries. Jasanoff compares India, Britain, and the United States to show how much the debates about science and technology differ in those countries. The focus on "civic epistemology" is crucial in that it emphasizes the role of the public in legitimizing or questioning science and technological commitments of the state or other private actors. Moreover, the idea of "civic epistemology" further emphasizes the importance of attending to context (in this case, place and culture) when drawing conclusions about the role of science in public decision making.

In this volume, I draw on comparative studies of science in policy making and on the concept of "civic epistemology" by paying specific attention to the ways in which context shapes interactions between science and policy. Rather than focus on national styles of policy making, however, I examine variations in science-policy interactions across a range of policy domains within the United States. By treating the policy domain explicitly, I demonstrate the extent to which the nature of science-policy interaction changes as the policy process matures. Though studies of national styles of decision making do not mischaracterize the nature of science-policy interaction at the level of nation-states, they suggest a uniformity that overlooks meaningful intra-national variations. Because I have moved the lens down to the level of within-state institutions, the findings I report here will necessarily be limited to those specific settings and will not necessarily apply to other arenas. The methodological approach of analyzing scientists' role in policy making across several settings in order to learn something about the effect of context is important for improving the generalizability of research findings.

Stages of the Policy Process

In order to highlight the role that context might play in shaping science-policy interactions, I draw on work that has roots in Harold Lasswell's division of the policy process into multiple stages (Lasswell 1956; Kingdon 1984; Polsby 1984; Nakamura 1975). Lasswell's attention to stages shifted scholarly attention to aspects of the policy process that had been largely overlooked by a discipline fascinated with congressional policy making.[6] Equally important, however, are studies that highlight distinctive features of each stage and contribute to a dynamic under-standing of the policy process in which actors, resources, and norms of participation change from one setting to the next (Kingdon 1984; Nakamura 1975).

Whereas the policy-stages approach has been criticized as imposing a linear view of policy making and as pointing scholars away from inter-branch cooperation (Jenkins-Smith and Sabatier 1993), more recent applications of that approach, sensitized to these criticisms, have avoided such over-simplification.[7] Notably, Kingdon's (1984) analysis of the policy process draws heavily on Cohen, March, and Olsen's (1972) concept of policy streams. For Kingdon, policy change occurs through the confluence of multiple streams of activity that connect ideas, solu-tions, and political will. This approach avoids the assumption that policy making necessarily proceeds from problem identification to selection of alternatives to implementation, and it acknowledges that activities in each stage can occur in parallel.

The policy-stages approach provides a framework for examining variation in scientists' participation in the policy process across settings. I begin this study by asking whether contradictory findings in existing research reflect actual differences in the roles that scientists play in the policy process from one stage to the next. To test for these differences, I begin with a longitudinal approach and divide the policy process into three stages that correspond to specific institutional settings: agenda setting, legislation, and implementation.[8] In addition, I compare scientists' participation in two environmental policy debates, one concerning acid rain and one concerning climate change. The research design, therefore, has both longitudinal and cross-sectional components. The longitudinal analysis offers insights into changes that occur over time. These involve (1) changes in knowledge—i.e., reductions in scientific uncertainties and innovations with respect to policy options—that shift the balance of supporters and opponents of policy change and (2) changes in actors and institutions as a policy issue matures. The changes in the second set occur whether or not there are significant changes in knowledge about the problem or about potential solutions.

The longitudinal comparison reveals notable variation in the roles played by scientists in each setting. This cross-sectional component of the research design allows for comparison across the two issue areas and demonstrates that longitudinal variation occurs in each case. This variation appears to be connected to structural features of the policy process that alter the terms of engagement for scientists. Specifically, as the policy process evolves, one sees a trend of increasing procedural formality.[9] Agenda setting is the least structured stage of the policy process and is notable for the lack of an obvious institutional home. In spite of the difficulty that the lack of a formal setting poses in studying agenda setting, a number of analyses set out the major components of the agenda-setting process (Cobb and Elder 1983; Polsby 1984; Kingdon 1984; Stone 1989; Baumgartner and Jones 1993). This stage is dominated by actors who advance policy ideas through information gathering, story telling, argument, and persuasion. Odén's characterization of acid rain as Europe's "chemical war" is a striking example. The discursive practices that appear during agenda setting are present in later stages of decision making, but they are joined by structures and procedures that reinforce preferred roles for participants.

Of course, Congress and the rules of engagement that apply there dominate the legislative stage of decision making in the United States. This stage of policy making is more formalized than agenda setting in that stable rules exist that make much of the activity of legislative politics predictable and repeated—congressional hearings, for example, follow a typical format and are orchestrated in advance by the committee's chair and his or her staff.[10] Certainly, if one wants to see legislative politics in action, there is a place where one can view legislative activities such as congressional hearings, floor debates, and, voting.[11] Comparing the legislative stage to agenda setting draws attention to the lack of a dominant institution in agenda setting and to the difficulty of identifying the locus of agenda setting.

The implementation stage of decision making is the most formally elaborated stage. Both the specific dictates of legislation that create and guide policy programs and the general rules of administrative procedure shape implementation. Once a policy issue has been given formal status as a policy program, that program will be housed in one or more organizations within the federal government.[12] This, of course, provides a setting in which to view the process of implementation. The process of administering a policy program is relatively open, formal, and well documented.[13] In addition, multiple opportunities for review of that process, and often for participation in it, are set out in the Administrative Procedures Act, which governs the process of regulatory rule making.

Dividing the policy process into three stages imposes a simplifying framework on a fluid and dynamic process. For example, Congress clearly dominates legislative policy making. At the same time, committees have an important role in overseeing policy implementation. Likewise, although issue framing and agenda setting often predate congressional attention to an issue, Congress has its own internal dynamic whereby the limits of congressional attention necessitate efforts by members to move issues onto and off the formal congressional agenda in pursuit of their own policy goals.[14] This means that agenda setting occurs within Congress as members use their institutional resources to try to gain the attention of the larger body. Moreover, actors who are involved in policy implementation often appear during legislative hearings. Thus, the norms they are accustomed to in agency settings are mixed with norms established during congressional procedures.

The goal here is not to draw too rigid a boundary between stages or to impose a false linearity on the policy process. Rather, the goal is to take note of systematic differences in policy dynamics across a range of settings. This involves conceptualizing the policy process broadly in order to capture interactions that normally are left out of analyses of science-policy interactions. Though this research relies on distinctions among the three stages of policy making, it also recognizes that these stages overlap and that they are more porous than the labels might suggest. I address this fluidity throughout the book, especially where the distinctions between stages become most blurred.

Having set out a framework that highlights stages of the policy-making process, one might apply that framework to the existing literature rather than conduct an additional study. There are, for example, excellent studies of scientists' participation in agenda setting (Miller and Edwards 1999; Takacs 1996; Yearly 1991) and in legislation (Zehr 2005), and there is a considerable literature on scientists' involvement in policy implementation, specifically focusing on regulatory rulemaking (Brickman, Jasanoff, and Ilgen 1986; Bryner 1987; Crandall and Lave 1981; Daemmrich 2004; Greenwood 1984, Guston 1999, 2000; Irwin et al. 1997; Jasanoff 1990; Landy, Roberts, and Thomas 1994; Melnick 1983; Nelkin 1979; Powell 1999; Salter 1988; Wagner 1995; and Weinberg 1972).[15]

Though a meta-analysis of the existing research might lead one to an important set of conclusions regarding how scientists' role in policy making changes with the stage of policy making, the literature contains enough potential confounding variables—e.g., the different issue areas studied—that any such conclusions would be provisional. For example, is Takacs's (1996) finding that conservation biologists were able to argue that "biodiversity" was a new way to understand nature a consequence of a specific public regard for conservation biologists? Equally, does the status of toxicologists in society drive Jasanoff's (1990) finding that scientists had difficulty closing down a controversy over food additives and environmental toxins? Apart from the respective status of the experts involved in these cases, could there be something else, specific to the cases, that drives the conclusions of the above-mentioned studies?

Studies of scientists in policy implementation tend to draw similar conclusions about the limitations of science in resolving political controversies (Bryner 1987; Crandall and Lave 1981; Greenwood 1984; Irwin et al. 1997; Jasanoff 1990; Landy, Roberts, and Thomas 1994; Melnick 1983; Nelkin 1979; Powell 1999; Wagner 1995; Weinberg 1972). The findings of studies treating agenda setting and legislation are less consistent. For example, whereas Takacs's study (1996) and the studies published in the volume edited by Miller and Edwards (2000) view scientists as important actors in shaping the agendas of biodiversity and climate change, respectively, Yearly's 1991 review of several environmental policy issues cites advocacy organizations as the primary agenda setters. According to Yearly, scientists may provide information that can be useful to advocacy organizations in advancing their environmental campaigns. However, Yearly does not find that scientists are prominent agenda setters. Yearly's findings are consistent with Kingdon's (1984) contention that experts are influential in devising policy alternatives but have little role in shaping which issues are on the public agenda. (Kingdon does not consider scientists *per se*.) One can find similar debates in the literature regarding the role of expertise in legislation. Edelman (1974), Huitt (1954), and Weiss (1989) argue that structural features of congressional decision making limit the role of expertise; Polsby (1969), Jones (1976), Schick (1976), Bimber (1996), and Esterling (2004) note the increase in sources of expertise available to Congress and argue that expert knowledge is a valued commodity in congressional settings.[16]

Despite the fact that existing studies cover scientists engaging in the three stages of decision making treated here, variations in method, in focus of study, and in conclusions make it difficult to use the existing case material as a basis for a coherent, dynamic theory of scientists' role in policy making. The present study, by selecting two comparable cases and treating scientists' participation over time within each case, provides unique insight into how the context of decision making affects scientists' participation without the risk that variation in method or in issue area is producing the results. This approach makes an important contribution to the literature in that it offers a systematic, novel argument about how the institutional settings for policy making in the United States shape scientists' participation. The present study adds to our understanding of how and why context matters in explaining the role of scientists in policy making. Specifically, it finds that the degree of formalization affects scientists' participation from one institutional setting to the next. Though the findings are specific to the United States, the argument about formalization might also explain variation in other countries. The generalizability of this study's findings is explored in detail in the conclusion.

Scientists and Role Expectations in the Policy Process

Comparing scientists' participation across stages of decision making exposes significant differences in their self-presentation in the policy process. These differences correlate with changes in level of formalization. During agenda setting, scientists do not appear to be bound by typical role expectations that tend to accompany scientists' participation in policy making. There is little evidence that the science/policy boundary that establishes distinct roles for scientists and policy makers acts as an effective constraint on scientists at this stage of the process. Scientists establish their credibility by claiming membership in the broader scientific community and speaking for that community. This implies that asking one scientist about the current state of knowledge is just like asking any other scientist about it. To the extent that scientists communicate to policy makers findings that are widely accepted in the scientific community, this claim might be justified. However, scientists do more during agenda setting than transmit scientific research findings.[17] Specifically, scientists create simple stories about human impacts on the environment. These stories, or "science narratives," have a causal component that encapsulates scientific knowledge about the problem.[18] In addition, science narratives contain normative elements that read policy implications into the causal argument. Science narratives, by definition, cross the science/policy boundary. Scientists in this position rarely indicate which aspects of their arguments are specifically supported by the broader scientific community and which aspects fall outside that community's jurisdiction. This is problematic in that scientists who agree on a body of scientific research often do not agree about the policy implications of that research.[19] In agenda setting, then, there is a potential for scientists to trade on the status they enjoy as spokespersons for the environment without being forthright about the more normative, extra-scientific aspects of the arguments they advance.

The terrain for scientists who participate in legislative policy making differs from that of agenda setting. During agenda setting, scientists face few challenges from policy actors regarding whether they have observed an acceptable division between science and policy. This is not the case during legislation, when both policy makers and scientists devote considerable time and attention to whether scientists are participating objectively.[20] In the more formalized setting, where they speak "on the record," scientists begin to respond to role expectations that are implicitly and even explicitly invoked. Specifically, participants in policy making tend to view scientists as having a legitimate role in the policy process when they speak objectively about the current state of scientific knowledge. A scientist responds to this role expectation by adopting either the role of an unapologetic boundary crosser, the role of an apologetic boundary crosser, or the role of a boundary observer. Unapologetic boundary crossers, like scientists in agenda setting, give little or no explicit attention to the boundary between science and policy. When asked about their political views on the issue at hand, they simply offer them. Apologetic boundary crossers are willing to engage in normative discussions, but only after disclaimers such as "Well, the issue of policy implications falls outside of the domain of science, so I will give you my opinion about that as a citizen, not a scientist." Boundary observers refuse to engage in any discussions outside the realm of their scientific expertise and, even when pressed, will not share their views about the policy choices faced by decision makers. As in agenda setting, scientists who participate in legislation invoke the support of the broader scientific community to establish their credibility. In addition, however, they begin to invoke the role of "objective expert," which suggests that they are responding to the expectation that scientists should refrain from voicing judgments about policy.

Scientists who participate in implementation are at the other end of the spectrum from their counterparts in agenda setting. The science/policy boundary shapes much of the daily life of a scientist who is participating in implementation. The freedom of scientists to participate in agenda setting without mentioning the science/policy boundary is long gone. Two related factors raise the salience of the science/policy boundary in this stage relative to other stages. First, scientists who participate in implementation work closely with decision makers. Because they regularly interact with those who exercise political power, expectations about the potential for technocracy or for the politicization of science come into play. Second, to protect against adulteration of science by politics or of politics by science, actors in the policy process establish specific roles and procedures to separate science from policy making. Chief among these is the distinction between risk assessment (the scientific part of risk analysis) and risk management (which involves political judgment).[21] Scientists, and those relying on science to justify public decisions, can be held to account if they do not adhere to the rules that govern policy implementation. Whereas during legislation role expectations are often implicit and vaguely defined, allowing scientists some leeway in deciding how they will negotiate the science/policy boundary, during implementation the role of scientists is codified and explicit.[22] Scientists who participate in implementation are in a constant struggle to demonstrate their objectivity and the credibility of the science they apply to policy making. These scientists call attention to the science/policy boundary in order to show that they are observing that boundary in a way that other policy participants will accept as legitimate. In addition, they expend substantial amounts of energy demonstrating that the science they rely on is in good standing with the science community, in order to show that their proximity to centers of decision making has not undermined their objectivity. Table I.1 summarizes the characteristics of the stages of decision making that affect scientists' participation in the policy process.

By dividing the policy-making process into three stages, I draw attention to the institutions that dominate each stage and to the level of formalization that characterizes each. Formal rules about participation signify agreement, albeit temporary, about appropriate conduct in making policy decisions and implementing policy programs.[23] Though the policy-making process is not necessarily linear,[24] the shift from agenda setting to implementation involves an increase in formalization of the

Table I.1
Characteristics of stages in decision making.

	Dominant institution	Level of formalization or visibility	Salience of science/ policy boundary	Techniques of securing legitimacy
Agenda setting	None	Low	Low	Community membership
Legislation	Congress	Medium	Mixed	Negotiation of boundaries
Implementation	Executive Branch agency	High	High	Negotiation of boundaries; explicit demonstration of method

rules of participation. Formal procedures give structure to the policy-making process and render several aspects of the process predictable. From the standpoint of scientists who participate in policy making, the level of formalization is important because it is an indicator of the salience of the science/policy boundary; the more formalized the rules of engagement, the more salient the boundary. To date, structural constraints have attracted little attention in studies of science in policy making, in part because they are fairly weak mechanisms for policing scientists' ability to advance normative commitments in their role as scientists.[25] The longitudinal perspective here, however, demonstrates that these mechanisms affect scientists' mode of engagement in the policy process, even though they fail to establish an uncontested science/policy boundary.

Though the emphasis on institutional setting calls attention to structural features of the policy process, this approach relies on both structure and agency in explaining differences across stages of decision making. Scientists, therefore, face structural constraints, but are also able to make choices about how they respond to those constraints.[26] These choices are most apparent during the legislative stage of decision making, in which scientists adopt one of three stances when pressed to make policy claims during congressional hearings. But scientists also choose whether to participate in the policy process and, if they do participate, at what stage. Thus, over the course of the public debates on both acid rain and climate change, it is rare to find a scientist who has been active in all three stages. In order to explain scientists' role in the policy process, it is important to attend to the institutional settings in which scientists participate and to scientists' motivations and choices when confronted with the constraints of a particular setting.

Settings matter in explaining participants' behavior because actors who enter the policy-making process are purposive and will adapt their behavior to the setting in order to maximize their goals. This is certainly the case for actors seeking specific policy outcomes. It is also true, however, for actors whose participation is motivated by less specific goals, such as a desire to fulfill one's civic duty or simply to have the experience of participating. Even in these cases, actors will seek to understand the norms of participation that characterize a particular stage of decision making in order to navigate those norms successfully.

Studying the "Public Face of Science"

In this book, I compare interactions between scientists and policy makers across stages of decision making. The central argument is that the norms that guide such interactions differ systematically among policy stages. But I do not follow a single set of scientists throughout the policy process for each issue. In fact, it is rare to find a scientist who participates in all three stages of policy making. If one were to study the few cases in which this happens, one would be defining the preponderance of interactions between scientists and policy makers as beyond the scope of study. Instead, I take as the unit of analysis the interactions between scientists and policy makers at a particular stage. This approach makes use of any selection bias that might be at work. Specifically, scientists seem to move toward or away from stages of the process according to the norms they find most agreeable or disconcerting. This suggests that interactions between scientists and policy makers look different when one is comparing stages because a particular type of scientist is more likely to participate in one stage than in another.

From the standpoint of those who observe policy making across stages, what is changing is *the public face of science* rather than the behavior of a specific group of scientists. The nature of the interaction between scientists and policy makers, therefore, is notably different when one is comparing any two stages of the process. And this difference matters specifically with respect to scientists' capacity to make persuasive arguments while retaining their rhetorical status as neutral participants. As a consequence, a policy maker who interacted with scientists only in agenda setting would have a different experience than a policy maker who interacted with scientists only in the implementation stage. Even though stages of the policy process are not necessarily eliciting different behavior in the same scientist, there is still notable variation in the interactions between scientists and policy makers according to stage. It is also important to note that there is variation in scientists' behavior within stages of the policy process. To the extent that structural features of policy making constrain participants' behavior or select for certain types of participants, these factors do not entirely determine interactions among participants. My analysis suggests, however, that the differences across stages are larger than the differences within stages.[27]

Scientists and Policy Makers

An analysis of the role of scientists in the making of policy necessarily focuses on the actions of scientists and policy makers. One might conclude from the talk about "scientists" and "policy makers" that it is easy, when studying the policy process, to determine who is a scientist and who is a policy maker. In practice, however, the actors who shape science and policy often have multiple roles and titles and are not easily characterized by these seemingly straightforward labels. Distinguishing scientists from policy makers is an exercise in classification, an exercise that is never neutral.[28] In the context of environmental policy making, the use of the label "scientist" is particularly interesting in that participants turn to scientific expertise as a way to bolster policy positions that those participants advocate. Under these circumstances, participants in policy debates may disagree about who counts as a scientist and about which accounts of the scientific record are most accurate or objective.

To clarify how I will use the terms "scientist" and "policy maker," I will draw from several works that provide guidelines for how to think about scientists in society and in policy settings. First, Jasanoff (2005b) argues that institutions that wish to integrate science and policy face a "three-body problem": they must account for science as a body of knowledge, for scientists as individuals, and for scientists acting in concert through expert committees. Jasanoff labels these, respectively, "good science," "unbiased experts," and "balanced committees," all of which might be used to defend one's particular application of science to policy decisions (ibid.: 211). My study focuses on scientists as individuals, recognizing that they often invoke a body of scientific knowledge as the basis for their policy claims and that they often speak for a committee of scientists who, together, are intended to represent a balanced view of how that body of scientific knowledge relates to a specific policy question. This approach leaves open the question of whether claims regarding scientific knowledge or objectivity are accepted by their intended audiences.

Don Price, characterizing the roles that individuals can occupy on a continuum from scientist to policy maker in his 1965 book on science and policy making, describes four "estates": scientist, professional, administration, and policy maker. For Price, movement from one estate to the next necessarily implies a tradeoff between freedom from state intervention and influence on public policy. There are prerequisites for membership in any of the estates, but these may overlap such that any individual has a choice about which estate he or she might occupy. A shortcoming of Price's approach is the lack of recognition of the potential for those in the science estate to affect the outcomes in the policy estate. By Price's logic, outputs of the science estate should be mediated by the intervening estates before influencing policy. This allows Price to overlook paths from science communities to policy communities that are much more direct than the image he portrays with the four estates.

Karen Litfin, in her 1994 analysis of the role of science in policy pertaining to ozone depletion, nominates an intermediary between the scientist and the policy maker: the "knowledge broker." This role, Litfin argues, is necessary in that the "producers of knowledge" conducting the basic research on ozone depletion are not effective in framing and interpreting that knowledge for policy makers.[29] Moreover, policy makers lack either the time or the literacy to turn scientific research findings into good public policy (Litfin 1994: 4). The knowledge broker—typically a low-to-middle-level bureaucrat—has a knack for framing science in policy-relevant terms and is institutionally well positioned to make such arguments. Litfin views the results of scientific research as a collective good that can be used by any actor with the skill to frame and interpret the knowledge in new contexts. However, like Price, Litfin discounts the likelihood that scientists will affect policy outcomes without relying on intermediaries.

In this book I explore the potential for scientists to engage directly in policy making, with a particular interest in the status that comes with the label "scientist" in environmental policy settings. I do not mean to diminish the role of non-scientists in policy making, nor do I mean to suggest that only scientific expertise is relevant to settling environmental policy disputes. Instead, I seek to examine how the label "scientist" is mobilized by actors in environmental policy making. I attempt not to prejudge how that label is applied.

Such an empirical approach leaves the definition of the term "scientist" to the actors who use it in environmental policy making. Thus, in this work, "scientist" refers most often (though not exclusively) to an individual who has a PhD in the natural sciences and is employed as a PhD scientist. A "scientist" is typically employed by a university or some other academic institution, but one may be employed by the government, by a corporation, or by a non-governmental organization. Though there are other routes to having a professional role in the sciences, the empirical evidence presented in this book shows that having obtained an advanced degree in the natural sciences and having gained professional employment on the basis of that degree characterizes the majority of actors who appear in policy settings under the label of "scientist." This label may be advanced by the individual who is acting as a scientist or by someone else. In addition, claims that someone is a scientist may be readily accepted by others engaged in a policy debate or may become an additional point of conflict among participants.

As used in this volume, "policy maker" refers to actors in the American policy process who are elected to public office or who are appointed to the Executive Branch of the federal government and who have the formal capacity to shape public policy. In the United States there are numerous avenues for individuals to influence policies through activities such as agenda setting and lobbying. These actors, however, have an informal role in shaping policy outcomes and are not generally considered policy makers. Instead, in this work, "policy makers" refers to individuals who routinely vote on policy in legislative settings or who have executive authority to shape policy implementation, such as setting out regulatory rules to fulfill the obligation of a congressional statute. Actors who have the formal capacity to carry out these duties are considered policy makers, with the caveat that these are not the only actors who shape policy outcomes.

If the terms "scientist" and "policy maker" are used as specified here, there is the potential that one individual will fill both roles. Specifically, the federal government employs scientists in multiple agencies of the Executive Branch. These actors certainly shape the course of policy implementation—for example, by deciding which research should be funded by federal grants, what standards of air quality should be met by American cities, and how workplace exposures to hazardous chemicals should be limited. In addition, there are members of Congress who hold doctoral degrees. They are not employed professionally as scientists, yet their scientific expertise may be germane in their policy-making roles.

Not surprisingly, the term "scientist" appears to be more fraught in environmental policy making than the term "policy maker." This suggests something about the work that each label can do in policy settings. It may be that the formal power granted to elected officials makes informal claims less threatening, whereas the lack of such clear delineation between the scientist and non-scientist almost guarantees debate. Any attempt to define the term "scientist" must come to grips with the fact that people often do not to agree on the definition of the term. In this sense, the term "scientist" can act as a "boundary object" between two communities—or social worlds—whose understandings of the term are likely to diverge (Star and Griesemer 1989). The common terminology, thus, can mask discrepancies in meaning across the two social worlds. In fact, ambiguity can be productive in that it can allow interactions among groups that might otherwise come into conflict.

At issue in who can act as a scientist is the issue of credibility. Steven Chapin, in his analysis of credibility, argues that there are no simple, formulaic rules for establishing the credibility of any truth claim. Instead, Chapin argues that the specifics of the case are likely to affect the resources and tactics used to establish credibility (1995: 261). In trying to set out a systematic approach to the study of credibility techniques, Chapin examines interactions among scientists and argues that credibility is established through familiarity and the absence of distrust. Chapin acknowledges the view that, in place of familiarity, scientific credibility is communicated to the lay public through things like institutional affiliation and expert consensus (ibid.: 270). He also cites Theodore Porter's argument (1995) that quantification signals credibility in public settings. Ultimately, however, Chapin concludes that beliefs about credibility come down to interpersonal relationships and argues that he learned his own beliefs about what is true from "familiar others" (1995: 271).

Stephen Hilgartner's analysis, in spite of Chapin's argument about the role of familiarity, points to impersonal communications as the centerpiece of the National Research Council's repertoire for establishing the credibility of its reports. These include references to the education and institutional affiliation of committee members who produce reports, established knowledge, the reputation of the National Academy of Sciences, and formal procedures governing scientific practice (2000: 45–52). Hilgartner's analysis centers on the discrepancy between the pubic face that the Academy shares with its audience, and the less visible "backstage" elements of report production. His discussion of the National Research Council's credibility (ibid.: 23) demonstrates that even an institution that "enjoys a longstanding reputation for expertise and objectivity" must still do work to convey and maintain that reputation. This suggests that the labels "science" and "scientist" often have to be clarified and defended in the public setting.

Steven Epstein's 1996 analysis of AIDS epistemology adds a crucial piece to the study of credibility claims in public settings. Epstein treats a case in which lay participants directly engage in the process of generating public knowledge about AIDS in spite of their lack of ability to make use of impersonal communications such as those used by the National Research Council to establish their right to participate. His interest in AIDS has to do with the *"multiplication of the successful pathways* to the establishment of credibility and *diversification of the personnel* beyond the highly credentialed" (1996: 3). He implies that credentials are a typical pathway to establishing credibility in public settings. However, in his introduction he sets up the AIDS case as atypical for the breadth of participants involved in knowledge production. More typical are cases in which who is expert is established through references to more typical markers of expertise, such as educational credentials and professional affiliations.

In the cases presented below, participants often rely on impersonal communications such as those used by the National Research Council to make claims regarding scientific credibility. These include having a PhD in a relevant discipline and being professionally employed on the basis of one's educational credentials. These claims attempt to make something that is complex—who speaks for science—appear simple. These impersonal communications suggest that scientists participate in environmental policy debates because of their access to specialized, relevant knowledge. In addition to listing credentials and institutional affiliations, participants often assert scientists' capacity to communicate specialized knowledge *objectively*. Porter (1995) argues that objectivity is linked to fairness in public domains and that it leads to a tendency for those exercising political power to demonstrate their objectivity through a reliance on quantification. This tendency, though a general one in democratic governance, is especially prominent in debates about environmental policy. Following Porter, I will highlight where the notion of objectivity is advanced without assuming that scientists are objective participants in policy debates.

So as not to exhaust the reader, I will use the terms "scientist" and "policy maker" in the text without noting at each use that these terms have contested meanings and can cover a range of actors and activities.[30] At the same time, I will call attention to the tendency of actors involved in environmental policy making to behave as if these terms are not contested, especially when the concept of "objective science" or "objective scientist" is used to bolster a political position or argument. Actors may shy away from defining the terms specifically as a way to try to avoid conflict. Additionally, though some actors are aware of the potential for contests to arise over who can act as a scientist in environmental policy making, some actors may genuinely believe that the terms are fixed and well understood by other participants.

Selection of Cases

The comparison of acid rain and climate change provides a mechanism for identifying the peculiarities of each case and highlights consistencies in scientists' experiences that may be general across a range of environmental policy issues. Acid rain and climate change are selected primarily for their visibility and longevity as policy issues. Both provide numerous observations at each stage of the policy process, since each case spans more than 20 years. The public became aware of acid rain in the late 1960s, and Congress first addressed the issue in 1975 (HCST 1976b). A federal research program to study acid rain was created in 1980, and a formal regulatory program to limit acid rain was created in 1990.[31] Climate change made its first congressional appearance in the 1950s, when scientists requested federal funding for the International Geophysical Year.[32] Congressional attention resumed in the 1970s and became commonplace in the mid 1980s. The issue was tracked moderately but consistently in the media from the 1950s until the early 1980s.[33] In 1986, media coverage expanded considerably, an indication of the arrival of the issue in the public consciousness. Climate change policy reached the implementation stage with the US Global Change Research Program (USGCRP), created in 1990.[34] Whereas the Clinton administration created voluntary programs to reduce carbon dioxide emissions, in more recent years the Senate and the G. W. Bush administration have opposed the Kyoto Treaty.[35] In the face of federal inaction on climate change, two groups of states are considering regional agreements for reducing greenhouse gases. In addition, California passed legislation in 2006 aiming to reduce greenhouse gas emissions by 25 percent by the year 2020.[36]

Another reason to study acid rain and climate change is that the two cases have a number of characteristics common to environmental policy issues. Both involve the spread of pollutants into the environment, which, through a complex set of interactions, causes damage that is both geographically and temporally dispersed. A substantial scientific record supporting the theory behind the respective mechanisms of effect substantiates both issues. In addition, the scientific understandings of acid rain and climate change, respectively, are limited by large scientific uncertainties about the timing, the magnitude, and the location of anticipated effects. The policy options implied in the definition of these issues have mobilized both vigorous support and organized and effective opposition. Finally, both issues tap into a broadly held view that advances in environmental protection create economic inefficiencies for regulated industries.

The selection of cases, however, carries with it an important limitation in that scientists' role in domains outside environmental politics may differ in important ways. The findings here cannot be generalized outside the domain of environmental politics. Because a number of environmental policy issues are not apparent to lay observers, the public and policy makers depend on scientists to keep them informed about the state of the environment. All other things being equal, this dependence would increase the role that scientists play in the development of environmental policy. Studies of scientists in this domain are, then, selecting on the dependent variable; these are cases in which one would expect scientists to have a special role in framing policy issues.[37] In spite of this weakness, "most likely" cases are theoretically important when they show that an expected relationship does not hold. Such a finding casts doubt on the likelihood of finding the relationship in less likely settings (Eckstein 1975). Because researchers remain divided about scientists' influence in environmental policy domains, additional research on this topic is warranted. Moreover, because the outcome of interest—the potential for erosion of democratic decision making norms—is an important finding wherever it occurs, a focus on environmental policy domains is justifiable even if study results cannot be generalized to other policy domains.

The focus on environmental policy is further justified by the ease with which an environmental issue's origins can be traced. In his study of agenda setting, John Kingdon points out the difficulty of locating an issue's inception. Kingdon is interested in the actors who command sufficient attention in the political arena to place something on the public agenda. Notably, he eschews the question of where such powerful actors get their ideas, referring to this as an exercise of "infinite regress" (1996: 72–73). Insofar as the issue areas he presents—transportation and health care—have been recurring agenda items for more than 70 years, Kingdon's approach is sensible.[38] For such issues, the question is not where an idea originated, but who has been able to return the issue to the political spotlight. Actors who can capture national attention—e.g., senators and presidents—are, according to Kingdon, most likely to fulfill this role.

The analytical problem of "infinite regress" often disappears in the arena of environmental policy, where issues can be traced to their earliest inklings in scientific research and journal publications. For example, in the fall of 1973 the chemists Mario Molina and F. Sherwood Rowland discovered the that chlorofluorocarbons destroy ozone molecules.[39] The initial research on acid rain and climate change are similarly traceable, respectively, to Robert Angus Smith's publication in 1872 and Svante Arrhenius's work published in 1896. Recognition of potential environmental problems and subsequent attempts to generate publicity around those problems can be documented fairly easily. Though research on agenda setting should not be restricted to cases whose origins are known, such cases provide an opportunity to trace policy issues from their earliest inception to their arrival on the political agenda.

Organization of the Book

In chapter 1, I discuss theoretical issues pertaining to the role of science in policy making. Each subsequent chapter is devoted to a stage of the decision making process—agenda setting, legislation, and implementation. Aspects of scientists' participation particular to certain stages are highlighted and explored in detail. In addition, I analyze the potential for scientists' participation to have long-term effects on the overall development of policies that address either acid rain or climate change.

In chapter 1, I discuss theoretical debates about the role of science in policy making and the particular status that science has in society. I also review the concept of boundary work and trace its intellectual roots. The literature demonstrates the social nature of interactions that take place in arguing for a recognizable boundary between science and non-science. This boundary, though fluid and elusive, produces status and confers authority. As such, it is materially important in policy-making settings, and its rhetorical status is important in developing norms that define legitimate engagement in the policy process.

I take up the issue of scientists' influence in the early development of policies on acid rain and climate change in the next two chapters. In chapter 2, I explore the policy process of agenda setting and examines the factors particular to environmental policy settings that might generate deference to scientists. I then conduct a careful analysis of the policy frames or "science narratives" that scientists offered for both acid rain and climate change. In each case, the scientists who spoke publicly about the respective issues incorporated into their discussion several normative commitments that were embedded in what came to be dominant policy frames for each issue. In chapter 2, I focus specifically on aspects of the early science narratives that generated little public debate.

That scientists involved in debates about acid rain and climate change blended their normative convictions with their discussions of the scientific record is not such a surprising finding. The lack of policy debate about those normative commitments is. In chapter 2, I examine the extent to which the two science narratives were read as "correct" (i.e., scientifically supported) by policy makers interested in the issues. Though both issues generated substantial debate about the prospect of adopting mitigation strategies, several of the normative commitments embedded in the science narratives were rapidly institutionalized in the public response to each issue. The respective federal research programs on acid rain and climate change are classic examples of institutionalized science narratives. My analysis demonstrates significant ways in which policy developments around acid rain and climate change followed in line with scientists' policy views. In addition, my analysis shows how these frames were stabilized by institutions that grew up around them, even in the face of incoming information that showed these frames to be suspect.

In chapter 3, I extend the inquiry into the institutionalization of the science narratives for acid rain and climate change by examining political debates carried out in legislative settings. I also address a set of general questions about the role of scientists in legislative setting, a topic that has received little attention in the "science in policy" literature. I examine the motivations of legislators in calling for scientists to participate in legislative debates and the reasons for scientists to accept such invitations, especially because many scientists do not. I point to a tension in scientists' role: legislators want scientists simultaneously to be neutral and to register their normative interpretations of the scientific record. These contradictory demands speak to the need for actors who can link science to policy choices in ways that are persuasive and emphasize the difficulty of maintaining distinct roles for scientists and policy makers in the policy process.

In chapter 4, I examine the effects of a formal science/policy boundary on scientists' participation. I highlight the extra efforts scientists must make in order to be understood as objective actors in the policy process, and I call attention to scientists' relative reluctance to engage in actions or discourse that might be perceived as political. Though scientists who participate in policy implementation inevitably cross the science/policy boundary, they work hard to give the appearance that they have not done so. Because engaging in persuasive argumentation about policy outcomes is not consistent with presenting an image of neutral expertise, scientists cede much of this role to other participants in the policy process. Scientists' actions in this setting appear to be supported by three not necessarily consistent models for setting the science/policy boundary. These three models, which emerge as a function of the heightened salience of the science/policy boundary in policy implementation settings, are explored in detail. Each sets out a different mechanism for protecting the credibility and therefore the authority of science when it is applied in political arenas.

In the conclusion, I return to the question of scientists' role in shaping environmental policy outcomes. In making claims about scientific issues that should become matters of public policy, scientists are constructing political arguments. These arguments start with scientific findings but give meaning to those findings by associating them with a particular set of values. If, in engaging in this process of establishing meaning through values, scientists are understood as providing an objective assessment of the state of science with respect to an environmental policy issues, scientists use their credibility as objective researchers to advance political commitments not specific to that research. My analysis raises particular concerns about scientists' role in agenda setting during which extra-scientific commitments seamlessly accompany the expert information they bring to the table. The potential for technocratic outcomes is certainly higher under these circumstances than it is in settings characterized by more open exchanges between policy makers, scientists, and stakeholders about where and how science should enter the process. While focusing on scientists' efforts in policy making, I also review the broader set of actors and social forces that help support the establishment and the stability of science narratives and emphasize the multiple pathways by which scientific meaning is constructed in public settings.

1

Theories of Science in Policy Making

... the conception of the social nature of fact perception should be useful to political science. In regard to policy, it suggests one of the limits to the usefulness of uncommitted social intelligence to the politician.
—Ralph K. Huitt (1954)

Early studies of the role of science in policy making tend to frame the central problem of using science for policy decisions as an issue of maintaining proper boundaries between the work of science and the work of politics.[1] The idea of a clear separation between science and politics, in theory, might guard against two potential failure modes in democratic decision making: technocracy and the politicization of science. Technocratic outcomes arise when scientists dominate decision making to the exclusion of other legitimate participants in democratic processes[2]; politicization occurs when individual or group interests in policy outcomes introduce bias into scientists' actual work or their representation of their work in policy settings.[3] For a number of scholars, setting the boundary between science and non-science correctly can lead to better decision making.

Interest in boundaries between science and non-science has continued in more recent studies of science in policy making.[4] However, this more recent work contains a notable turn in the analytic approach to the boundary.[5] Instead of assuming that science and non-science can be objectively separated and pursuing the "correct" separation, those engaged in analysis of boundary work ask how such separations are made and whom they serve (Gieryn 1983, 1995, 1999; Jasanoff 2004a; Jasanoff and Wynne 1998; Star and Griesemer 1989). This approach emphasizes the social and contingent aspects of drawing a distinction between science and non-science. Further, it addresses the allocation of power that accompanies setting such a boundary, and it focuses the analytic lens on how actors work to achieve, stabilize, and, on occasion, destabilize such settlements.

I begin this chapter with an overview of the traditional approach to separating science from policy in the policy process. Next, I present several analyses of decision making that do not rely on the notion of a clean division between science and politics and view persuasion and negotiation as irreducible elements of the policy process. These analyses demonstrate the impracticality and even the impossibility of settling the question of the proper boundary between science and policy.

At the same time, I explore the extent to which the idea of science as objective—descriptively inaccurate as that idea might be—continues to have rhetorical weight in that actors involved in decision making use it, sometimes convincingly, to make their case.[6] In this chapter, without assigning objectivity to science in policy making, I consider the work that "claims of objectivity" can do in closing off political debate. Further, I address why such claims retain persuasive power in light of scholarly work that demonstrates the social nature of science/non-science settlements. This exploration of science in decision making lays the groundwork for subsequent chapters in which the interplay between the social elements of science and the frequent rhetorical claims of scientific objectivity are examined. That these idealized images of science and scientists continue to circulate in policy-making settings suggests that analysts must attend to the actual workings of science in policy making while also being attentive to the persuasive potential of the invocation of "objective science" in policy debates.

Boundaries between Science and Non-Science

The idea of creating a boundary between science and policy as a way to preserve the norms of each is based on a rationalist conception of science. According to the rationalist perspective, science is a useful resource in decision making because of its capacity for connecting means with ends. The ability of science to provide causal explanations for events, both current and future, improves policy makers' ability to achieve desired outcomes. Reliance on science is successful when scientific information enables policy makers to choose a policy solution that (a) brings them closer to their stated policy goals and (b) outperforms other solutions in achieving those goals. Science, under these circumstances, should not help policy makers define their goals. Rather, science is applied *after* those goals have been agreed upon and is merely used as an aid in finding the most effective, efficient means to of achieve them.[7] Ideally, this method of drawing science into decision making preserves democratic norms in that it protects against an elite minority—i.e., scientists— substituting their policy judgments for those of the majority. Further, according to the rationalist account of science, a boundary between science and policy making does double duty in that it protects science from political bias that would undermine its capacity to provide decision makers with reliable, valid information.

The rationalist view of the role of science in policy making is given institutional expression in the policy process through a number of structures and procedures designed to preserve a boundary between science and policy.[8] Ideally, such a boundary will define formal and controlled situations in which science and policy will interact. Most prominently, the boundary has been expressed through a supposed division of labor between Congress and administrative agencies such that Congress manages the political aspects of policy making and then turns to Executive Branch agencies for their expertise in implementing congressional decisions. This view of administrative agencies has its roots in the Progressive-era effort to create "neutral competence" within the bureaucracy (Knott and Miller 1987).[9] Although the idea that bureaucracies are apolitical and have no policy-making role has been overturned, a number of procedures established in bureaucratic agencies still draw on a conception of politics and scientific expertise as separate and separable endeavors.[10]

A second model of science in decision making that also finds institutional expression in the policy process conceives of the relationship between science and policy somewhat differently. This model views science as a resource in resolving policy controversies and is based on a logical positivist perspective that scientists' description of reality corresponds exactly with that reality. According to this view, technocracy might be not a failure mode but a desired outcome, in that science can offer a definitive answer about the efficient allocation of resources. The assumption here is that what is missing in cases of persistent political conflict is information. If scientific uncertainties are resolved, political debate will follow suit. According to this view, by introducing information that is consonant with reality and fact, science can bring erstwhile opponents into agreement over policy choices and even goals. Starting from this perspective, democratic norms of decision making are not necessarily violated when a scientific elite dominates decision making because science is truth-based and therefore is not subject political debate. If science reveals truths about the world, anyone with the proper training and the proper methodological tools would arrive at the same incontrovertible endpoint.

A softer version of this view assumes that, though science does not eliminate value conflict, it can limit its scope. Scientific information, by explaining our physical surroundings and our relationship to those surroundings, delineates plausible and implausible courses of action. Value debates remain, but they must be carried out in light of existing scientific realities. This softer version of the logical positivist position is consistent with the argument that conducting scientific research is an important preliminary step in resolving policy controversy, an argument that is made routinely in environmental politics.

The interaction between scientists and policy makers according to the soft-positivist perspective differs from the model above, in which ends are selected through a democratic process and science is used to find efficient, effective means. Instead, science is viewed as a mechanism for *understanding* political goals (for example, whether ozone depletion poses risks for humans and the environment). This perspective still relies on a boundary between science and politics, in that science must be unadulterated by politics in order to come to the truth. However, the orientation toward the potential for technocracy is different in these two models specifically regarding how each model conceives of the role of science in decision making. Efforts in the political process that seek to avoid technocratic outcomes clearly carve out space for the legitimacy of the judgment of non-scientists in decision making, whereas policy mechanisms that advance science as a way to contain or reduce policy debate rely on the putative link between science and truth to skirt the worries that come with technocracy.

A second important distinction between the rationalist and positivist views of science in decision making is when science should enter the process. Rationalists view science as helping find means to achieve goals once the policy process has selected a set of goals. The positivist view invokes science as a prerequisite for policy debate such that science defines the terrain that is factual and uses that to circumscribe issues that remain open for debate.

Both the rationalist and the positivist models of decision making make use of the idea of a science/policy boundary to address the problem of using science in setting policy. However, that solution has been discarded resoundingly by scholars of the policy process.

In this chapter, I present several critiques of the rationalist and positivist models of science in decision making. These critiques differ in their views of the potential for technocratic outcomes. At issue is the power that actors claiming scientific insight have to shape policy debates in terms that encourage reliance on scientists or science in shaping public policy outcomes.

The Limits of Rationalism in Decision Making

Alvin Weinberg's concept of "trans-science" offers a practical criticism of the rationalist approach to decision making. Weinberg (1972) applied the term "trans-science" to policy-relevant questions that have scientific or technical components but cannot be resolved through scientific means. This is the case, for example, in using scientific experiments to judge the health risks associated with low-level radiation—as Weinberg argues, the numbers of mice required to have confidence in experimental results is on the order of 8 billion (ibid.: 210). In general, trans-scientific problems can be *approached* through scientific methods, but irreducible uncertainties make reliable *conclusions* unlikely. Weinberg argues, instead, for a type of science-policy interaction—"trans-science"—that is separate from what we normally think of as science (ibid.: 209). The role for scientists in approaching trans-scientific questions, according to Weinberg, is to point out irreducible uncertainties, thereby noting the limits of science in settling policy debates. Here Weinberg implies that an identifiable boundary between science and policy would be helpful in decision making. This approach is consistent with soft positivism, in which science sets the terms of debate by demonstrating what is known and what remains uncertain. At the same time, Weinberg argues that scientists themselves do not agree about these limits and suggests that, for better or worse, both scientists and non-scientists will argue about the applicability of science in policy making. Weinberg lays out a model for how science might be useful in policy making. On the other hand, he does not offer much guidance on how debates about the role of science will be settled or who might settle them.

A more radical departure from the rationalist model comes from Charles Lindblom, who, in one of the most cited works in political science, argues that the synoptic approach to decision making is both descriptively inaccurate and normatively misguided (1959).[11] Lindblom rejects the idea that policy alternatives are evaluated in light of their ability to maximize stated goals and thereby to lead to the selection of the most effective and efficient means by which to achieve collective ends. Instead, decision making proceeds through an analysis of only a limited set of options that represent incremental changes from current policy.

Lindblom's criticism of the synoptic model of decision making is largely practical. First, decision makers lack the time and resources to evaluate systematically all possible solutions to a stated policy problem. A second and related point is that by considering small policy changes decision makers *decrease* the knowledge requirements associated with predicting outcomes of new policy options. By limiting the uncertainty that participants face about likely future outcomes, decision makers *increase* the chances of forming consensus among participants in support of proposed policy options. Third, Lindblom argues that the ability to judge a policy option as good or bad, in rationalist terms, depends on agreement about the goals. If participants to do not agree about goals, there are few objective criteria by which to evaluate a particular policy option—for example, is it better to balance the budget than to expand a program that provides health insurance to children? Lindblom argues that goals are not judged independently from means. Instead, he argues, valued outcomes are discovered and elaborated through examination of a set of policy options that make explicit necessary tradeoffs that are inherent in choosing one option over another.

Lindblom's description of the policy-making process rejects both the rationalist and the positivist models of decision making. For Lindblom, a rationalist approach would be time-consuming, would inevitably be incomplete, and might suggest a route that strays too far from the comfort zone of participants in the policy process. Equally, Lindblom defines the quality of a policy decision not by its consonance with reality or truth, as the positivists would, but by the process that led to the decision. Lindblom's more practical approach allows for learning by participants who can make small policy changes and then evaluate the extent to which those changes achieved desired policy outcomes. Scientists might play a role in Lindblom's decision making by providing insights about the outcomes associated with a policy or by making persuasive arguments about policy alternatives. However, Lindblom carves out no value-neutral place from which scientists can or should operate.

Lindblom simply casts aside the need for a boundary between science and policy.

A comparison of Lindblom's view of decision making with Alvin Weinberg's illustrates Lindblom's nuanced rejection of rationalist and positivist views. Whereas Weinberg falters on the issue of who should demarcate science and trans-science, Lindblom is able to skirt the issue of the proper boundary by arguing that decision making can proceed without resolving major uncertainties. Through evaluation of successive, limited comparisons, decisions are made without stretching participants past their willingness to proceed. Participants learn by evaluating outcomes associated with existing policy settlements and can re-engage policy decisions as needed. In addition, rather than viewing stakeholders as a force that distorts otherwise sensible policy choices, Lindblom sees interested actors are crucial pathway by which pertinent information reaches decision makers. For Lindblom, the approach is not a step away from rationality toward relativism. Instead, it is a practical way to proceed despite inherent uncertainties.[12] This allows Lindblom to conceive of a decision-making process in which the decision makers are neither all-knowing nor operating without any helpful information.

Notably absent from Lindblom's model is a role for objective information. Good decisions are not judged on the basis of objective criteria such as efficiency, effectiveness, or truth. Instead, a good decision is one on which participants can agree. This model posits democratic decision making as a solution to the problem of irreducible uncertainties. Rather than democratic decision making being an irrational process that needs to be propped up by science in order to avoid going hopelessly astray, it is a practical way of proceeding in the face of uncertainty.

Deborah Stone, in her more recent account of the policy process (1997: 8–13), attacks the rational model of decision making as descriptively inaccurate. However, in contrast with Lindblom's view of the policy process, science is a specific and useful resource in Stone's view. Stone rejects the rationalist model because it does not acknowledge that actors involved in policy actively attempt to alter the ways in which other actors perceive the contest. Instead, the rational model of decision making takes for granted public consensus about "the way things are" or presumes that consensus can be produced through the provision of facts and information. Stone argues, to the contrary, that facts are always contested in policy making such that the consensus that information is supposed to produce is elusive (ibid.: 310). Instead, actors mobilize ideas with the intent to provide accounts of events that are more persuasive than other actors' accounts. Stone asserts that ideas, as tools for influencing the policy process, are "more powerful than money and votes and guns" (ibid.: 11).

For Stone, one of the most important ways to integrate ideas into policy making is through the construction of policy narratives and causal stories. Stone finds two routine story lines that shape most policy narratives: (1) a story of decline, in which some previously happy state of affairs is slipping away, and (2) a story of control, in which a tolerated but unwanted state of affairs can now be alleviated through newly available courses of action. Problems of environmental policy, for example, often are framed in terms of decline and often imply the need for intervention to halt or slow a looming crisis. The idea of addressing poverty through federal housing projects fits a control plot line. The availability of a solution—i.e., low-income housing as a basis for economic development—brings a long-standing problem onto the political agenda not as a function of a perceived change in the severity of the problem, but in response to the claim that there is a course of action that might address the problem. In this way, policy narratives make a case that action is warranted and feasible.

In addition, policy narratives can contain more precise descriptions of policy problems that Stone calls "causal stories." Causal stories draw clear links between problems and solutions, assign blame, and suggest more likely and less likely options for remediation. Stone's (1989, 1997) analysis of causal stories turns on the flexibility one has in locating a problem in the realm of accident and fate versus locating it in human agency. If a policy problem is understood to be within the realm of human control, arguments about the need for government action are more likely to be convincing. Stone's work on causal stories highlights the need to persuade in order to have one's view of a policy problem accepted. But Stone also emphasizes a subtle trick of the causal story; its persuasive element is masked. Political actors, Stone writes, "use narrative story lines and symbolic devices to manipulate so-called issue characteristics, all the while making it seems as though they are simply describing facts" (1989: 282). In Stone's view, the attempt to present a causal story as if one is merely presenting "the way things are" is an important component of that story's persuasive power. If the audience accepts the claim of the causal story—i.e., "this is, in fact, the way things are"—the members of the audience do not see themselves as having been lobbied. Instead, they view the interaction as one in which they learned something new.

Stone recognizes social and cultural norms that place limits on how much flexibility one has in creating a convincing policy narrative or a causal story. For example, her emphasis on familiar plot lines implies that an innovative policy entrepreneur who diverges from such plot lines might risk his or her credibility with the audience.[13] In addition, Stone emphasizes that policy narratives invite counter-narratives. Contestants in a political process are often anything but passive recipients of one another's framings. Stone conceives of such struggles in terms of battles over boundaries:

> Each mode of social regulation draws lines around what people may and may not do and how they may or may not treat each other. But these boundaries are constantly contested, either because they are ambiguous and do not settle conflicts, or because they allocate benefits and burdens to the people on either side, or both. Boundaries become real and acquire their meaning in political struggles. (1997: 13)

For Stone, a boundary between science and policy is crucial in that it sets out the space of what can be contested and what will be left out of the arena of policy debate because participants view some features of the world as factual and therefore beyond debate. Rather than trying to argue about where the boundary should be drawn, Stone is interested in the resources policy adversaries use to advance their claims about what is factual and therefore not open to debate.

Unlike the rationalists and positivists who would carve out a safe space for scientists to create and provide relevant information to policy makers, Stone sees science, or at least the rhetoric of science, as a resource that participants use in the game of persuasion. Successful participants create a boundary between science and policy when they convince other actors that their view of reality is correct. By implication, there is no fixed boundary between science and policy, or at least not one that participants in the policy process will agree on. Stone's approach differs from the soft positivist approach in that she views efforts by participants in the policy process to persuade others as the normal and legitimate currency of political engagement rather than an undesirable process that interrupts a more objective approach.

Science plays a more visible role in Stone's account of policy making than in Lindblom's. The causal story, a crucial resource in Stone's policy world, borrows heavily from the idiom of science, i.e., the notion of identifiable causality. In addition, one of the marks of success of the policy story is its ability to present its normative framing as if it is factual. To do this, proponents of causal stories often draw on scientific studies to bolster their claims. Stone characterizes science as being able to "command enormous cultural authority as the arbiter of empirical questions" (1997: 204). At the same time, Stone does not argue that science or scientists carry the day. Instead, she characterizes science as useful but certainly not sufficient in convincing others to accept one's policy narrative (1989: 295).

Sheila Jasanoff's 1990 study of science advisors in regulatory policy making offers an empirically grounded assessment of the tenuousness of boundaries erected between science and policy and draws on theoretical contributions from science studies scholarship to elucidate the processes she observes in regulatory decision making. Jasanoff considers two models that address the problem of science in decision making: (1) technocracy, in which the application of sound science can rationalize policy making, and (2) democracy, in which broader participation by stakeholders improves outcomes (1990: 15). Jasanoff argues that the presence of science advisors in regulatory decision making and the need for regulators to consult scientists and to maintain strong ties to the science community are evidence of the dominance of the technocracy model (ibid.: 229). At the same time, Jasanoff highlights, throughout her book, the weakness of technocratic solutions in policy debates. Jasanoff provides detailed examples of the complex negotiations involved in trying to develop consensus around scientific evidence in order to use that evidence to legitimize regulatory decisions at the Environmental Protection Agency and the Food and Drug Administration. Jasanoff finds that scientists often cross the presumed boundary between science and policy by incorporating subjective judgments into the advice they offer while maintaining their authority as experts. Likewise, agency administrators face incentives to redraw the boundary between science and policy from one regulatory decision to the next as a consequence of the contingencies associated with a particular instance of agency rule making. Administrators in the study have an array of institutional mechanisms available to them—for example, contracting with independent advisory groups versus relying on in-house advisors—for incorporating scientific information into decision making.[14]

For Jasanoff, efforts on the part of participants to create a reliable boundary are not only elusive but also misguided. Jasanoff argues that efforts to draw science into decision making in ways that blur the boundary between science and policy often lead to policy outcomes that are *less controversial* than efforts that attempt to maintain an unrealistic division between expert advice and democratic decision-making authority (1990: 231). Her analysis suggests that a rejection of the myth the rationalist model of decision making could lead toward a more productive, if less defined, relationship between science and policy. The lack of a clear boundary between science and policy should not be troubling if, as Jasanoff argues, the balance between democratic and technocratic forms of decision making are kept in a "creative dialectic" by actors on either side of the science/policy boundary (ibid.: 228).

A notable feature of Jasanoff's treatment of science advisors in policy making is that political contests over the role of science in the formation of policy have not limited the tendency to rely on science advisors, in spite of scientists' limited capacity to close off political debate. "Consultation between agencies and [science] advisory committees," Jasanoff writes, "has become almost routine, even when not required by law." (ibid.: 1) The cases she presents do not lead easily to the conclusion that scientists are shaping outcomes. At the same time, the recourse to science advisors has not abated.

There is a notable consistency between the perspectives offered by Stone and Jasanoff, in spite of the differences in their approach to the subject matter. Neither of their treatments requires *a priori* agreement about how to draw the science/policy boundary, nor, in view the stakes involved in demarcating this valuable political terrain, should such agreements be expected. Thomas Gieryn, who has made substantial contributions to the literature on boundary work, predicts repeated efforts to demarcate science from non-science, not only in policy domains, but in any domain where science is held out as a distinct form of knowledge (1983, 1995, 1999). "Boundary-work abounds," Gieryn writes, "simply because people have many reasons to open up the black box of an 'established' . . . representation of science—to seize another's cognitive authority, restrict it, protect it, expand it, or enforce it." (1995: 407) Gieryn goes on to argue that, because such boundaries are continually contested, there is little stability in what is considered scientific:

. . . neither actual scientific practice and discourse in labs or journals nor earlier maps showing the place of science in the culturescape *determine* how the boundaries of science will get drawn next time the matter comes up for explicit debate. . . . In this sense, then, the space for science is empty because, at the outset of boundary-work, nothing of its borders and territories is given or fixed by past practices and reconstructions in a deterministic way. (ibid.: 406)

This picture of science in policy making, in which actors must continually renegotiate what constitutes "sound science," raises the issue of how society can cope with such indeterminacy. Gieryn offers a clue when he acknowledges the potential for stability in negotiated settlements around science. In a move that sounds somewhat akin to Stone's approach, Gieryn argues that there is a repertoire from which participants draw from when they articulate science/non-science boundaries, and that some demarcations are easier to defend than others. He clarifies that some representations of science "achieve a provisional and contingent obduracy that may preempt boundary-work" (ibid.: 407).

David Guston's (2000) analysis of the administration of grants given by the National Institutes of Health offers a concrete example of how such "obduracy" might be achieved. Guston explores changes in the rhetoric describing government support of basic scientific research from World War II to the end of the twentieth century, focusing specifically on the erosion of the laissez-faire model that dominated postwar public funding. This erosion arose from an increasing willingness on the part of legislators in charge of the purse strings to ask whether basic research was in fact benefiting society in a way that justified the costs. Researchers who had assumed that basic science was inherently worthy and who bristled at the idea that non-scientists might exercise any oversight of their domain found their behavior in policy domains increasingly scrutinized. Guston develops the concept of the "boundary organization" to explain how the dual expectations of scientists and policy makers have been managed within the National Institutes of Health in order to keep the relationship from breaking down.[15] Guston describes the NIH as a boundary organization that is able to internalize negotiations along the science/policy boundary and to stabilize them in ways that allow actors on each side of the boundary to protect their interests. In this case, the routine of a bureaucracy helps create the obduracy that Gieryn posits.

When comparing Guston's analysis against Jasanoff's, one can see that the policy setting is likely to have a substantial influence on the ability to create stable boundaries around science. Arenas of distributive politics, of which NIH grant giving is a clear example, are relatively non-competitive when compared with regulatory policy settings (Lowi 1964, 1972). That Jasanoff finds few routinized boundary settlements in Food and Drug Administration and Environmental Protection Agency regulatory decision making is consistent with expectations about politics in regulatory versus non-regulatory domains.

Notably, none of the scholars treated here endorses a relativist approach. Rather, each of them explores the persistent role of science in policy making. It is this persistence that is of interest. If we accept the social underpinnings of science and accept the frustratingly infrequent examples we have of science being instrumental in resolving political debate, we must wonder why we have not revised our view of the importance of science in the policy process. This calls attention to the work that "the idea of science" can do in society. A central argument in the present volume is that participants in politics cling to the idea of applying science for policy making because of the appeal of finding the "correct" or "best" answer, especially if one assumes that the alternative is endless debate. The idea of using "sound science" to inform policy decisions creates an incentive for participants to demonstrate that science supports their positions.

Here we can see two orthogonal currents running in the arena of science in decision making. On a scholarly level, researchers advocate for solutions that dispense with the traditional notion of separating science and policy (Jasanoff 1990; Sarewitz 1996; Guston 1999, 2000). At the level of practice, recourse to the traditional notion of scientific objectivity as a powerful epistemological basis for resolving political debate remains in high currency. Perhaps, as a function of these two currents, recent scholarship is divided about the trajectory of science in policy making, with some researchers decrying the decline of science while others cite its pervasiveness.

Trends in the Recourse to Science in Decision Making

Yaron Ezrahi (1990) makes a strong case that scientific norms are in decline and argues that, because of this decline, ideology will supersede rationality as the basis for legitimate state action. In a vast work tracing the links between Enlightenment views of science and democracy, Ezrahi argues that political action, once justified in rational and instrumental terms, is increasingly understood in moral, emotional, and symbolic terms. Ezrahi demonstrates convincingly the foundational role Enlightenment thinking had in the creation of modern democracies and explores how visions of industrialization and mechanization have been used to articulate the rationale for legitimate state action.

Ezrahi makes his case by arguing that rationalist thinking during the Enlightenment led to a concept of democracy such that citizens could hold leaders accountable for their actions. This accountability, according to Ezrahi, stems from the capacity to judge an action of the state in light of its consequences. Citizens, by observing the state's action, assess the extent to which state officials achieve their goals.[16] This notion, according to Ezrahi, relies on a visual culture that assumes that state policies are goal oriented and can be "measured" with reference to their ability to reach those goals (1990: 75; 89). Ezrahi argues that the visual culture of politics and the idea of constraining state action on the basis of instrumental expectations about outcomes are now in decline.

Ezrahi's account, however, captures at least two trends that turn out to be moving in opposite directions rather than changing together. Certainly trust in scientists, and in professionals more generally, has declined in the United States since the 1950s. But one can argue that this decline in trust is the consequence of citizens *exercising* rather than rejecting the visual, attestive culture that Ezrahi argues is the foundation of democratic politics. Society's experience with technological developments since World War II has been one of glowing promise followed by disillusionment as the public experiences unforeseen costs that accompanied many technological advances. For example, promoters of pesticides promised an increase in agricultural production, but now face a public that is wary of the costs to the environment and public health that have accompanied widespread pesticide use (Baumgartner and Jones 1991). A similar account can be made of nuclear power, whose proponents argued it would provide "energy too cheap to meter" without focusing on the costs associated with maintaining safety in such complex, large technical systems and with managing the waste (Baumgartner and Jones 1991; LaPorte and Keller 1996). A more recent example concerns claims about the ability of stem-cell research to provide cures for several degenerative diseases; such predictions do not include an accurate picture of the long time horizons involved before such treatments will reach medical clinics. These examples suggest that expert claims about the promise of science and technology may well have been judged in instrumental terms such that a decline in scientific and technical authority has occurred as a consequence of a visual, attestive culture. Declining trust in scientists may be evidence that that culture is alive and well.

Further evidence that scientists are subject to increasing scrutiny that has its underpinnings in Enlightenment thought comes from Guston's analysis of changes in the administration of NIH grants (2000). Guston provides evidence that a laissez-faire approach to scientific research has been replaced with specific rules of accountability that govern publicly funded grants. Moreover, members of Congress initiated this change in response to questions regarding whether the "social contract for science" articulated after World War II was, in fact, accurate—i.e., did public support of basic scientific research reap benefits for society? Guston's analysis shows the visually attestive culture that Ezrahi describes in action. Moreover, it was this culture of observing and judging outcomes that eroded the social contract for science and placed scientists under increasing scrutiny as a condition of accepting pubic funding for their research.

Curiously, the erosion in the social status of scientists has been matched by an increase in the use of analysis in policy making. Although a number of political scientists point to the limits of science in guiding political decisions or resolving political controversy, policy making in the United States has seen an increase in recourse to expertise since the 1970s. Jasanoff's 1990 study responds to the proliferation of science advisory boards around agencies involved in environmental and health-related regulatory decision making. A number of scholars have noted a similar trend with respect to Congress, the branch of government that, according to classic political science, faces institutional incentives that make recourse to analysis and expertise unlikely.[17] During the 1970s, Congress created a number of offices (including the General Accounting Office, the Congressional Research Service, the Congressional Budget Office, and the Office of Technology Assessment) to provide expertise to its members (Bimber 1996). Legislators, eager not to be outflanked by the Executive Branch in policy making, created these new sources of congressional expertise (ibid.). Independent "think tanks" have increased in number over a similar time period, equally suggesting a market for policy expertise (Jenkins-Smith 1990; Ricci 1993; Smith 1991). Moreover, several scholars argue that both status and congressional access are allocated to interest groups who have reputations for being scientifically informed (Carpenter, Esterling, and Lazer 1998; Esterling 2004; Heclo 1978). Similar trends are occurring among state legislatures (Hird 2005). It is difficult to acknowledge this proliferation in sources of expertise across arenas of policy making while accepting the notion that rationalist justifications for decision making are in decline.

One approach to understanding science and policy making that captures elements of the two seemingly orthogonal trends in science in policy making is that of "co-production" (Jasanoff 2004a; Jasanoff and Wynne 1998). The term "co-production" refers to the notion that natural and social orders are produced together, a notion that avoids both natural and social determinism in explaining outcomes of interest (Jasanoff 2004a: 3). More important than avoiding the pitfalls of the "science wars," however, those advancing the idiom of co-production challenge the social sciences to address more directly the role of science and technology in culture and politics. Jasanoff (ibid.: 1) charges that the social sciences have "[retreated] into a conspiracy of silence" on the question of the relationship between science, technology, culture, and power. The co-production framework can address cultural and social elements of the advancement of "technoscientific" objects without discarding science and technology as powerful symbols of social order in current society.

A powerful application of the co-production framework comes from Clark Miller's (2004a) analysis of the role of the Intergovernmental Panel on Climate Change as a site for the renegotiation of scientific and political orders within a "global" context. Miller shows how the notion of global climate change altered the status of nation-states as capable actors in confronting global environmental problems. At the same time, Miller argues that scientists' representation of the environment in global terms gained credence only through institutional mechanisms that supported the notion that such claims were representative of broad, even global perspectives. Thus, the ability of scientists to argue that their understanding of climate change was universal depended on the creation of an institution that could advance that notion in a convincing framework of global representation.

Co-production addresses, among other things, the emergence and stabilization of new scientific/technical framings (Jasanoff 2004a: 38). This echoes Gieryn's discussion of the "obduracy" of certain science/non-science settlements, and it touches on one of the central themes of the present volume. Jasanoff argues that political order is expressed through institutions, and that institutions provide societies with "tried-and-true repertoires of problem-solving, including preferred forms of expertise, processes of inquiry, methods of securing credibility, and mechanisms for airing and managing dissent" (ibid.: 40). The co-production framework alerts us to the cultural and scientific underpinnings of such institutional arrangements and cautions against attending to only one of these in addressing an institution's origins.

Science for Environmental Policy Making

The above examples from political science and from the more interdisciplinary field of science and technology studies are consistent in their broad rejection of rationalist and positivist descriptions of the application of science in policy making. At the same time, although science does not seem especially useful in resolving policy debates, the availability of expertise and analysis is on the rise in several arenas of public decision making. Moreover, both the rationalist and the positivist conception of the role of science in policy making continue to have rhetorical significance among actors involved in policy making. Work by Jasanoff (1990) and by Stone (1989, 1997) point to the continued appeal of the notion that science will simplify policy making by clarifying what is true and beyond the realm of political debate, in spite of the fact that that notion is not supported by repeated experience.

The persistent view that science will simplify policy choices raises an important question about the role of scientists and science in policy making. If actors believe, or act as if they believe, that science produces reliable, objective information that may be of use in resolving policy debates, this belief will continue to be relevant for understanding policy-making processes. Such reliance on rationalist and positivist models of science in policy making can certainly be instrumental, as Stone points out. At the same time, some participants in policy making may turn to science because of an earnest belief in its objectivity and neutrality. If the idealized image of science informs participants' understanding of the role of science in decision making, then the rationalist and positivist models, though inaccurate, must be recognized for their symbolic importance in shaping actors' expectations and, potentially, in shaping outcomes. This may be especially true in domains, such as environmental policy, where participants view scientific and technical information as central. From an analytical standpoint, the challenge is to demonstrate the extent to which the rationalist and positivist accounts motivate interactions in the making of environmental policy without also suggesting that such accounts are accurate descriptions of science in society.

My analysis starts with the puzzle of the unique cultural authority of science. Though it cannot be adequately explained in rationalist or positivist terms, the authority of science is materially relevant through its expression in policy making. Though the status of science is invoked rhetorically, when that rhetoric is persuasive it becomes materially significant through the creation of public policy which allocates resources toward some goals and away from others.

In the next three chapters, I focus on negotiations of the science/policy boundary and examine the extent to which the negotiations themselves become the subject of policy debate. The capacity to keep such negotiations out of political discourse is a major concern of this analysis in that a lack of debate signals participants' acceptance of a particular settlement of the science/policy boundary.

2

Scientists and Agenda Setting

... the definition of alternatives is the supreme instrument of power; the antagonists can rarely agree on what the issues are because power is involved in the definition. He who determines what politics is about runs the country, and the choice of conflicts allocates power.
—Elmer Eric Schattschneider (1961: 68)

Because both time and resources limit the number of policy issues that will receive serious public attention, agenda setting is a competitive activity in the policy process with substantial consequences. Attention given to one issue naturally implies that some other issue will be overlooked. In view of the limits of the public agenda, the ability to place an issue on the agenda constitutes real political power (Schattschneider 1961; Cobb and Elder; 1983). Equally important is the ability to keep some issues from receiving serious attention in the public domain (Bachrach and Baratz 1962; Cobb and Ross 1997). If powerful actors' interests are served by denying agenda access, agenda setters can anticipate an uphill battle.

In this chapter, I consider the extent to which scientists play a role in agenda setting by analyzing scientists' early articulations about the policy ramifications of acid rain and climate change, respectively. Though scientists' initial statements typically made clear links between environmental degradation and the need to regulate energy use, scientists' agenda-setting activities were not met by a set of powerful actors seeking to undermine scientists' claims in order to keep acid rain and climate change out of public view.[1] Instead, policy makers accepted scientists' claims and moved quickly to give those claims institutional expression in the policy process without notable opposition or even significant deliberation. Once public officials granted formal agenda status to the respective issues, stakeholders—including scientists who disagreed with the early issue framings—began to debate the extent to which each issue posed an environmental problem and to clash over efforts to create regulatory programs to mitigate expected environmental effects.[2] Evidence cited in this chapter suggests that any study that started with the respective congressional debates over regulatory action on these two issues would miss the crucial period of early policy-making activity when scientists' claims were rapidly translated into policy action.

In this chapter, in order to understand this period of relative quiescence around the eventually contentious issues of acid rain and climate change, I examine scientists' claims about the two policy issues and analyze those claims in light of the idealized view of scientists as contributing to the policy process by providing objective information to decision makers. To the extent that scientists stepped out of their prescribed role, however, they were subject to little scrutiny that might expose boundary crossing that was not consistent with participants' expectations—idealized as they are—regarding scientific objectivity.

In this chapter, I consider features of agenda setting that make such accounting difficult. In comparison with other stages of the policy process, agenda setting stands out for its lack of an obvious institutional home and for its lack of structure or even semi-formal rules for participation. In this chapter, I focus on the effects of participation in a setting with such fungible norms for participation. In this more freeform environment, explicit conflicts over the science/policy boundary appear to be less common than they are in the more formalized venues for policy making.

In the first section, I present current theoretical approaches to the study of agenda-setting activities and explore the importance of focusing on those political activities that help place issues on the formal policy agenda. This section also introduces several tools that scholars who study agenda setting use to elucidate this crucial but under-studied stage of decision making. I then present empirical evidence from the cases and analyze the emergence of the science narratives for acid rain and for global warming up to the point that each issue is established on the formal policy agenda. The empirical evidence demonstrates that, for a period of time, scientists articulated science narratives for each issue, respectively, and were met with remarkably little criticism or counternarratives. I then draw on Baumgartner and Jones's concept of "Downsian mobilization" and Gieryn's exploration of "obduracy" to explain these respective periods of quiescence. I conclude the chapter with a discussion of the implications of the relatively uncontested institutionalization of each policy issue.[3]

Tools of Agenda Setting: Policy Narratives and Science Narratives

"Agenda setting" refers to the collection of activities that policy entrepreneurs engage in when they want to direct the attention of public officials—a decidedly scarce resource—toward a particular problem. The goal of agenda setting is to convince powerful policy actors to consider an issue and to consider that issue in a specific way. Getting the attention of public officials is a first step in convincing those officials to reallocate resources toward a desired policy outcome. However, as Cobb and Elder argue (1983: 172), agenda status is more than that:

> In giving an issue formal agenda status, government conveys important messages about who and what are socially important, about what is and is not problematic, and about what does and does not fall within the legitimate purview of government. Because these messages bear the imprimatur of public authority, they serve to define winners and losers in a social and political sense just as the more material allocations of government define them in an economic sense.

Scholars who study agenda setting focus primarily on discourse and framing. As Baumgartner and Jones (1993), Cobb and Elder (1983), and Stone (1989, 1990) show, the way an issue is framed can affect the likelihood that the issue will receive public attention and can shape the course of subsequent policy debate. The potential to influence subsequent events makes agenda setting a particularly important activity from the standpoint of understanding the exercise of political power.

Unfortunately, agenda setting is inherently difficult to research.[4] In spite of this, scholars have developed a number of concepts that facilitate to the study of agenda setting. Cobb and Elder (1983) began to conceptualize agenda setting by distinguishing between the systemic agenda and the formal agenda. "The systemic agenda" refers to the issues that the public and the news media consider pertinent to policy. "The formal agenda" refers to issues that are up for active consideration by public officials. This distinction clarifies the fact that issues can occupy space in one of these domains without attracting attention in the other. The systemic agenda may have room for more issues than the formal agenda in that the public can pay attention to any number of issues that do not receive formal consideration from elected officials. At the same time, elected officials are important agenda setters in their own right and can place on the formal agenda issues that had not been circulating in the systemic agenda (Kingdon 1996: 44).

Cobb and Elder's concept of different types of agenda status provides insight into what success in agenda setting might look like. Deborah Stone, in describing the tools used by agenda setters, gives scholars a way to analyze the activities that might lead to success. For Stone, the building blocks of agenda setting are persuasive stories that signal to other actors how to approach a particular policy issue. Stone calls these stories "policy narratives." Narratives tell us how to view a set of events and place those events into a meaningful context. When applied to policy making, a narrative can establish an event as a policy problem, allocate blame for that problem, and point to plausible solutions.[5] Policy narratives also argue for a policy response. In taking this step, a narrative contains not only descriptive elements, but also prescriptive ones. Not only does it make causal claims about a problem; it tells us how we should judge the events linked to that problem. Events that do not support the normative orientation of the narrative are often downplayed or disregarded in order to preserve the integrity of the narrative (von Meier, Miller, and Keller 1998: 29). In this way, a narrative can shape the interpretation of incoming information such that the narrative "entails or even imposes *a priori* pattern, rather than either revealing an intrinsic structure of events or accepting their contingency" (Paulson 1994: 12).

A narrative introduced into the policy arena must compete with other narratives for prominence in guiding the conceptualization of a policy problem. In this sense, narrative is argumentative; it asserts that the conceptualization of the issue it provides is the correct one. As a tool in policy debate, a narrative becomes "the medium through which actors try to impose their view of reality on others, suggest certain social positions and practices, and criticize alternative social arrangements" (Hajer 1993: 47). In forwarding a particular conceptualization of a policy problem, narratives rely on rhetorical devices (Litfin 1994: 39) and familiar plot lines (Paulson 1994: 12; Stone 1988: 108) that tap into deeply held values or beliefs. Narratives that combine these elements successfully are more readily accepted into the policy process.[6] In addition, the ability to portray a policy issue as resolvable is a crucial step in gaining status as an important problem on the public policy agenda (Cobb and Elder 1983: 176; Stone 1989: 284). Once accepted, decision makers often take for granted that the narrative is the appropriate way to view the policy problem. A policy narrative gains stability through institutional arrangements that grow in response to the narrative. Such arrangements consolidate the policy narrative as institutional activities reproduce and reinforce that particular view of the issue (Cobb and Elder 1983: 184; Baumgartner and Jones 1993; Hajer 1993: 46).[7]

Scientific claims made in the policy arena inevitably rely on narrative as a vehicle for transferring those claims. Without explanation or grounding, the implications of scientific findings are often elusive. Science narratives[8] provide this context and facilitate the transfer of information from the scientific community to the policy community.[9] Science narratives are interesting, first, because science is not typically associated with the more normative practice of story telling. Secondly, science narratives attract attention because of the particular status of science in policy debate.[10] Science narratives have an advantage in the policy arena in that reliance on scientific information is, itself, legitimizing. Narratives are often presented as if they are entirely factual, resting on the authority of science to advance a set of claims about policy making (Stone 1989: 282; Litfin 1994: 30). Science narratives, because they carry the implicit endorsement of the science community, are more likely than other narratives to be accepted as factual. Moreover, stating a policy problem in scientific terms suggests that that problem is within the realm of human control. The very act of explaining a problem through the application of science demonstrates that the problem is subject to the power of science (Paulson 1994: 19–20). In addition, by recognizing an event as a policy problem, scientists almost inevitably define themselves into the issue as part of its solution (Latour 1983; Hajer 1993; Zehr 1994a). Attention to science narratives is crucial in assessing the role that scientists play in the policy process in that it is through the science narrative that scientists provide a conceptual map that, if they are successful, establishes the relevance of their policy claims.

Another crucial theoretical framework is necessary to make sense of the activities that scientists engage in during the early phases of agenda setting in each case. The co-production framework argues strongly against assuming that meaning is produced in scientific settings and is then offered, neatly packaged, for non-scientists to consider. The co-production approach rejects such a simple, linear conception of how scientific ideas come to have status in non-science settings (Jasanoff and Wynne 1998: 4). A more realistic account, they argue, acknowledges contingency in the production of meaning and insists on including such contingencies in descriptions of how socially relevant scientific claims are produced. Evidence of co-production can be found in the case of climate change, where scientists' arguments about the reasons for studying climate change shift with prevailing social norms.[11] This serves as an important reminder that "science narratives," though actors in the policy process might wish to portray them as if they are objective products of scientific research, derive their meaning from social context and from shared societal values. That is, science narratives do not emerge fully formed from a politically and socially insulated scientific world. Rather, scientists, as the publicly visible actors who articulate science narratives, are inevitably anticipating and reacting to non-science actors who have a role in conferring or denying status to circulating science narratives.

The following sections present the empirical evidence for the early science narratives for acid rain and climate change. Before presenting empirical evidence from each case, the scope of agenda setting must be defined. Agenda setting, in view of its amorphousness in the policy-making process, is difficult to delineate. Here, scientific reports, articles published in journals and newspapers, and even statements made about the issue in early congressional hearings are considered. Because the goal of agenda setting is to place an issue on the formal policy agenda, consistent congressional attention is a powerful signal that agenda status has been achieved. However, the transition from agenda setting to legislative policy making does not occur at some obvious, identifiable point. Thus, in this chapter I will consider early public discussions concerning acid rain and climate change and point to the sporadic congressional attention that accompanied each issue's appearance on the systemic agenda. News media coverage of each issue provides a basis for examining public discussion of the issue that occurred prior to sustained congressional attention.

Acid Rain

Science and the Development of a Policy Problem
Perhaps the earliest statement of trans-boundary air pollution comes from the English writer John Evelyn. In his 1661 book *Fumifugium*, Evelyn reported that French farmers attributed crop damage in France to smoke coming from England (Gorham 1991: 19, Cowling 1982: 111A). Considerably later, in 1872, Robert Angus Smith coined the term

"acid rain." Smith used this term to label the phenomenon that he discovered 20 years earlier in his research of precipitation in and around Manchester, England. In a report he published in 1852, Smith noted that three types of rain—acid sulfate, sulfate of ammonia, and carbonate of ammonia—were associated, respectively, with the city's center, its suburbs, and the fields beyond the suburbs (Gorham 1981: 15; Cowling 1982: 111A).

Research both before and after Smith's work is characterized by a series of isolated findings that were produced in the absence of a self-conscious research community.[12] Awareness of a growing body of inter-related research began in the field of atmospheric chemistry. E. J. Conway, an Irish scientist, conducted the first modern review of the literature on precipitation chemistry in 1942. In 1948, a Swedish scientist, Hans Egnér, started the first large-scale precipitation chemistry network in Europe (Cowling 1982). These efforts to collect information published on precipitation chemistry and to coordinate data collection for continued study represent early instances of a research community working toward the accumulation of knowledge on a specific topic. This research community, however, did not extend beyond the field of atmospheric chemistry. In addition, there is no evidence that these researchers were aware of Smith's work.[13]

The genesis of a self-conscious acid rain research community began with the work of Svante Odén, who drew together insights from limnology, atmospheric chemistry, and agricultural research to articulate a modern understanding of the causes and potential effects of acid precipitation (Gorham 1981: 19; Cowling 1982: 114A). In 1967, Odén captured public attention with an article in the Swedish newspaper *Dagens Nyheter* in which he referred to acid rain as a "chemical war" among European countries (Cowling 1982: 114A). In 1968, Odén published his research in a more scientific publication, Sweden's *Ecology Committee Bulletin*. With these two publications, Odén addressed two distinct audiences: the public and scientists. Reactions from both audiences began to shape the subsequent mobilization around the issue of acid rain.[14]

Up to the point of Odén's work, the term "acid rain" had no resonance outside of a relatively small set of researchers.[15] Once Odén published his research, however, public officials took up the issue and gave it life in non-science settings. The Swedish government was the first to respond to Odén's articles by conducting a case study of acid rain that was presented at the United Nations Conference on the Human Environment (Gorham 1981: 19; Cowling 1982: 115A). The Swedish case study (Bolin et al. 1972) led to two major research efforts into acid rain. The Norwegian Interdisciplinary Research Programme, also know as the SNSF Project, conducted a study in order to establish the effects of acid rain on forests and fish (Gorham 1981: 19; Cowling 1982: 115A–116A). The Organization for Economic Cooperation and Development organized the second research effort (1973–1975), which focused on the transport and deposition of sulfur dioxide in Europe (Cowling 1982: 116A; VanDeveer 1998: 10–12). These research efforts placed institutional weight behind the issue of acid rain in Europe and brought increased attention to acid rain beyond the community of researchers involved. The involvement of the OECD and the United Nations, in particular, provided the basis for considering political action to curb trans-boundary air pollution (VanDeveer 1998).

Scientific attention to acid rain in North America can be traced to a Canadian study of the effects of metal smelting on the environment surrounding Sudbury, Ontario (Gordon and Gorham 1963). Though this study did not create the same kind of mobilization around the issue in Canada that Odén's publications did in Sweden (and in Europe, more generally), it did establish that the problem was not limited to Europe. In 1971, Odén contributed to increased awareness about the issue in the United States through a series of lectures delivered in various parts of the country (Cowling 1982: 117A). Though several studies on precipitation chemistry had been conducted in the United States starting in the 1920s, the first US publication to address acid rain in Odén's terms, connecting trans-boundary air pollution to ecosystem damage, was Likens, Bormann, and Johnson 1972. Likens, along with several colleagues, followed this study with a series of publications throughout the 1970s that provided a firm scientific base for the issue in the US context (Cowling 1982: 117A).

By the late 1970s, a number of coordinated efforts to study acid rain in the United States had emerged. In 1975, the US Forest Service sponsored the First International Symposium on Acid Precipitation and the Forest Ecosystem. In 1978, a number of American scientists established the National Acid Deposition Program (NADP), which enlisted the efforts of approximately 100 scientists in coordinating research on acid rain's effects and setting up a system for monitoring its occurrence (Galloway et al. 1978; Cowling 1982). One year later, NADP scientists were asked by the Carter administration to draw up a plan for a federally funded and organized program of research into the causes and effects of acid rain. Congress turned this plan into law through the National Acid Precipitation Assessment Act of 1980, which established a ten-year research effort—the National Acid Precipitation Assessment Program (NAPAP)—to study acid rain. An analysis of the science narrative made public by Odén and his colleagues sheds light on the rapid uptake of this issue among governmental actors.

The Acid Rain Science Narrative

Consistent with Stone's discussion of policy narratives, the science narrative for acid rain contains a causal story. In addition, however, that causal story is embedded in the politically relevant stories of decline and control. An example of the causal story for acid rain taken from the National Acid Precipitation Assessment Program presents scientifically grounded information without interpreting that information in terms of its potential policy relevance:

Sulfate and nitrate are the two primary negatively charged ions (anions) in acidic deposition. When these anions are balanced by hydrogen ions, an acidifying chemical compound (sulfuric and/or nitric acid) results. The major concern about the aquatic effects of acidic deposition is that surface waters will lose ANC (acid neutralizing capacity), which would result in increased acidity (lower pH)[16] and increased inorganic aluminum, which is toxic to aquatic organisms. (NAPAP 1991: 13)[17]

When presented without any interpretation of its political import, this statement generated remarkably little controversy among scientists or policy makers. It also provided very little guidance.

Scientists who participated in creating a science narrative for acid rain, beginning with Odén, rarely presented acid rain only in terms of this causal argument. Notably, Odén called acid rain Europe's "chemical war," clearly offering a political orientation toward what otherwise might be a scientifically defined problem. Though few scientific statements are as provocative as Odén's, most contain both decline and control stories and makes an unequivocal case for policy action. The National Academy of Sciences' first report on acid rain provides an example of a science narrative that embeds the causal story in a larger framework of decline:

Ecologists, geochemists, and climatologists are beginning to discover that in many respects man is now operating on nature's own scale, particularly through the heavy use of fossil fuels to supply the energy that runs our industrial civilization. Because the uncertainties associated with such large-scale operations are very great—for good or for ill—it behooves us to exercise restraint in our present intensive use of energy, and to mitigate where possible the ill effects that air pollution imposes not only on us but also on the ecosystems that make up our life support system. . . . Perhaps the first well-demonstrated widespread effect of burning fossil fuel is the destruction of soft-water ecosystems by "acid rain," which has been caused by anthropogenic emissions of sulfur and nitrogen oxides that are further oxidized in the atmosphere. Major effects include destruction of many species of fish and their prey and acidification of surface and ground waters to the point where toxic trace metals reach concentrations undesirable for human consumption and for aquatic animal habitats. (NRC 1981: 2–3)

This quotation contains the causal story: sulfur dioxide and nitrogen oxide emissions, further oxidized in the atmosphere, create deposition that acidifies aquatic systems. The NAS statement, however, goes considerably beyond the simple explanation of acid rain and offers a particular understanding about why the public should care and respond to the threat of acid rain. In particular, the National Academy takes a clear policy position on acid rain by arguing that we should act to mitigate the effects of air pollution to protect humans and ecosystems.

The control story also surfaces in the science narrative for acid rain. Specifically, scientists often call for scientific research as a prerequisite for political action. Scientists argue not only that there is a problem to confront, but also that, through science, we can reverse or mitigate the problem.[18] According to the science narrative, investment in continued scientific research will facilitate the work of policy makers by providing them with better information about the causal mechanisms and the effects of acid rain. The following statement is a typical example of the view that scientific research will provide answers to policy makers:

Research [on acid precipitation] is the key to improved understanding. Improved understanding is the key to wiser public and private decisions that relate to the use of energy and to the quality of life in our society. Let us get on with the job of learning so that the challenge of managing acid precipitation and its effects can begin as soon as possible. (Cowling 1982: 121A)

Calls for governmental support of scientific research on acid rain are routine in the public statements that scientists make about the issue and reflect a relatively common view that such research will produce information that will be useful to decision makers.

Multiple instances of scientists' statements about acid rain and media treatments of the issue are consistent with the examples cited above in that they contain the causal story and interpretation of that story. The interpretation might be focused on discuss ecosystem degradation or on the capacity of scientific research to guide policy makers in responding to the science-identified problem.[19] Often, statements from scientists include all three of these elements: (1) a causal story, (2) an interpretation of harmful effects on ecosystems, and (3) a statement about the role of science in mitigating the problem.

An additional theme that emerges in the acid rain science narrative is uncertainty in scientists' understanding of acid rain. The element of uncertainty is important in stabilizing the science narrative in that it allows for learning and adjustment as new information is incorporated into scientists' and society's collective understanding of the problem. By highlighting uncertainty, scientists signal to their public audience that elements of the science narrative can be expected to change. Claims that forests and agricultural production were at risk from acid rain were common in early statements about acid rain. However, both of these claims were eventually revised in light of evidence showing that forest decline is caused by multiple stressors, one of which might be acid deposition. High-elevation red spruce forests, however, did appear to be susceptible specifically to acid rain (NAPAP 1987: I-27–I-30; 1991: 45–46). Research also suggested that most crops either were resistant to acid rain or benefited from the natural fertilizer delivered through the deposition of nitrogen oxides (NAPAP 1987: I-25, 1991: 45–46).[20] In addition, early discussions of possible effects on human health focused on the potential for heavy metals to be leached into waterways such that humans could be exposed to heavy metals through drinking water or through consuming fish from acidified lakes (NAPAP 1987). While subsequent research did not substantiate fears about increased human exposure to heavy metals, there is evidence that the pollutants that cause acid rain have negative effects on human health (ibid., 1991).

Comparing scientists' statements about acid rain made in the 1990s with those made in the 1970s, there is consistency in how they discuss damage to aquatic systems from acid rain, damage to buildings and materials, and decreased visibility. Scientists' emphasis on their uncertainty about effects of acid rain created room for the science narrative to evolve in light of scientific research. In spite of refinements in scientists' claims about the effects of acid rain, there appears to have been sufficient consistency over time to substantiate the idea that scientists were producing reliable information about the environmental policy problem. Moreover, the idea of acid rain as a policy problem and the view that scientific research would help solve that problem were sufficiently convincing to spark a period of institution building that provided a supportive venue for the acid rain science narrative over the course of a ten-year period of legislative debate.

Consequences of the Acid Rain Science Narrative

The agenda status of acid rain was uncertain in 1968, when Odén published his newspaper article. However, by 1972 public officials were already conducting research on acid rain that would test Odén's claims (Bolin 1972). In the United States, the first government action was taken in 1975, when the Forest Service and the National Science Foundation convened a conference to gather researchers to study the impacts of acid rain on forests in the United States (USDA 1976).[21] In the same year, acid rain made its first congressional appearance in a hearing on the human health effects of automobile emissions. Although most of the witnesses did not mention acid rain, this hearing gave scientists involved in acid rain research their first opportunity to discuss the problem in a formal appearance before elected officials (HCSST 1975a). Acid rain quickly achieved systemic agenda status. Formal agenda status was not far behind, when public officials took up the issue and decided to devote money to research. Prior to congressional action, individual Executive Branch agencies, on their own initiative, were conducting small-scale, isolated research projects.[22] Ultimately, however, President Carter called for a coordinated and systematically funded federal effort and encouraged Congress to pass legislation to create a National Acid Precipitation Assessment Program. Congress obliged in 1980.

Although major features of the science narrative traced here became subjects of considerable debate, especially in the context of proposed regulations to curb acid rain, the acid rain science narrative received little if any public criticism before 1980. In fact, in the first three congressional hearings that mentioned acid rain, not one witness challenged the science narrative that was presented (HCSST 1975a, 1979, 1980). The *New York Times*'s coverage of acid rain in the years 1972–1980 was similarly uncritical of the science narrative, the first sign of opposition appearing more than 10 years after Odén's first newspaper publication (figure 2.1).[23] There is ample evidence that acid rain was on the systemic agenda during this period. Specifically, newspaper coverage began before congressional hearings were held on acid rain and well before it became an established topic of congressional debate (figure 2.2). Moreover, several agencies produced reports concerning acid rain during the period of early

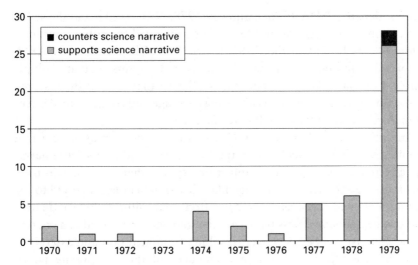

Figure 2.1
Number of stories on acid rain in *New York Times* by year, 1970–1979. Source: Historical *New York Times* Database. N.B.: Stories that advanced the idea that long-range transport of sulfur dioxide and nitrogen oxides produced acidic deposition that had the potential to damage forests, soils, surface waters and aquatic life were coded as supporting the science narrative. Stories that countered this understanding of the causes or consequences of acid rain were coded as countering the science narrative.

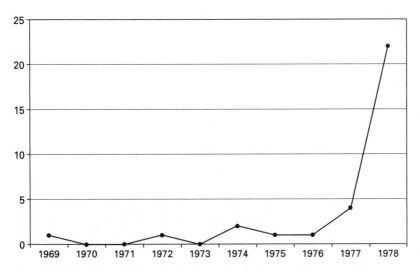

Figure 2.2
Number of newspaper stories mentioning acid rain by year, 1969–1978. Source: LexisNexis database of "general news" in "major papers." Articles were located by searching for the term "acid rain" in the full text.

public debate (USDA 1976; Galloway 1978; NRC 1981), and the scientific community began to produce reports intended for public consumption (Likens 1972; Cowling 1982; D'Itri 1982). The creation of NAPAP signified definitive formal agenda status in Congress in that multiple elected officials had to support the legislation that created the research program. After this period, both media coverage and congressional attention to the issue intensified (figures 2.3, 2.4).

Scientists—including Svante Odén—were instrumental in creating public awareness of acid rain in the 1980s. The acid rain science narrative contains the argument, implicit or explicit, that the acid rain issue merits a place on the political agenda. This argument is connected to the causal link made between ecosystem effects and sulfur dioxide and nitrogen oxide emissions. This basic causal argument is packaged in a context that emphasizes negative effects resulting from acid rain and asserts the role of scientific research as a component of the appropriate policy response. In this regard, the science narrative about acid rain is much

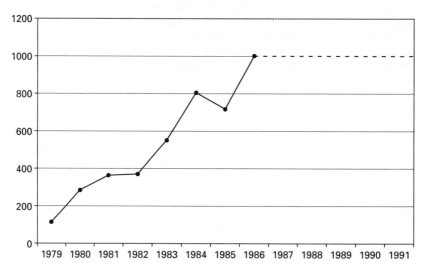

Figure 2.3
Number of newspaper stories mentioning acid rain by year, 1979–1991. Source: LexisNexis database of "General News" in "Major Papers." N.B.: From 1986 to 1991, the database contains more than 1,000 entries per year. Specific figures for these years are, therefore, not available, as the LexisNexis search engine will not return search results for searches that yield more than 1,000 stories. Thus, the dashed line indicates that there are at least 1,000 stories per year from 1986 to 1991.

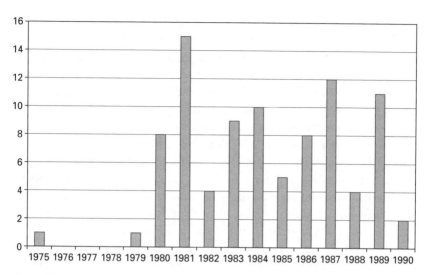

Figure 2.4
Number of hearings on acid rain by year, 1975–1990. Source: LexisNexis Congressional Publications

like other policy narratives in that a scientifically grounded causal argument is placed within a larger story of decline and control. What is particular about the science narrative for acid rain is that it was so quickly adopted by policy makers, who, with little deliberation, allocated substantial federal resources to the study of acid rain and initiated discussions in Congress about a regulatory program to limit acid rain's precursors. Though interests groups and legislators subsequently engaged in protracted negotiations and spent the better part of a decade battling over the potential for a federal regulatory response to the problem, the initial period of agenda setting was notably free of debate. Moreover, policy makers created an institutional home for the science narrative in the form of NAPAP, an organization that, once created, communicated three consistent messages to the public: (1) that there was enough scientific evidence to support viewing acid rain as a pressing environmental problem, (2) that the problem warranted the active attention of policy makers and the expenditure of public resources, and (3) that additional scientific research would provide decision makers with necessary information and thus merited investment.

In looking back at this period of easy institutionalization of scientists' claims, we must not overlook the subsequent period of protracted debate, during which several components of the acid rain science narrative were challenged.[24] At the same time, the creation of NAPAP not only signaled that the issue quickly achieved formal agenda status; it cemented that status and ensured that regular attention would be paid to the issue after the appearance of each NAPAP publication. NAPAP, though it was ultimately criticized for not providing policy-relevant information, played a role in the process that has been largely overlooked. NAPAP provided a stable venue for the idea of acid rain as a policy problem, thus acting as a powerful symbol of the original science narrative. The creation of NAPAP provides a clear example of Cobb and Elder's argument about the role of the government in conferring status and legitimacy on a topic by giving that topic formal agenda status. The creation of NAPAP signaled broad congressional interest in acid rain, and its statutory authority ensured that the Congress would be formally visiting and revisiting the issue for at least the 10 years of NAPAP's initial authorization.

Climate Change

Science and the Development of a Policy Problem

In 1896, in an attempt to explain the driving force behind ice ages and interglacial periods, the Swedish chemist Svante Arrhenius predicted global warming.[25] Arrhenius coined the term "the greenhouse effect" and argued that higher levels of carbon dioxide in the atmosphere would trap solar radiation, thereby increasing temperatures by 5 or 6 degrees Celsius (Weart 2003: 5–8). Arrhenius's prediction did not attract much attention, in part because the idea of warming, in and of itself, did not seem threatening, but also because several questions about the theory remained unanswered. Specifically, experiments showed no increase in absorption of infrared radiation when more CO_2 was added to air samples. In fact, these experiments demonstrated that the atmosphere was basically saturated with heat-trapping gases, and that additional gas produced no additional infrared absorption. Fifty years later, however, Gilbert Plass showed that that the atmosphere's absorption potential was only saturated at lower altitudes. The upper atmosphere, in contrast, could absorb more infrared radiation if concentrations of heat-trapping gases increased (Plass 1956). Plass's research demonstrated that the changes in the chemical composition of the atmosphere could alter the energy balance of the planet and lead to an increase in its average temperature.

A second potential flaw in Arrhenius's prediction was the expectation that CO_2, because of its potential to be absorbed into the oceans, would never accumulate in the atmosphere. Two crucial advances in scientific understanding of the CO_2 in the atmosphere turned global warming from a far-fetched theory into a reputable topic for scientific research. First, Roger Revelle and Hans Seuss (1957) demonstrated that the oceans would not absorb anthropogenic CO_2 fast enough to prevent increases in atmospheric concentrations of the gas. Second, Charles Keeling (1960) developed a technique for measuring concentrations of CO_2 in the atmosphere and showed definitely that they were increasing. With these discoveries, scientists were inclined to believe that industrialization could significantly change the chemistry of the atmosphere. At this point, Revelle introduced the public to the idea of climate change.

Climate Change in the 1950s and the 1970s—Two Instances of Framing

Roger Revelle was the first scientist in the United States to argue publicly for federal funds for research on global warming. Revelle appeared before Congress to discuss the goals of an international scientific research effort called the International Geophysical Year. Researchers created the IGY to facilitate coordination of geophysical research during an 18-month period in 1957 and 1958.[26] Revelle testified about the IGY at a congressional hearing in 1956 (HCoA 1956). Though global warming was not the central focus of the IGY, Revelle presented global warming to make his case for congressional funding. During his testimony, Revelle uttered his now-famous characterization of global warming, calling it a "tremendous geophysical experiment" (ibid.: 467).[27] Curiously, Revelle did not frame global warming as an environmental problem. He began his testimony that day by comparing the effort of scientists to secure funding for the IGY to Christopher Columbus asking "the sovereigns of Spain" for money to support his exploration (ibid.: 465–466). Later in his testimony, Revelle posited that, as a consequence of global warming, the Arctic Ocean might become navigable and open Russia's Arctic coastline for shipping. In a written statement that is included in the hearing record, Revelle notes that adding CO_2 to the atmosphere might have "a very large effect," but he never says whether the effect will be good or bad (ibid.: 468). Revelle does mention one potential negative impact when he suggests that climate change could result in changing weather patterns and gives the example of hurricanes along the East

Coast of the United States (ibid.: 479). Overall, his discussion of the "experiment" suggests more scientific curiosity than fear of the consequences of climate change.[28] In light of the fact that global warming is now considered a pressing environmental problem, Revelle's characterization is noteworthy in that he framed the issue largely in scientific terms and argued for federal dollars to advance knowledge for the sake of knowledge. This framing was consistent with a prevalent view in the 1950s that the federal government should support basic research.[29] Revelle's comments regarding the vast "geophysical experiment" may have influenced members of Congress in their decision to fund the IGY, which they did through special appropriations. Then, except in two follow-up hearings on the progress and accomplishments of the IGY, global warming disappeared from the congressional agenda for more than 10 years.[30]

When global warming reappeared on the congressional agenda in the early 1970s, it was framed in decidedly more negative terms. Three factors might account for the reemergence of the issue and for its more negative framing. One, scientists began to explore the idea of significant and rapid changes in the climate.[31] This research led to theories of positive feedbacks in the climate system according to which a small change in the climate would trigger further changes that would enhance the original effect. In response to these scientific discussions of rapid climate change, scientists began, at least sporadically, to discuss the potential for climate change to have negative environmental effects. For example, in 1963 the Conservation Foundation sponsored a conference of climate scientists and produced a report that predicted significant warming from an increase in atmospheric CO_2 and linked that warming to potentially harmful effects, including a rise in sea level (Conservation Foundation 1963). The National Academy of Sciences subsequently convened several panels to address climate change. The report from the first panel argued that climate change was possible, but suggested that there was no immediate threat from warming (NRC 1966). However, several panels convened in the 1970s listed a number of potentially negative consequences, including disruptions in food supplies (NRC 1976), water shortages (NRC 1977a), substantial warming (NRC 1977b: 24), changes in patterns of ocean circulation (ibid.: 25), and melting of polar ice in the Artic Ocean (ibid.: 125).

Although worry about negative environmental effects mounted in the 1970s, it is not as if these outcomes were completely unknown in the mid 1950s. For example, Revelle discussed the possibility of melting polar ice during his testimony in 1956 (HCoA 1956). For Revelle, melting polar ice might open more ports in Russia, an outcome that does not necessarily carry negative connotations. Notably, the shift in how scientists presented climate change followed the surge in environmentalism that occurred in the United States after Rachel Carson's book *Silent Spring*, published in 1962, became a best-seller. Although discussions of the impacts of global warming may have increased awareness of the potential for human harm to the environment, the timing suggests that scientists were reacting to environmentalism more than environmentalists were reacting to the predictions of climate scientists. Environmentalism was gaining social ground in the United States in the 1960s, but not until the 1970s did it begin to become routine for scientific reports about climate change to list its possible environmental effects.[32]

A revision of the social contract for science may have been a third factor in the change in how scientists discussed climate change in public settings. In particular, public officials began in the 1960s to demand better accounting practices among researchers receiving federal funds and to assess the extent to which federally funded scientific research produced useful applications (Guston 2000: 72–81). This shift toward a more instrumental justification for public funding of science may have affected how scientists saw their own work, or at least how they justified their research publicly. Certainly, this more instrumental approach appears in scientists' discussion of climate change research in the 1970s. In particular, after a number of droughts and crop failures in the early 1970s, Congress brought climate change back to its agenda in a 1976 hearing on a proposed research program on climate (HCSST 1976).[33] This proposal culminated in the National Climate Program Act of 1978. During the hearings, scientists were much more likely than their counterparts testifying in the 1950s to discuss the expected negative effects of climate change. Though many scientists testified in the 1970s that it was important to establish a national research program to learn more about the role of fossil fuels in climate change, most of the witnesses discuss the potential for climate research to facilitate weather prediction in a way that would support agricultural production and water resource management.[34]

It is certainly possible that all these forces were acting together in such a way that scientists had a more negative view of climate change in the 1970s than they did in the 1950s. Alternatively, scientists in the 1970s might have learned to present the practical implications of basic research to policy makers. What is important to note is that the shift in framing does not seem to come from new findings that led scientists to understand the consequences of climate change differently. This transformation in the framing of climate change in public settings demonstrates the extent to which such framings are products of the social and political context in which they originate. At the same time, in each period, scientists were able to act as legitimate spokespersons in arguing that for climate change was an important policy issue.

The Climate Change Science Narrative
The fact that there were two distinct periods in which scientists "went public" with information about climate change is instructive in that the science narrative for climate change was not the same in the second period as it had been in the first. The causal story for climate change was largely unchanged from its initial public appearance (that is, when Revelle argued that atmospheric increases in CO_2 were likely to cause global warming). An important caveat is that if Revelle were testifying today he would undoubtedly include a longer list of greenhouse gases that, like CO_2, have heat-trapping potential and are increasing in the atmosphere.[35] The addition of the longer list of greenhouse gases, however, would require no additional adjustment in Revelle's discussion of the phenomenon. Surprisingly, this even extends to Revelle's examples of likely effects of global warming, including his prediction of the loss of sea ice in the Artic and the potential for an increase in the frequency of hurricanes experienced by the United States—two present-day phenomena that most scientists now link to global warming.[36]

Likewise, scientists are fairly consistent in the application of a control framing when comparing the 1950s with the 1970s and later years. In fact, Revelle's characterization of the increase in CO_2 to the atmosphere as an "experiment" is a quintessential example of a control story in that experiments are successful when they are able to exercise control over conditions in a way that allows scientists to separate causation from correlation. Revelle, in a turn of phrase, summarily reduces one of the consequences of industrialization to a phenomenon that fits in the confines of the laboratory and can be manipulated by scientists through the scientific method.

Although the causal story for climate change and the control framing were stable from the 1950s onward,[37] the idea of climate change as an environmental problem requiring a societal response did not emerge until the 1970s. This framing contains the "decline story" that was common in the acid rain science narrative articulated in the same period. For example, the potential for disruption of ecosystems and the role of scientists in preventing such disruptions are evident in a 1971 report written by an international group of atmospheric scientists:

The implications of inadvertent climate modification, both in terms of direct impact on man and the biosphere and of the hard choices that societies might face to prevent such impacts, are profound. Should preventive or remedial action be necessary, it will almost certainly require effective cooperation among the nations of the world. [The Study of Man's Impact on Climate] was developed to assist in this process by providing an international scientific consensus on what we know and do not know and how to fill the gaps. It is hoped that this consensus will provide an important input into planning for the 1972 United Nations Conference on the Human Environment and for numerous other national and international activities. (SMIC 1971: xv)[38]

Likewise, a report from the National Research Council published in 1977 contains both decline and control framings:

The results of the present study should lead neither to panic nor to complacency. They should, however, engender a lively sense of urgency in getting on with the work of illuminating the issues that have been identified and resolving the scientific uncertainties that remain. Because the time horizon for both consequences and action extends well beyond usual boundaries, it is timely that attention be directed to research needs and to the anticipation of possible societal decision making now. The principal conclusion of this study is that the primary limiting factor on energy production from fossil fuels over the next few centuries may turn out to be the climatic effects of the release of carbon dioxide. This conclusion follows from a review of the models that transform increased carbon dioxide in the atmosphere into an associated rise in global temperatures. (NRC 1977b: viii)

A similar framing is used in an article published in *Nature* in 1987:

The inhabitants of planet Earth are quietly conducting a gigantic environmental experiment.[39] So vast and so sweeping will be the consequences that, were it brought before any responsible council for approval, it would be firmly rejected. Yet it goes on with little interference from any jurisdiction or nation. The experiment in question is the release of CO_2 and other so-called 'greenhouse gases' to the atmosphere. . . . Although we don't know nearly enough about the operation of the Earth's climate to make reliable predictions of the consequences of the build-up of greenhouse gases, we do know enough to say that the effects are potentially quite serious. (Broecker 1987: 123, 126)[40]

These negative framings represent an important shift in the science narrative for climate change.

In discussing the climate change science narrative, one must not overlook a crucial shift in the locus of expertise and the techniques developed for the study of climate change—in particular, the shift from studying local weather to modeling global climate (Edwards 2001; Miller 2004a). Initially, data collection regarding climate was based on statistical analysis of local weather data (Weart 2003: 10–12; Edwards 2001: 32). The development of computer models, however, offered a tool for analyzing the climate on a planetary scale (Edwards 2001: 33). Miller argues that this shift was necessary before the idea of an international response to climate change might be mounted (2004a). In spite of this, there is evidence that a number of scientists were thinking in global terms before the late 1970s, when general circulation models were initially developed. Weart, for instance, argues that the scientists who pressed for increased scientific attention to global warming were outsiders to the field of meteorology and were motivated by the unsolved mystery of what drove the shift in climate from ice ages to interglacial periods (2003: 9–19). The scale of change involved in the shift from an ice age to an interglacial period is much greater than what we traditionally think of as "weather." This suggests that conceptualizations of "planetary physics" predated the use of computer models to study climate.

Also noteworthy is that some scientists who were active in publicizing the issue of climate change beyond scientific circles articulated the issue as a planetary one well before the use of general circulation models (GCMs). Revelle statement regarding the "tremendous geophysical experiment" characterizes the problem at the level of the planet rather than at the level of regions of the Earth or ecosystems. (HCoA 1956: 467–468). His characterization is not surprising when one considers that his scientific contribution to the field centered on the capacity of the oceans to absorb atmospheric CO_2—something that is measured on the planetary scale.

The National Research Council, in its earliest report on climate change, discussed both "weather and climate modification" and included a focus on the "macrodynamics of the worldwide atmospheric circulation" (1966: 88). Miller points out that this report, in spite of its appreciation of global-scale phenomenon, emphasized local effects and made no argument for an international response (2004a: 53). Five years later, a group of scientists centered at MIT wrote a report to encourage policy makers to raise the issue of climate change (SMIC 1971). That report distinguished between "weather" and "climate" (9) and emphasized the need for research that would capture global-level phenomena (ibid.: 6, 15). Importantly, it also called for an international response and for international organizations, such as the UN, to implement the report's recommendations (ibid.: 4–5).

These early examples of scientists "going public" with the issue of climate change do not undermine the importance of the shift from the study of weather to the study of climate, insofar as it was not certain at the time that the planetary focus would eventually dominate. However, these early public statements did include a planetary framing of the issue, and they ensured that the shift in the scientific community with respect to the techniques for studying climate change did not require any significant re-articulation of the problem of climate change.

The science narrative articulated for climate change, like the acid rain science narrative, plays an important role in policy making in that it argues that the public should be concerned about human-induced climate change and that scientists, through further research, will be able to shed light on the problem and enable enlightened decision making. Also similar to the acid rain case is the fact that scientists' public statements about climate change often highlight uncertainties. The focus on uncertainties sensitizes the audience for the science narrative to the potential for scientists to make revisions and refinements to the science narrative over time.

The Consequences of the Climate Change Science Narrative

During the 1980s, climate change occupied a more permanent place both on the congressional agenda and in the print media than it did after its first congressional appearance in 1956.[41] In fact, 1983 was the only year between 1980 and 2006 in which Congress did not hold a hearing that addressed climate change.[42] Moreover, climate change, instead of being raised in the context of other policy concerns, became an issue in its own right. In fact, the first hearing to portray climate change as an environmental issue in which the climate itself becomes the "environment" needing protection, occurred in 1980 (SCENR 1980). After the 1970s, hearings on climate change did not address the issue primarily in terms of downstream effects, such as water or food shortages.[43] Instead, the post-1980 hearings routinely addressed the current state of scientific

knowledge, the need for more federal research, and the likely policy
options for mitigating climate change.[44]

Although there is a gap in congressional attention to climate change
from the 1950s to the 1970s, the print media covered the issue continually from the 1950s onward. However, the *New York Times*'s coverage
of the issue during this period is characterized by a marked shift in tone.
From 1951 (when its first story on climate change appeared) to 1979,
the *Times* ran nearly 50 stories on climate change. Many of the early
stories do not mention effects other than warming itself. In addition,
warming is not framed either positively or negatively in those stories.
After 1968, however, the preponderance of stories mention negative
outcomes associated with warming (figure 2.5). This shift in tone is
consistent with an increase in popular attention to environmental issues
in the United States.

The number of newspaper stories on climate change from the 1950s
through the 1970s suggests that climate change generated sufficient public

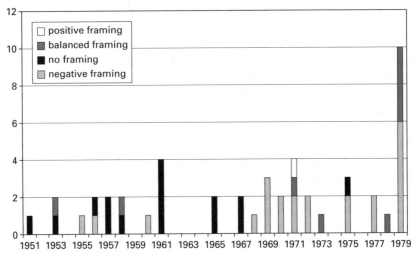

Figure 2.5
Number of stories on global warming in *New York Times* by year, 1951–1979,
categorized by framing. Source: Historical *New York Times* Database. Stories
that mentioned positive impacts were coded as "positive framing," stories mentioning negative impacts were coded as "negative framing," and stories mentioning both positive and negative impacts were coded as "balanced framing." Stories
that did not discuss possible impacts were coded as "no framing."

interest to warrant consistent, if low-level, media coverage. Formal agenda status for the issue was episodic before the 1980s. Then, following two reports produced by working groups of international scientists, congressional and media attention increase dramatically. The first report was published by the International Council for Science, the United Nations Environment Program, and the World Meteorological Organization after a conference of climate scientists in Villach, Austria in 1985 (ICSU, UNEP, and WMO 1986). The Senate Committee on Environment and Public Works discussed the recommendations of the that report in its hearing on global warming in 1985 (SCEPW 1985b). A second report, coordinated by National Aeronautics and Space Administration, collected the work of 150 scientists from eleven countries and argued that the increases of greenhouse gases in the atmosphere constituted a "totally uncontrolled experiment with no kind of knowledge of where we are going in the end" (Shabecoff 1986). In that phrase, the NASA report drew from language from Revelle and Suess's 1957 publication, but added a negative tone by suggesting that the "experiment" engendered a loss of control.

The *New York Times* first covered the NASA report in January of 1986 (Shabecoff 1986). Print-media stories on global warming that same year totaled 59, whereas there had been only 22 in 1985.[45] Congressional attention made a similar leap. The NASA report was covered in a congressional hearing held in 1986, the only hearing on global warming in that year. Seven hearings were then held in 1987 (figure 2.6). Many

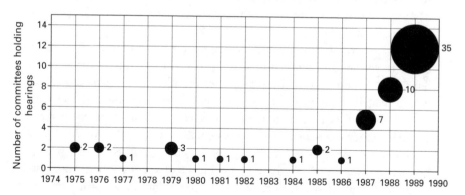

Figure 2.6
Number of hearings covering climate change by year, 1974–1990. (Size of "bubble" represents number of hearings.) Source: LexisNexis Congressional Publications.

scholars attribute attention to global warming to the extremely hot summer in 1988. The scientist James Hansen declared before a Senate committee that he was 95 percent confident that the summer's heat was attributable to anthropogenic increases in greenhouse gases (SCENR 1988a).[46] Hansen certainly helped to fix global warming in the minds of policy makers and the public, but clearly the increase in congressional attention predates his testimony.[47]

The institutionalization of global warming as a policy problem took notably longer than the similar institutionalization of the acid rain issue. Not until 1989, after the issue had been on the systemic agenda for at least 10 years, did President George H. W. Bush organize the United States Global Change Research Program to support climate change research.[48] The USGCRP was enacted through congressional statute the following year—a clear sign of formal agenda status.[49] However, in a parallel with the acid rain issue, the climate change science narrative was rarely countered in the period preceding formal agenda status. From 1976 to 1990, the climate change issue was addressed in 66 congressional hearings. The first instance of a witness with scientific credentials offering a framing of climate change that countered the science narrative presented here occurred in 1989 during a hearing before the House Committee on Merchant Marine and Fisheries: a statistician argued that only slight warming had been detected and that it could not be definitely linked to increases in greenhouse gases (HCMMF 1989: 23–26).[50] Reviewing the hearings during this time period, we find that witnesses reinforced scientists' framing of climate change rather than challenging it.[51]

Scientists' framing of climate change also dominated media attention to the issue. The story here is less straightforward than the story of what happened in congressional hearings, yet the idea that greenhouse gases would lead to an increase in global average temperature with negative consequences for the environment and society accounts for 90 percent of the coverage the issue receives between 1975 and 1988, overwhelming the counter-narratives (figure 2.7).[52] This finding is especially surprising because during the 1970s there was evidence of slight cooling. Scientists who were predicting warming had to contend with an empirical record that was not clearly substantiating their story. Though there were relatively few stories about climate change in the media during the 1970s, even during the period when the temperature record might have called the greenhouse warming theory into question, 83 percent of the news-

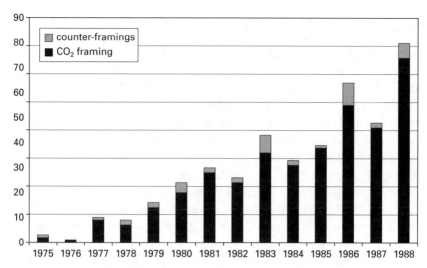

Figure 2.7
Number of newspaper stories on climate change by year, 1975–1988. Source: LexisNexis database of "General News" in "Major Papers." Stories were coded as supporting or as countering the idea of CO_2-induced warming. Ideas countering CO_2-induced warming included warming caused by solar activity, natural variation in climate, volcanoes as a source of warming, and global cooling.

paper stories about climate change cited warming as more likely than cooling or no change in global average temperature. During the 1980s, when global average temperatures started once again to climb, the percentage of stories that presented climate change in terms consistent with the science narrative jumped to 91. These data illustrate the overwhelming tendency of the media to reinforce the existing science narrative that linked increases in greenhouse gases to an increase global average temperature that would ultimately have negative environmental and social consequences.[53]

Though members of Congress and the news media accepted and reinforced the climate change science narrative, others shaped the science narrative by offering more specific interpretations of its likely social and environmental consequences. Miller shows that a number of agencies interested in climate change during the 1970s framed the issue in ways that suited their respective organizational missions—for example, the Central Intelligence Agency framed climate change in terms of its potential to affect national security, while the Department of Energy saw an opportunity to oversee the development of technological solutions to the problem of climate change (2000: 214–215). Miller's analysis illustrates the flexibility of the decline story used to frame climate change. The science narrative did argue that climate change was a problem that should be studied (and, it was hoped, averted). But the decline story for climate change did not specify that the problem was one of water shortages, one of interruptions in food production, or one of threats to national security; it might be all of these. Like the acid rain narrative, the climate change science narrative often touched on uncertainty in predicting outcomes. This created room for the narrative to evolve and created room for interpretation of the narrative across multiple organizational contexts. What the science narrative did specify was that further research was needed to create a more precise picture of the expected negative effects. In this sense, the organizations that were interpreting climate change within the context of their respective organizational missions were adding meaning to the problem while accepting scientists' claim that there was a problem and reinforcing the idea that the problem called for additional research and government involvement. Miller's analysis demonstrates that treating the science narrative as if scientists had found an environmental problem and simply communicated that to policy makers leaves out the important role of non-science actors in grounding the science narrative organizationally, politically, socially, and culturally.

Scientists' dependence on public officials is further demonstrated by the fact that scientists, when relying on their own resources, cannot create a venue for an issue in the policy arena. Policy venues are most likely to be established and institutionalized as a consequence of decision makers dedicating public resources to an issue. Through that process, policy makers add their own interpretations of what an issue "means" in policy terms. The activities on the part of agencies writing about climate change in the 1970s do not appear to have been efforts to argue against one another's framings of climate change or against the early scientific framing of the issue. For example, the National Research Council report cited by Miller comes from a series of NRC reports intended to provide policy makers with pertinent information about geophysics, including a report on water and climate (NRC 1977a) and one on energy and climate (NRC 1977b). The report on water and climate includes the following statement on "deliberate and inadvertent" climate change:

'Leaders in climatology and economics are in agreement that a climatic change is taking place, and that it has already caused major economic problems throughout the world.'— CIA, 1974

The CIA report from which the above quote was extracted must surely rank as one of the most widely publicized and discussed documents in the history of climatology. . . . What appears to separate this age from its precursors is that for the first time in history mankind has sufficient power to upset the world's climate or, at least, to trigger changes that might have occurred at a later date without mankind's modifications. (NRC 1977a: 13)

In this passage, the NRC report is not arguing against the framing of climate change offered by the CIA. Instead, it is relying on the CIA report to add weight to the NRC's own argument about the links between CO_2-induced climate change and concerns about stable water supplies (NRC 1977a: 13). The fact that a number of governmental and quasi-governmental organizations sought to establish themselves as important participants in a public conversation about the issue demonstrates the success that scientists had in creating a space for climate change on the systemic policy agenda.

Explaining Quiescence

The empirical evidence presented above from congressional hearings and news media stories about acid rain and climate change shows that each issue was drawn into the policy-making process with few explicit challenges. Given the debates that typically arise during congressional policy making, the lack of criticism of the respective science narratives during agenda setting and the lack of explicit contests over the science/policy boundary as drawn by the two narratives both call for some explanation.

One likely explanation for the onset of debate is that congressional attention to an issue signals to other participants that competition over scarce resources is underway. This is especially true if members of Congress show interest in finding a regulatory solution to the respective problems, given that regulatory policies bring with them heavily contested politics. Beginning in the 1960s, Theodore Lowi argued that policies created politics rather than politics generating specific policy outcomes. Lowi distinguished between distributive and regulatory policies and argued that the politics associated with these two kinds of policies were quite distinct (1964, 1972). Distributive policies are those that allocate funding for a specific project and are often decided at the level of congressional committees with the larger chamber—i.e., the House or the Senate—deferring to the committee's judgment. Distributive policies are carried out by subdividing federal spending among innumerable recipients. Because the recipients are not pitted against one another (benefits are concentrated among recipients, whereas costs are distributed widely through general taxes), distributive politics rarely spur opposition (Lowi 1964, 1972). Allocating money for federal research fits under this heading. Stakeholders behave differently, for example, in the case of regulatory policies, where concentrated costs are applied in very specific ways—e.g., the effects of acid rain controls on states producing high-sulfur coal. When a policy issue implies regulatory policies, mobilization of opponents is likely. And, in fact, once congressional policy makers take up the idea of creating regulatory programs to address acid rain and climate change, respectively, the expected opposition turns out in force for each issue.

Had the acid rain and climate change science narratives been arguing only for research programs to study the issue, a lack of debate would be consistent with Lowi's framework. However, scientists' argument about the respective issues went considerably beyond the goal of conducting more research. In most cases, distributive policies are ends in themselves. Funding allocated to build a dam or a highway in a particular district, or funding for research on a particular disease, is the goal of the policy. The science narratives for climate change and acid rain are different in that the distributive policy goal is a preliminary step in the larger science narrative. Ultimately, the control story articulated in each case is one in which scientific research will inform policy makers about how to *act* in response to the two policy problems.

The importance of the early policy steps for acid rain and climate change is supported by Baumgartner and Jones's analysis. Their central argument rests on the capacity of policy actors to reframe issues and to shift policy venues, sometimes decades after the primary venue has begun its policy work. At the same time, Baumgartner and Jones highlight the importance of venue construction when a policy problem is first articulated—what they refer to as a "Downsian mobilization."[54] In particular, they argue that when a novel policy issue gains agenda status it typically does so in the context of marked enthusiasm for governmental action. Such a political environment is ripe for the formation of new institutions. The design of such institutions can have long-term consequences for subsequent policy development:

Waves of popular enthusiasm surrounding a given issue provide the circumstances for policymakers to create new institutions to support their programs. These institutions then structure participation and policymaking, often ensuring privileged access to the policy process for those who helped set them up. After public interest and enthusiasm fade, the institutions remain, pushing forward with their preferred policies. (Baumgartner and Jones 1993: 84)

Although politics normally is beset by struggle and debate, Baumgartner and Jones point out that there are periods of relatively contest-free institution building. This might occur because the framing of an issue is sufficiently persuasive that most engaged actors accept the proposed policy action as in their interests. Alternatively, stakeholders might not be aware that institution building has occurred or will occur in a way that can shape their ability to participate in subsequent policy making. In either case, the policy narratives constructed during early periods of agenda setting do not necessarily stimulate significant opposition, in spite of the institutional building that occurs in each case.

In view of the importance that political scientists accord to agenda-setting activities and the long-term effects that institutionalized policy frames can have on subsequent policy making (Schattschneider 1967; Baumgartner and Jones 1993), the easy uptake of the respective science narratives begins to look more surprising. In addition, even assuming that those actors who become opponents of each science narrative are unlikely to expend resources opposing policy programs before they have actually been proposed in Congress, one still has to explain the quiescence around the science/policy boundary, given the fact that scientists, in articulating science narratives, are engaging in what some political scientists view as the most politically powerful act in the policy process (Schattschneider 1961: 68). This is a dramatic break with the idealized role for scientists that is routinely articulated in the more formal legislative and implementation policy settings.[55] Specifically, both scientists and policy actors invoke the idea that scientists are useful in policy making when they contribute objective information to decision makers. Scientists' objectivity, according to this view, allows them to contribute uniquely reliable information that is derived from their ability to use empirical verification to separate facts from mere claims. Accordingly, scientists contribute stable stories about how the world works and what we can expect in the future.

In both the acid rain case and climate change case, however, it is not difficult to find in the respective science narratives views that are not clearly supported by the evidence that scientists call on to support each narrative. For instance, because the effects of acid rain were uncertain during initial discussion of the issue, scientists were unable to make definitive statements about the likely outcome of continued sulfur dioxide emissions. The effects that were anticipated were damage to aquatic life in lakes and streams, damage to soils and to terrestrial vegetation, damage to crops, and damage to materials and monuments.[56] In spite of the uncertainty in predicting the extent of damage, scientists' statements called attention to the potential for damage in all cases.[57]

The bias in this interpretation of effects becomes more apparent when we look at what additional research showed about the effects of acid rain. Lakes and streams were being acidified, and aquatic life in these water systems was damaged as a consequence (NAPAP 1991: 11–12). However, the number of lakes and streams showing damage as the result of acid rain was smaller than originally predicted. Research into the effects of acid rain on forests was unable to show a clear link between acid rain and forest damage, except for high-elevation red spruce (ibid.: 301). The main cause of forest decline in both the western and the southeastern region of the United States was ozone pollution rather than acid deposition.[58] Agricultural research showed that some crops *benefited* from exposure to acid rain owing to the "free fertilizer" provided by nitrogen deposition (ibid.: 154–155).[59] The effects on materials were borne out by research that showed, in particular, damage to buildings of carbonate stone (ibid.: 76). These research findings demonstrate that original guesses about the effects of acid rain overstated a number of effects; wherever there was uncertainty in predicting outcomes, that uncertainty was interpreted through the lens of ecological conservatism, which saw damaging effects as more likely than neutral or positive ones—a typical decline story.

Further exemplifying the interpretive nature of the decline story is the fact that Odén's initial framing did not simply call attention to the potential for destruction of ecosystems. Odén interpreted this destructive capacity in terms of the geopolitics of Europe. In calling acid rain a "chemical war," Odén placed the issue in the context of diplomacy, where nation-states must address issues of territory and sovereignty. The variation among the framings suggests that the way to read the importance of the core of the science narrative is not fixed, but requires interpretation.

Now let us turn to the control story. Scientists' assertions that scientific research will help policy makers in their decision making were only partially fulfilled in the case of acid rain.[60] Certainly this aspect of the science narrative on acid rain was accepted and implemented with little debate in the form of the National Acid Precipitation Assessment Program.[61] However, NAPAP produced findings that were heavily criticized as both irrelevant to policy makers' concerns and untimely (in that the major report produced by the research program was published the year after regulatory controls were voted into law). The second criticism is largely unfounded given that drafts of NAPAP's report were available to policy makers in advance of their passage of the relevant legislation[62]; the first is not so easily dismissed. The charge of irrelevance was made on the grounds that NAPAP findings were not clearly linked to policy implications and that policy makers had difficulty relying on NAPAP findings in making policy decisions (Herrick 2000; Roberts 1991).[63]

Scientists who present climate change to the public engage in a similar exercise in interpretation. The central claim of the science narrative about global warming is that an increase in the concentration of certain gases in the atmosphere will lead to a higher average global temperature.[64] In order for this claim to merit the attention of the policy community, scientists must tell a story about the effects of climate change. The view that global warming is problematic is an important part of the science narrative. Scientists base their predictions about the negative effects of global warming on empirical evidence and on the conviction that rapid change is inherently bad for humans and ecosystems.

For empirical evidence, scientists begin with the greenhouse effect, or the theory that global temperature rises with an increase in atmospheric concentrations of certain heat-trapping gases. This theory is remarkably well established.[65] However, the Earth's climate system is extraordinarily complex. An increase in atmospheric concentrations of CO_2 will set in motion a number of changes, each with a different effect—either damping or magnifying the extent of the temperature increase.[66] Because of the complexity of the climate, it is hard to predict exactly what the planet Earth will look like after a doubling of atmospheric CO_2.

Current predictions about the effects of global warming are based largely on simulations of the climate using large-scale computer models or general circulation models. However, the accuracy of the predictions of GCMs remains uncertain, owing in large part to the complexities of modeling clouds and humidity (Houghton et al. 2001: 484, 486, 511). However, substantial improvements have been made in GCMs since the time of the Intergovernmental Panel on Climate Change's first assessment report.[67] These improvements include the ability to model seasonal climate cycles and reproduce the observed twentieth-century warming (Houghton et al. 2001: 473).[68] The resolution of these projections remains fairly rough in that the information is specific only to the level of subcontinents.[69] The notion that global warming would have adverse effects, however, predates these improvements in the model and is evident in a number of prominent reports published under the auspices of the scientific community during the 1960s and the 1970s that listed expected negative effects associated with rapid and significant warming.[70] Moreover, in spite of the acknowledgement that the complexity of the climate system makes prediction difficult, scientists are still likely to view the pace and scale of change as a threat to humans and ecosystems.[71]

A second element of the science narrative that has its roots in normative commitments rather than scientific expertise is the assertion that additional scientific research is needed to make policy decisions about climate change. The success of the science narrative rests, in part, on the belief that the problem is within the realm of human knowledge and, therefore, human control (Stone 1989). Scientists, in presenting the issue of global warming to policy makers, portray the problem as ultimately subject to scientific explanation. This places scientists in a position of authority relative to policy makers, who have few ways to evaluate the credibility of scientists' claim. Though additional scientific research often does produce information that is important to policy makers, this is not always the case.[72] Scientists' commitment to their profession, however, predisposes them to argue for their relevance in devising policy solutions (Zehr 1994a).[73]

Scientists' commitment to research as a foundation for policy decisions gains institutional expression through the US Global Change Research Program.[74] As in the acid rain case, the assumption of the importance of scientific research for environmental policy making is an endorsement of the climate change science narrative.[75] The USGCRP itself makes a strong case for the link between scientific knowledge and policy development.[76] Its annual report argues for the general need for increased scientific understanding of global change for the purpose of addressing policy concerns. As an example of "a successful partnership between science and policy making," the USGCRP cites the Montreal Protocol on Substances That Deplete the Ozone Layer (USGCRP 1997: 5). In support of the science side of this partnership, the USGCRP argues as follows:

Over the past decade, scientific research has greatly advanced our understanding of global change. The growing understanding that the current and future state of the Earth system is inexorably linked to human activities, and the increasing societal concern about the implications of global environmental change, under-score the need for and importance of these scientific efforts. Science continues to improve our understanding of global change. Research supported by the USGCRP is providing answers to important questions about the Earth system, how it is changing, and the implications of global environmental change for society. (ibid.: 5–6)

The USGCRP's research agenda is broad, covering seasonal to inter-annual climate variability; climate change on the scale of decades to centuries; changes in ozone, ultraviolet radiation, and atmospheric chem-istry; and changes in land cover and in terrestrial and aquatic ecosystems (ibid.: 23–24). The USGCRP, as a justification of the money spent on its programs, promises to increase the ability to predict effects on both natural and socio-economic systems from climate change.

In spite of the research community's conviction, it is not a given that more precise knowledge about the effects of climate change will aid policy making or that more precise knowledge is actually a reasonable goal.[77] It is true that advances in the science of climate change have been made that are relevant to policy makers. One crucial advance has been the willingness of the Intergovernmental Panel on Climate Change to argue that "the balance of evidence suggests a discernible human influ-ence on global climate" (Houghton et al. 1996: 4–5). This statement is tied to the increasing ability of GCMs to reproduce roughly the climate during the twentieth century (Houghton et al. 1996: 35–39).[78] This raises confidence in the outcomes GCMs predict as a result of elevated levels of greenhouse gases.

The ability to predict changes in climate on a regional scale, the ability to account for ecosystem-level effects, and even the ability to predict socio-economic consequences of climate change pose much greater chal-lenges.[79] For example, the ability to predict accurately inundation of cities as a result of sea-level rise might enable city governments to prepare. However, the level of certainty required before resources would be committed to such a project are likely to exceed what science can produce, at least on such a localized level. Moreover, accurate predic-tions of regional-scale outcomes are as likely to produce conflict over responses to climate change as they are to produce policy movement. Those who believe that changes in climate will have regional benefits such as an increase in agricultural productivity may be less willing to undertake costly efforts to alter their energy-use patterns. Scientists, because of their professional commitments, may not be the best judges of the limitations of scientific information in contributing to difficult policy decisions. In spite of this, there is a willingness to defer to scientists' claims about the relevance of the knowledge they can produce.[80]

It is notable that the science narratives for both acid rain and climate change contain arguments that are political or cultural in nature and are not directly read from the empirical evidence that makes up the causal argument for each one. As a consequence, each science narrative might, in other settings, have ignited opposition or sparked contests over the proper boundary between science and policy. The lack of such challenges during this early stage of policy making requires explanation.

Thomas Gieryn, though he emphasizes the incentives for actors to challenge any given science/policy boundary, offers some guidance for understanding periods when boundary work is likely to be suspended. First, Gieryn argues that the claims that achieve the status of "science" are selective representations of a larger set of activities intended to present a convincing picture of the cognitive authority of science. Gieryn views science as "maps" which direct our attention in order to achieve pragmatic ends—i.e., establish the cultural authority of science. For Gieryn, these maps are created through boundary work were multiple actors with a stake in the outcome negotiate what counts and science and what does not. At the same time, Gieryn raises the concept of "obduracy" in this process of negotiating science/non-science boundaries:

Interpretative flexibility in the boundaries of science need not imply infinitely pliable [sic]; some maps of science are easier than others to defend as bona fide representations. . . . Indeed, some maps achieve a provisional and contingent obduracy that may preempt boundary-work. Borders and territories of cultural spaces sometimes remain implicit, matters of personal belief or of such apparent tacit intersubjective agreement that people working together need not explicate "what everybody knows" about the meaning of science. (1995: 406–407)

Gieryn's analysis suggests that, to the extent that there is broad agreement about scientists' role in environmental policy making, scientists who invoke the familiar map of scientific work in the environmental policy domain may not be challenged. Taking Baumgartner and Jones and Gieryn together, enthusiastic institution building and the quiescence around the proper boundary between science and non-science might not be atypical for this stage of the policy process. Evidence here suggests that scientists are accepted as sentinels for environmental policy problems, even when that involves communicating normative commitments along with scientific theories and empirical evidence. More specifically, the idealized image of scientists as neutral actors in policy making is not strongly invoked during agenda setting. This does not mean that boundary work is not occurring. Rather, the boundary work that is taking place is not sparking explicit debates.

Without an obvious setting, and without any formal rules of engagement, agenda-setting activities may be hard to recognize except in hindsight. This limits the extent to which agenda setters are, themselves, likely to provoke opposition. Formal agenda status and indications of congressional intent, specifically with respect to potential regulatory action, offer the counter-example that highlights the distinctiveness of policy making during agenda setting.

Policy Implications of the Two Science Narratives

The concern with agenda setting hinges on the long-term consequences of a successful policy framing. If policy narratives provide the basis for institution building around a policy issue, the ability to articulate a successful narrative can bring with it significant influence over subsequent policy outcomes. Both the acid rain case and the climate change case are instructive given the extent to which policy actors adopted the science narratives for each as appropriate conceptualizations of the respective policy issues. The evidence in this chapter does not examine the extent to which opponents challenged each narrative during the respective periods of legislative debate. Rather, it elucidates a period during which actors established each narrative under highly favorable conditions that then influenced the subsequent lifespan of the narrative.

NAPAP collected scientists under a common label and funded research over a sustained period. Through NAPAP activities, government officials were exposed to acid rain research and to a network of scientists conducting that research. NAPAP operated throughout the 1980s in an uneasy tension between congressional leaders who wanted to see regulatory action on acid rain and the Reagan administration, which did not. Though a number of critics of the research program correctly charged that it was a stalling tactic by the recalcitrant Reagan administration, critics and strategists alike overlooked the institutional inertia created by the research program that enabled the acid rain issue to outlast attacks against the science narrative that framed it.[81]

The climate change case, like the acid rain case, illustrates the considerable amount of institutional inertia that can develop around publicly funded research. The science narrative is based on the conviction that global warming is a problem that can be surmounted through scientific research. Acceptance of this framing has led to large budget outlays for climate change research under the assumption that research is policy-neutral. However, establishment of a research program has created organizational weight behind climate change as a policy issue. For example, the USGCRP distributes research money across eleven Executive Branch departments and agencies. The number of organizations that have a stake in the government's research on global change is substantial. These organizations can be expected to defend vigorously their programs and budgets.[82] In fact, organizational commitment to the issue of climate change initially emerged in a symbolic competition among agencies over who would control a presumed regulatory program that would be implemented if the Kyoto Protocol was ratified.[83] Symbolic or not, agency competition over a presumed regulatory program was sufficient to raise concerns among members of Congress who opposed ratification of the Kyoto Treaty. Congress reacted by adding a provision to an appropriations bill to forestall any "premature implementation of Kyoto" and prevent any Executive Branch activities consistent with the Kyoto Protocol in advance of Senate ratification (Morrissey 1999).

Although legislative debate over global warming stalled in the face of a lack of Senate support for the Kyoto Treaty,[84] opponents of a regulatory program for climate change have been unable to kill the issue, which has stayed on the agenda for more than 25 years. Moreover, a number of policy actors are leading sub-national efforts to address climate change by creating coalitions of states that will work collectively to reduce greenhouse gas emissions (DePalma 2005). The most concrete effort to date is California's decision in 2006 to cut CO_2 emissions by 25 percent by the year 2020 (Barringer 2006).[85]

The argument that a research program creates a stable venue for nurturing a policy narrative runs counter to a number of perspectives offered in the existing literature. Many have criticized the creation of a research program as evidence of policy failure, i.e., the unwillingness of decision makers to make any firm policy commitments.[86] Some studies that treat the climate change issue have echoed that sentiment through pessimistic predictions of the likelihood of policy commitments to reduce greenhouse gases (Litfin 1994: 191–194; Ungar 1992).[87] These perspectives overlook the legitimacy accorded to the issue through the creation of a research program and the recurring opportunities to bring the issue back on the formal agenda as scientific reports are published and new evidence proffered to policy makers.

As in the case of acid rain, the creation of a research program on climate change represents a policy commitment. It is also clearly a policy commitment that accepts the science narrative as the appropriate framing of the issue. While the evolution of climate policy in the United States remains uncertain, the institutionalized commitment to the problem and recent state-level activity suggest a certain amount of staying power that is likely to outlast opposition articulated by an administration or a congress.[88]

Conclusion

According to the literature on agenda setting, the potential for a policy narrative to frame the way participants in the policy process understand an issue can concentrate an important source of influence in the hands of those who construct a successful narrative. Science narratives are especially important to consider in view of the legitimacy scientists carry in environmental policy making. The present study traces policy makers' response to scientists' respective claims about acid rain and climate change and notes that the creation of research programs in each case came fast and with little contest.

The description of scientists' role in agenda setting offered in this chapter serves as a benchmark against which their roles in later stages of decision making will be compared. During agenda setting, scientists participating under circumstances face few structural and procedural constraints. The lack of formal procedures in this policy venue gives scientists leeway to meet public expectations rhetorically while engaging in boundary work that would be likely to invite scrutiny in other policy-making settings. In later chapters we will see the policy-making process become increasingly formalized. Though scientists are engaged in boundary work in every stage of policy making, the salience of scientists' boundary efforts appears to increase, in part as a function of both formal and informal procedures that make it difficult to avoid debate about objectivity and bias. In the next two chapters, I examine the increasing constraints placed on scientists in pursuit of legitimate science-policy interaction. In connection with this, I explore the increase in explicit attention that actors in the policy process devote to the science/policy boundary.

3

Scientists and Legislation

SEN. CHAFEE: Well, if you were sitting up here, what would you do? Would you worry and do anything, or say well, let's wait a little while longer?

MR. CHRISTY: I have never been a senator before.

SEN. CHAFEE: Well—

MR. CHRISTY: And, I suspect—

SEN. CHAFEE: —you can pretend you're one. A lot of people do. (Laughter.)

MR. CHRISTY: I suppose what will be done is that which is politically feasible from your point of view.

SEN. CHAFEE: No, don't put it on that basis. Let's say we're trying to do the right thing up here, and we've tackled things like the, long before it was popular, we got into the chlorofluorocarbons, the CFC's, and as you just mentioned, I think we did some good work there. It wasn't immediately popular, but it was the right thing to do. So, just tell us what your recommendation would be to us.

MR. CHRISTY: . . . I'm not an expert on the economic issues, and things like that. I only know about pretty much one thing, and that's the satellite temperatures. So, it's hard for me to answer that kind of question. (SCEPW 1997)[1]

Scientists' mode of participation in legislative settings is notably different from their participation in the agenda-setting stage of policy making. During legislative hearings, scientists, as in the example above, express their policy preferences very gingerly, if at all. In fact, some refuse to step out of the role of "neutral expert" even in the face of considerable coaxing on the part of policy makers.[2] In congressional settings, scientists begin to demonstrate publicly that they are aware of the boundary between science and policy making. The contrast with scientists in agenda setting is pronounced.[3] The central claim of this book is that context shapes scientists' participation in policy making and that systematic variation across contexts has been overlooked in an attempt to reduce scientists' role to a single, generalized phenomenon. The comparison between agenda setting and the legislative stage of policy making provides the initial evidence that context does, indeed, matter.

In the previous chapter, I treated scientists who acted as agenda setters in the earliest stages of policy making for acid rain and climate change by constructing stories around each issue to make a case that those issues merited space on a limited public policy agenda. That members of Congress take up the respective issues might illustrate several dynamics in environmental policy making: (1) scientists are successful in attracting interest from elected officials in a set of ideas that, before scientists' efforts, were confined primarily to scientific circles, (2) policy entrepreneurs in congressional settings are actively scouting for issues illustrating the policy narrative of environmental decline, or (3) some combination of (1) and (2). Certainly, the frequency with which scientists are called to testify on the respective issues is evidence that members of Congress view scientists' framings as important to solidifying the place of an issue on the congressional agenda within Congress.[4]

A particularly interesting feature of legislative stages of environmental policy making is the fact that, as each issue finds a place on the formal policy agenda, scientists find themselves in a setting dominated by norms that are at odds with the idealized notion of how science informs policy.[5] During legislative hearings, scientists are often asked to fulfill two competing roles. The first role is symbolic and is consistent with an idealized understanding of scientists in policy settings—i.e., as neutral advisors. The second role places scientists in the position of interpreting findings of scientific research in policy-relevant terms. This pulls scientists out of the arena in which they can comfortably claim expertise. The analysis of the transcripts of congressional hearings presented in detail below provides considerable evidence that (a) policy makers routinely pressure scientists to make policy statements on the record and (b) scientists adopt one of three coping strategies in response to this pressure: they acquiesce, they answer policy questions as "citizens" rather than as "scientists, or they find a way to avoid responding directly to the policy question.

In this chapter, comparing agenda setting with legislative decision making, I assert that there are meaningful differences in the two domains that affect participants' behavior. In doing so, I do not suggest that activities that occur in legislative settings are all alike. Strategic actors who participate in congressional decision making choose from a range of options in pursuing their goals. The institution produces nothing like uniform behavior. And yet, researchers study Congress with the starting assumption that the institution itself matters and that norms and role expectations obtain in that setting that constrain actors' choices (Huitt 1954; Truman 1959; Fenno 1966, 1973, 1978; Mayhew 1974).

The distinction among stages in policy making calls attention to specific norms at play in each stage. This insight applies even though the stages of policy making are porous rather than airtight. When focusing on the legislative stage of policy making, we find processes that are similar to those found in agenda setting, but find that they have distinctive characteristics in this stage. For example, scholars who study Congress analyze agenda-setting efforts (DeGregorio 1992) and issue framing (Talbert, Jones, and Baumgartner 1995) within the institution. If agenda setting occurs within Congress and not merely before members in Congress begin to pay attention to an issue, then an important question for a study comparing stages of decision making is whether agenda setting outside Congress differs from agenda setting within Congress. Cobb and Elder's distinction between the systemic and formal agendas addresses this issue.[6] Cobb and Elder view the systemic and formal agendas as separate spheres and argue that the formal agenda "will always lag to some extent behind the more general systemic agenda" (1983: 14). For them, the specificity and intentionality of the formal agenda sets it apart from the systemic agenda. State officials signal the potential for formal state action when they place an issue on the formal agenda. The move from the systemic to the formal agenda is important, Cobb and Elder argue, because the public judges the legitimacy of a polity, at least in part, by its responsiveness to the systemic agenda (ibid.: 14–15). When an issue gains formal agenda status, elected officials are demonstrating some measure of responsiveness to the systemic agenda.

In studying policy making in legislative settings, we see aspects of agenda setting and even sporadic appearances of the norms established in implementation settings. This has to do with the metabolism within Congress as issues are pushed onto the formal congressional agenda and as actors from implementation setting periodically participate in legislative processes. The overlap between agenda setting and early congressional activity occurs because formal agenda status is not necessarily achieved the moment the first congressional hearing is held on the topic. Formal agenda status, in Cobb and Elder's terms, comes when political actors indicate the intention to consider state action. In the preceding chapter, I listed a number of early hearings in which committee chairs began to lay the groundwork for advancing either acid rain or climate change more forcefully on the congressional agenda. These early hearings demonstrate the first links between the systemic and formal agenda. Early congressional action has several characteristics in common with agenda setting in that members of Congress who are pushing a new issue or a renewed one must, like their counterparts in agenda setting, work to get the broader attention of the chamber. This early work typically does not include the analysis and the debate that accompany specific policy proposals, activities that are associated with formal agenda status. Cobb and Elder's idea of the formal agenda, by emphasizing the potential for state action, refers to a point in congressional policy making when an issue occupies more than the attention of a handful of members. It is at this stage that distinction in scientists' participation across agenda setting and legislative policy making is most pronounced. At the same time, data presented in this chapter demonstrate that scientists who participate in early congressional hearings tend not to voice policy positions, suggesting that the norm of scientific objectivity is present in the legislative setting even when an issue is new to the congressional agenda.

The data presented below also indicate that witnesses with scientific backgrounds who work for government agencies are much less likely than their academic counterparts to articulate policy positions, even after issues have been placed on the formal agenda. This suggests that these witnesses bring with them the norms of implementation settings when they appear before Congress and retain agency in deciding how they will negotiate the legislative setting. Were these witnesses the only ones to testify, there might be little reason to set apart the norms of legislative settings from the norms of implementation settings. Though legislative policy making can include actors who normally work on policy implementation, these actors are a relatively small subset of the individuals who influence the legislative process. Therefore, it would be unlikely for the norms of implementation to override legislative norms. In this chapter, I will detail the specific features of legislative policy making that create a distinct arena for scientists' participation. These differences are meaningful in that they provide real constraints on participants' behavior. At the same time, the differences exist in degree rather than in kind.

In studies of policy making in the legislative setting, the control that committee chairs and party leaders have over which issues are addressed and how they are debated is critical (DeGregorio 1992; Talbert, Jones, and Baumgartner 1995). Committee and subcommittee chairs dominate the hearings process and are able to exercise considerable influence over whether and what kinds of messages are transmitted. Witnesses of any stripe have less control over the timing and even the content of the messages they send when participating in a legislative setting. An actor who is successful in placing an issue on the systemic agenda may have limited success once that issue is taken up in Congress (Cobb and Elder 1983; Kingdon 1984). While an issue's framing is not fixed at the point at which a member of Congress places that issue on the congressional agenda, the number of individuals with the capacity to independently influence its direction declines precipitously because, in Congress, jurisdiction over an issue will only be shared among a few committees, each of which is dominated by a single committee chair.[7]

Aside from setting the congressional agenda and working on the specifics of legislation and budgeting, Congress also has a role in overseeing Executive Branch activities. Oversight activities are, of course, primarily carried out by congressional committees. Such interactions might involve written correspondence between committee chairs and agency officials, but oversight activities are also carried out through congressional hearings. The primary tools members have to influence agency decision making include writing or revising statutory language that governs agency activities and controlling agency budgets. When oversight takes this form, it begins to look very similar to normal legislative behavior on the part of members and committees. In addition, members of Congress may use hearings to create political pressure on agencies to change their behavior without having to go through the process of writing new legislation or changing budget authority. Several of the hearings included in this study are oversight hearings—for example, the hearings held to review the progress of the National Acid Precipitation Assessment Program (HCSST 1988). Scientists are included in these hearings, just as they are included in legislative hearings in which a specific bill is under review.

Without specifically addressing the idea of distinct types of policy making within the congressional setting, Talbert, Jones, and Baumgartner (1995) find distinctions between legislative hearings (in which a particular bill is reviewed) and non-legislative hearings (in which no bill is reviewed). Specifically, they argue that non-legislative hearings are more likely than legislative hearings to be biased toward the committee chair's preferred position. This is true whether the hearing is held for the purpose of agenda setting or for the purpose of oversight. Thus, it may not be very analytically useful to distinguish types of policy making within the legislative stage if these two functions do not appear to be notably different in practice. The overlap between agenda setting and oversight in the congressional setting can be traced to the fact that oversight hearings are often a prelude to revising existing statutes—a function that is a close cousin to congressional agenda setting and issue framing. In short, these two different functions appear to be accomplished through a consistent set of practices in Congress.

In all these cases, committee chairs have enormous discretion in setting up committee hearings. Research suggests that committee members differ in the degree to which they choose control the agenda of committee hearings and the selection of witnesses (DeGregorio 1992). Some chairs chose to cede power to members of the committee; others guard the prerogatives of agenda and witness selection jealously. The behavior of committee chairs in setting up hearings falls into predictable patterns according to the resources and constraints committee chairs face (Huitt 1954; DeGregorio 1992; Talbert, Jones, and Baumgartner 1995). Witnesses appear in Congress at the pleasure of the members who dominate such interactions (DeGregorio 1992; Talbert, Jones, and Baumgartner 1995). Although committee chairs may have any of several different goals (agenda setting, bill markup, oversight), their ability to orchestrate interactions among participants is pronounced and is unlike anything we see in systemic agenda setting.

In this chapter, I examine structures and practices that influence scientists' participation in legislative hearings. While there are a number of studies that examine the use of expertise in Congress,[8] studies that focus directly on science or participation by scientists are rare. This lack of attention may result from a common conception that Congress does not rely heavily on science, which would make the study of scientific inputs a low research priority.[9] However, there are attempts both within Congress and by outside groups to review and improve the way scientific expertise is drawn into congressional processes.[10] These efforts demonstrate that actors close to the institution are concerned with the role of science in legislative decision making. This places in relief the relative lack of attention on the part of political scientists to the role of scientists in legislative politics.

Specifically, political science has not explained why scientists often participate in legislative hearings. A number of researchers argue that actors other than scientists—interest groups, knowledge brokers, policy entrepreneurs—are more effective than scientists in communicating expertise to members of Congress and their staff (Esterling 2004; Litfin 1994; Kingdon 1984). To the extent that these arguments are correct, we still must explain the fact that scientists are frequent participants in legislative hearings.[11] If knowledge brokers are reliable conduits for scientific research, why do members of Congress bother asking actual scientists to participate? In posing this question I do not presume that scientists shape legislative policy outcomes. Rather, in this chapter I explore the nature of scientists' participation in congressional hearings without assuming that participation necessarily implies a central role in the legislative process.

In the chapter's first section, I review the literature that establishes the importance of hearings in larger legislative processes. Next, I present the research opportunities available when studying hearings. In the following section, I analyze incentives that members of Congress have to seek scientific expertise in pursuing their legislative goals and consider why scientists accept invitations to act as witnesses at congressional hearings. I then give an overview of the political events that defined the legislative stage of decision making for each case and highlight the debates that adversaries pursued in this public forum. The following section, the centerpiece of the chapter, is a detailed discussion of scientists' efforts in negotiating the boundary between science and policy when they act as witnesses before congressional committees. That discussion is followed by an examination of the resilience of the science narrative during the legislative stage of decision making.

Learning from Congressional Hearings

In order to study the role of scientists in the legislative stage of decision making, I rely heavily on congressional hearings held on acid rain and climate change. Scholarship on Congress has long argued that committees are central to the work of the institution (Fenno 1962; 1973; Jones 1961; Shepsle and Weingast 1981; Weingast and Marshall 1988; Krehbiel 1991, 1998). Less established in the literature on Congress is the role that committee hearings play in larger congressional processes. Scholars have enumerated a number of likely reasons why members of Congress hold hearings, the three most pertinent of which are learning, advocacy, and the provision of information to the larger chamber.[12]

Ralph Huitt, in an early study of the role of hearings, tackles the question of learning. In his study of the Senate Banking and Currency Committee's hearings on the price control and stabilization program of 1942, Huitt tests the idea that committee members learn from witness testimony in forming their judgments about policy options. Huitt finds that committee members left the hearings holding the same views they held at the start and concludes that committee members did not rely on information provided during the hearings in establishing their legislative positions. At the same time, Huitt does not view the hearings as congressional artifice. He argues that committee members are partisans participating in the debate over the correct policy to adopt rather than impartial actors who hear evidence and render a verdict. The hearings, therefore, served as a forum for that debate. Huitt argues that the hearings "made perfectly clear . . . that the groups opposing price control were both more numerous and more militant than the groups supporting it," and that "this was, of course, *crucial* information" (1954: 365, emphasis added). Huitt's study of one set of hearings does not rule out the possibility that learning occurred in hearings he did not study. More important, however, is Huitt's often overlooked conclusion that the lack of position change in the hearings he *did* study is not an indication that those hearings played an insignificant role in larger legislative processes. Huitt's research demonstrates that hearings can be relevant even if members do not change their positions as a consequence of participating in hearings.

Richard Cohen's analysis of Clean Air policy making in Congress, in contrast to Huitt's research, suggests that hearings can be a platform for learning. Cohen describes the early efforts by Senator Edmund Muskie to address air pollution. First, Muskie, who sat on the Senate Public Works Committee, urged that committee to create a subcommittee on Air and Water Pollution, which Muskie then chaired.[13] Muskie, reflecting on that period in his career, recalled: "None of us knew very much about air pollution. We educated ourselves in the subcommittee's hearings." (quoted in Cohen 1995: 14) Later, in his analysis of developments in clean air policy, Cohen locates Muskie's ability to dominate the conference committee leading to the 1970 Clean Air Act Amendments in Muskie's superior knowledge of the issues relative to the other conferees (ibid.: 18).

Comparing Muskie's reflections on hearings concerning air pollution with Huitt's study of the Senate Banking Committee raises an interesting question about the potential for learning during congressional hearings. If the Banking Committee's members were already well versed in the policy options available regarding price controls and stabilization, one would not expect them to modify their positions after a recitation of available options. Muskie, on the other hand, characterizes subcommittee members as not knowing very much about air pollution. Committee chairs may design hearings very differently depending on the novelty of the issue before the committee.

Another potential role that hearings play in legislative decision making has less to do with shaping committee members' views than with transmitting information between committees and the larger chamber (Krehbiel 1991; Diermeier and Feddersen 2002). Krehbiel agrees with Diermeier and Feddersen that hearings can provide information to the larger chamber; however, he suggests different conditions under which hearings can be informative. Diermeier and Feddersen argue that committees have incentives to specialize, a prediction that is supported by Hall and Grofman (1990) and by Londregan and Snyder (1994). Krehbiel, to the contrary, finds no incentives for committee specialization and predicts that information is only provided to the floor when committee preferences match those of the larger chamber. In the end, both Krehbiel and Diermeier and Feddersen suggest that the larger chamber relies on committees to provide information about upcoming policy choices.

Consistent across several studies of hearings is the finding that members use hearings for the purposes of advocacy (Huitt 1954; DeGregorio 1992; Talbert, Jones, and Baumgartner 1995; Diermeier and Feddersen 2002). DeGregorio finds that committee chairs control resources that make it possible for them to control committee agendas and issue framing. Specifically, committee chairs can limit hearings topics and select witnesses according to their own legislative goals. DeGregorio finds variation among committee chairs in how much control they exercise over what the hearings are about and who gets to testify. She also finds that some chairs feel a duty to the chamber to hold balanced hearings before they engage in advocacy through the hearings (1992: 979–980). This suggests that committee chairs recognize both advocacy and providing information to the larger chamber as part of their legislative responsibilities.

The framing of issues is central to Talbert, Jones, and Baumgartner's 1995 study of the hearings process. Talbert et al. want to explain changes in jurisdiction among committees and find that non-legislative hearings (i.e., those hearings not held for the express purpose of reviewing a bill) are used by committees to (a) establish their expertise in a certain area, (b) frame issues in ways that fit with that committee's jurisdiction, and (c) encourage future referral of bills. Moreover, they find that witness selection for non-legislative hearings is more likely to be skewed toward the chair's favored policy position. Legislative hearings (i.e., hearings convened to review a particular bill) have a more balanced, though still skewed, selection of witnesses. This finding suggests that committee chairs are responsive to pressures to provide information to the larger chamber in spite of the benefits that accrue to committees who are able to grab jurisdiction through biased non-legislative hearings.

These studies create a nuanced picture of the role of hearings in larger legislative processes. Certainly, advocacy is a central goal of committee chairs in picking topics for hearings and in selecting witness panels. At the same time, this research shows that chairs do not solely pursue advocacy; they also convene hearings to provide information to the larger chamber. The quality of the information provided to the larger chamber may be an issue, especially given committee chairs' propensity for biasing hearings toward their preferred views. And yet, the larger chamber is made up of an audience with a high degree of political sophistication. It is hard to imagine that members of Congress are not sufficiently skilled to draw useful information even from biased hearings. Though participants may not change their positions as the consequence of hearings, crucial information can be gleaned from the hearings process, including information about the potential for striking deals with potential collaborators, positions and strategies of adversaries, signals about controversy-inducing issues that are likely to kill an otherwise promising bill, and opportunities for "log rolling" (i.e., trading votes). When an issue is particularly novel to a committee or the larger chamber, it is likely that hearings can be a venue for learning. In short, the hearings are a central venue for staking out policy territory, advocating specific positions, and communicating to any one of several larger audiences about upcoming policy choices and battles.

Analysis of committee hearings can be defended on both substantive and methodological grounds. First, from a methodological standpoint, the hearings provide a partial but chronologically accurate picture of the debates as they happened.[14] Interview data, though such data might reveal crucial information that was not included in the hearings, would rely on participants' memories of events. Such accounts are likely to be unreliable over the time periods in question for the two cases. Personal reflections are also potentially affected by knowledge of legislative outcomes. The hearings do not have this flaw, since none of the participants in the hearings knew, at the time, what the ultimate policy outcomes of the respective debates would be.

Substantively, the hearings provide a window into how events both internal and external to Congress shaped legislative debates. Committee members' statements and witnesses' testimony provide partial accounts of relevant events linked to each policy issue. The hearings track new scientific findings, shifting analytic uncertainties, emerging regulatory approaches, developing compliance technologies, international negotiations, evolving political positions and arguments, and debates brewing between committees and between Congress and the White House.[15]

The most important reason to study the hearings is to learn about advocacy on the part of members of Congress. The hearings provide a window on of congressional activity. Though significant features of the legislative process may not occur in hearings, hearings are a purposive arena of legislative activity.[16] The reason to hold a hearing is to communicate something publicly. The audience for such communication can include other committees, the floor, the other chamber, an Executive Branch agency, the White House, or the public. By reviewing the hearings, one can analyze the ways that members of Congress incorporate scientists into this task of communication. Scientists' participation in this context is shaped by a group of very powerful actors who draw scientists into the process in pursuit of goals that may be at odds with scientists' own goals.

The data in this study cannot conclusively explain why members of Congress invite scientists to testify in hearings. Instead, the hearings only show us that members of Congress invite scientists.[17] Research on members' goals, however, points to several reasons why scientists might be useful participants in hearings. One crucial characteristic of congressional hearings is that they are costly (DeGregorio 1992; Krehbiel 1992; Diermeier and Feddersen 2000). They consume scarce resources. Only a limited number of hearings can be held in a legislative session. A committee chair who holds too many hearings can risk the attentiveness of the public, the larger chamber, and even members of the committee. In addition, only a limited number of witnesses can be included in a hearing. The more witnesses included, the longer a hearing will last. Committee chairs must consider the limits of audience attentiveness when constructing hearings. Under these circumstances, one must assume that when a committee chair invites a scientist to testify, the chair expects the scientist to play a role in meeting the goals the chair has for the hearing. This assumption is reasonable in that a scientist who holds a position on a witness panel takes a position that might have gone to someone else.

In general, it seems safe to assume that politicians' reliance on expert knowledge is instrumental—i.e., that it furthers their political goals (Bimber 1996: 21–22). Members might rely on scientists to learn about substantive areas of policy in which they have an interest (Cohen 1995: 14).[18] Members might invite scientists to testify to create the impression that the members are familiar with the latest scientific research (Talbert, Jones, and Baumgartner 2002). They might also bring scientists to Congress in order to add credibility to the policy positions they wish to advance. Some combination of these factors probably explains the impetus to invite scientists to participate in congressional hearings.

Equally important for the purposes of this research is to understand why scientists accept invitations to testify. Scientists face real risks in testifying before Congress. It is not a given that scientists, once invited, will testify. Because this study is interested in scientists' behavior over the course of the policy-making process, the potential for selection bias in explaining differences from one stage to the next is crucial. And there is evidence that selection bias is at work during this stage of policy making. Some scientists avoid Congress. Given that scientists can and do decline to participate in hearings, one must be careful not to generalize from the select group of scientists who do participate to the larger scientific community.[19]

Why, then, do scientists serve as witnesses at hearings? I will begin with the simple case. For a number of scientists, attending hearings is an expected part of their job. For instance, any scientist who is directly employed by the federal government may be asked to testify and is likely to accept the invitation as part of representing and advancing the program or programs with which he or she is affiliated.[20] Next, scientists employed by industry or by non-governmental organizations (NGOs) are likely to testify when interests of their parent organization are at stake.

For scientists who are not clearly linked to government, to industry, or to NGOs, the reasons for testifying are less clear. In fact, there are strong disincentives for academic scientists to testify before Congress, given that an association with a particular policy or with politics, in general, may mar their status as impartial researchers among their scientific peers.[21] It is not uncommon for scientists in academia to refuse to testify before Congress so as to avoid being perceived as politically motivated (interview, July 1, 1998).[22] Nonetheless, scientists from academia *do* testify before Congress. Certainly, if public funding has supported scientists' research, as is often the case, they may feel an obligation to testify. Another reason may be interest in the policy issue at hand. In addition, academic scientists may testify out of a general sense of civic duty in spite of any interest or lack thereof in the policy issue in question. Finally, scientists who have neither an interest in the policy issue nor a sense of civic duty may accept an invitation to testify because of the sense of recognition that comes from being called by the august body.

Because scientists can accept or decline an invitation to testify before a committee, the population of scientists who do appear at committee hearings is not a representative sample of scientists. The disincentives to testify probably mean that it is harder for members of Congress to secure participation by the most disinterested scientists, since these might be the very scientists who worry about protecting their reputations as apolitical. At the same time, evidence suggests that members of Congress want more from scientists who testify than a disinterested account of the scientific record. The neutral expert goes only part of the way to fulfilling House and Senate members' goals. This is clearly demonstrated when members press scientists into making political statements, as in the example given at the opening of this chapter.

Acid Rain at the Legislative Stage

Acid rain appeared on the congressional agenda in 1975 when the House Committee on Science, Space, and Technology took up the issue of the adequacy of the Environmental Protection Agency's research into the causes of "acid rains" (HCSST 1975a). In fact, most of the early congressional activity on acid rain focused on supporting scientific research. These efforts culminated in a substantial federal research effort established under the National Acid Precipitation Act of 1980.[23] Hearings on acid rain were conducted throughout the 1980s across a variety of committees in both the House and the Senate.[24] While 16 committees held hearings with a substantive focus on acid rain,[25] the bulk of the hearings held on acid rain were concentrated among four committees: the House Committee on Energy and Commerce, the Senate Committee on Environment and Public Works, the House Committee on Science, Space, and Technology, and the Senate Committee on Energy and Natural Resources (table 3.1).

When members of Congress initially placed the issue on the congressional agenda, advocates argued for the need to learn more about acid rain and, therefore, the need for additional research. These discussions provoked little controversy. In 1975, only two out of 20 witnesses took a position against acid rain controls. In 1979, none of the witnesses who appeared in the hearings took a position against acid rain controls. On the other hand, only one hearing was held in each of these years, suggesting that acid rain was not garnering major congressional attention. After 1979, the picture changes considerably. First, the number of hearings held on acid rain jumps from the sporadic hearing held in a given year to multiple hearings held every year. From 1980 to 1990, Congress held at least two and as many as 15 hearings per year on acid rain. Debate on acid rain also escalated. The annual percentage of witnesses during this period arguing against acid rain controls averaged 35 percent.[26] The increase in the number of witnesses taking positions against acid rain was almost certainly driven by the level of commitment that several prominent legislators devoted to the issue; as acid rain regulations began to seem likely, stakeholders whose interests would not be served by such regulations mobilized to counter the likely legislation. Discussions of the

Table 3.1
Committees holding hearings on acid rain, 1975–1990. Source: LexisNexis Congressional Publications.

	Number of hearings	Percentage of House or Senate acid rain hearings	Percentage of all acid rain hearings
House committees			
Energy and Commerce	26	48	28
Science, Space, and Technology	13	24	13
Interior and Insular Affairs	4	7	4
Agriculture[a]	3	5	3
Interstate and Foreign Commerce	2	4	2
Aging (Select Committee)	1	2	1
Banking, Finance, and Urban Affairs	1	2	1
Foreign Affairs	1	2	1
Merchant Marine and Fisheries	1	2	1
Small Business	1	2	1
Ways and Means	1	2	1
Senate committees			
Environment and Public Works	26	65	28
Energy and Natural Resources	11	28	12
Commerce, Science, and Transportation	1	2	1
Foreign Relations	1	2	1
Small Business (Select Committee)	1	2	1

a. Two hearings were held jointly between the House Committee on Science, Space, and Technology (HCSST) and the House Committee on Agriculture (HCA). One of the joint hearings is counted in the total for HCSST and one is counted in the total for HCA.

creation of a federally funded research program on acid rain did not produce similar opposition.

The shift in the discussion from funding for research to regulatory action mobilized stakeholders on both sides of the issue, creating a fertile environment for debate. These debates covered a number of scientific and political issues. Certainly, much of the debate centered on whether acid rain was, in fact, a threat to aquatic and terrestrial ecosystems. Debate among scientists that surfaced in media coverage and in congressional hearings did not focus on the fundamentals of acid rain; most scientists who participated in the public debate agreed that acid deposition was occurring and agreed upon the mechanism causing acid rain.[27] Scientists also tended to agree about the major sources of uncertainty—how much of acid rain could be attributed to natural sources, whether acid deposition was affecting forests, the extent and severity of surface water effects, the potential effects on crops and soils, the potential for acid deposition to leach heavy metals into ground water, the relationship (linear or nonlinear) between the volume of emissions and the consequent amount of acid rain, and whether particular sources of pollution could be identified and linked to specific locations being damaged by acid rain. Some scientists also posited that there might be important thresholds of acidification beyond which lakes and streams would not be able to recover.[28]

Broad agreements over acid rain and future research priorities, however, were bracketed by notable public disagreements among scientists. Scientists split, both in the media and in congressional hearings, over the severity of the problem (HCSST 1988; Shabecoff 1982a). In addition, scientists publicly debated whether policy action was warranted given the uncertainties with some scientists calling for immediate controls and others arguing for continued research (SCEPW 1982; Shabecoff 1982b; United Press International 1982). Scientists also differed publicly over how to translate research findings into policy recommendations (Mohnen 1983; Gould 1983).

During congressional hearings, witnesses of all stripes actively disputed the severity of the problem. Industry representatives predictably argued that it was insignificant (HCEC 1987) and/or that the costs of responding would outweigh any benefits (SCENR 1983; HCEC 1984, 1986, 1987, 1988a; HCSB 1989; HCBFUA 1990). Many argued that more research was needed before costly regulations should be adopted (SCENR 1980c; SCEPW 1981a; HCEC 1984, 1987). Industry representatives also argued that legislators should rely on forthcoming "clean" coal technology to decrease the pollutants leading to acid rain, rather than impose costly regulations (HCEC 1988a). Manufacturers of scrubber technologies designed to reduce sulfur dioxide emissions from coal-fired plants argued, with environmental interest groups, that regulatory action was called for (SCEPW 1987e). Industries' dislike for governmental regulation, in this case, could not override the potential for government action to create demand for scrubber technology. This demand would make those manufacturing scrubber technologies winners in the case of a regulatory program. Environmentalists, for their part, emphasized the potential for irreversible harm to forests and aquatic systems and argued that the problem was real, severe, and imminent (SCENR 1980d; SCEPW 1983a, 1985a, 1986c).

There also were heated disputes over the links between Midwestern coal burning and Northeastern acid deposition. This debate pitted senators from the Northeast against those from the Midwest. Those from Northeastern states pressed for a federal solution (SCEPW 1983a); those from the Midwest opposed new federal regulations that would disproportionately affect industry in their states (HCEC 1983, 1988a). West Virginia, a producer of high sulfur coal, was also interested in keeping acid rain regulations off the books (SCENR 1982, 1984). Canadian officials joined senators from the Northeast in pressuring Congress for action on what they viewed as something for which Canadians bore the costs but from which they experienced few if any benefits (HCFA 1981; HCSST 1981).

A number of congressional actors dominated the legislative scene during the acid rain debate. Richard Cohen, in his study of the Clean Air Act Amendments of 1990, focuses particularly on the activities of six members of Congress—Dingell, Waxman, Byrd, Stafford, Mitchell, and Baucus—to explain the long period of congressional debate leading up to the passage of the 1990 act. However, Cohen makes very clear that, in spite of the power and skill these men had in pursuing their interests in acid rain, the passage of the Clean Air Act Amendments occurred because of presidential leadership (1995: 48): "The key change between the 1970s and the 1980s happened at the White House: Nixon and Carter supported clean-air laws (1970 and 1977, respectively) and legislation went through. Reagan opposed it so nothing happened. With the election in November 1998 of George Bush, the self-proclaimed 'environmental president,' the gridlock of divided government would no longer be an excuse for inaction." Extrapolating from Cohen's analysis that members of Congress are less important than presidents in explaining the ultimate passage of Clean Air Act legislation, one can assume that scientists are somewhat farther down in this hierarchy of influence. Though there is a case to be made that scientists help place issues on the political agenda and are instrumental in the framing of those issues, it would be a significant leap to assume that scientists, therefore, have a direct role in shifting Congress from a period of protracted debate to the point at which a policy program is finally passed. Comparing the legislative outcomes in the acid rain and climate change cases demonstrates that formal agenda status, though necessary, is far from sufficient for generating policy action.

Climate Change at the Legislative Stage

Hearings on climate change have continued over a longer time period than the hearings for acid rain.[29] The first hearings that mention climate change were held in the 1950s in the context of scientists asking for funding for basic scientific research (HCoA 1956; SCA 1956; HCoA 1957, 1958, 1959). Then, after a 14-year silence on the issue, climate change reemerged in Congress in the 1970s (table 3.2). First, witnesses raised the issue of climate change in a handful of hearings only loosely related to climate (SCANF 1973; SCASS 1975; HCSST 1975b).[30] Congress then took up the issue of climate directly in two hearings (HCSST 1976, 1977). These hearings focused on funding federal research on climate as a way to improve weather prediction and, therefore, agricultural planning. In these hearings, scientists discussed ways in which humans might be causing global warming through increasing greenhouse gas concentrations and global cooling by spreading pollutants in the atmosphere that deflect incoming solar radiation.[31] Scientists' testimony in these hearings is notable for the lack of scientific consensus regarding why climate change should be a policy issue. During these hearings, many scientists discussed global warming in terms of food production; others mentioned threat to water supplies, and others talked about global warming as a problem in and of itself. This suggests that scientists who argued that government funds should be spent to study climate change were not necessarily in agreement about the rationale for tackling the issue. Still, scientists testifying before Congress in the 1970s were strongly united in their call for federally funded research and did reinforce the notion that climate change was a noteworthy policy problem (HCSST 1976, 1977). In keeping with the focus on scientific research, these hear-

Table 3.2
Committees holding hearings on climate change (CC), 1976–1992. Source: LexisNexis Congressional Publications. (While the coded data for the climate hearings includes only a random sample of 50 percent of the hearings in 1990, 1991, and 1992, respectively, these tables include a complete count of the committees holding hearings in these years.)

	Number of hearings	Percentage of House or Senate CC hearings	Percentage of all CC hearings
House committees			
Science, Space and Technology	26	42	20
Appropriations	13	21	10
Energy and Commerce	12	19	9
Foreign Affairs	5	8	4
Merchant Marine and Fisheries	3	5	2
Interior and Insular Affairs	2	3	2
Agriculture	1	2	1
Senate committees			
Commerce, Science, and Transportation	26	38	20
Energy and Natural Resources	14	20	11
Environment and Public Works	10	14	7
Appropriations	7	10	5
Governmental Affairs	4	6	3
Foreign Relations	3	4	2
Agriculture, Nutrition, and Forestry	3	4	2
Finance	1	2	1
Joint Economic Committee	1	2	1

ings led to the congressional action to create the National Climate Program, a research project that was the predecessor to the US Global Change Research Program (Pielke 2000a).

The first hearing to focus exclusively on global warming was held in 1980 in the Senate Committee on Energy and Natural Resources (SCENR 1980b). This hearing was convened in response to a report by the National Academy of Sciences on the climate effects of carbon dioxide (Charney et al. 1979). Between 1980 and 1986, members of Congress held seven hearings on climate change and framed these hearings in terms of the state of climate change research and the policy implications of climate change. Then, in 1987, the number of hearings held and the number of committees holding hearings took a significant jump (figure 2.6), with seven hearings held in that year alone.[32] Furthermore, there was more discussion of the policy implications of climate change, and there were frequent discussions of the policy responses that might be warranted. This shift spurred subsequent stakeholder mobilization which, in turn, sparked explicit debate about climate change.

As in the acid rain debate, the initial discussion of climate change laid out the potential for warming and the need for increased research to address uncertainties in order to provide a clearly picture of the problem to policy makers. This early period of hearings (1975–1979) generated little debate about climate change, in part because members of Congress were not seriously considering action beyond funding federal research. The preponderance of witnesses during this period did not take a position for or against action to mitigate climate change (69.6 percent); 8.7 percent argued against policy action, and 21.7 percent favored policy action (figure 3.1). Also striking during this period is the overwhelming

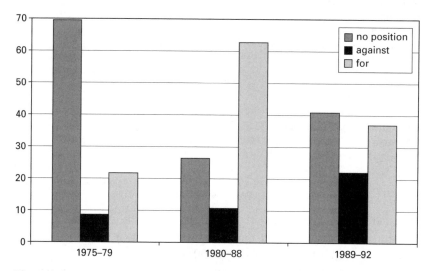

Figure 3.1
Witnesses' positions in three periods of climate change hearings. Witnesses who argued for a "no regrets policy," for climate change regulations, or for a stronger policy than that being discussed are coded as "for" policies to mitigate climate change. Witnesses arguing against such policies or against such policies as applied to their state or industry are coded as "against" policies to mitigate climate change.

representation of scientists holding PhDs in the natural sciences (77 percent of the witnesses who testified during the period of interest). Counting all witnesses between 1975 and 1979 who mention any advanced training, this percentage rises to 86 percent of witnesses (figure 3.2).

The next period of congressional activity, 1980–1988, began with the first hearing to focus exclusively on climate change (SCENR 1980b) and was capped by hearing in which James Hansen testified that he was, with 95 percent confidence, convinced that the world was getting warmer and that greenhouse gases were the cause (SCENR 1988a). When comparing this period of congressional debate to the earlier period, the number of witnesses who took a position on climate change relative to those who articulate no policy position changes dramatically (figure 3.1). Moreover, those who took positions during this period were much more likely to argue *in favor* of policy action to curb climate change, outnumbering those who argued against government action six to one. The hearings during this period were dominated by three committees: the House Com-

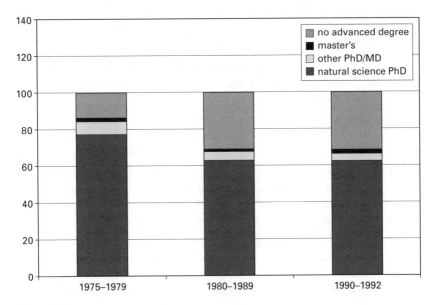

Figure 3.2
Educational distribution among witnesses attending hearings on climate change, 1975–1992. Data for the years 1990–1992 are taken from a random sample of 50 percent of the hearings held during these years.

mittee on Science, Space, and Technology, the Senate Committees on Energy and Natural Resources, and the Senate Committee on Environment and Public Works.[33] The dramatic shift in witness positions and the dominance of the issue by a handful of committees mark this period as one of congressional issue framing (Talbert, Jones, and Baumgartner 1995). In such a period, one expects bias in the hearings toward the favored position of the committee chair or chairs pushing the issue. The overwhelming majority of hearings held during this period are non-legislative (88 percent), a characteristic that is also consistent with issue framing in Congress.

Just as in the case of acid rain, an increase in the salience of the issue of climate change sparks a dramatic increase in the number of hearings held on the issue, an expansion of the number of committees holding hearings, and a notable increase in debate such that the hearings begin to look less one-sided. In particular, there is a significant increase—from 10 percent to 22 percent—in the percentage of witnesses who take a stand against government action to mitigate climate change (figure 3.1). While those arguing in favor of policy action still outnumber those arguing against, the discrepancy is not nearly as large. Figure 2.6 shows the number of committees holding hearings on climate change from 1975–1989 and includes a count of how many hearings are held each year.[34] The participation by previously silent committees is important in that it adds new venues from which to launch counter-narratives concerning climate change.

Also notable during this period was the appearance of "climate skeptics," or a group of scientists who publicly argued against the position forcefully articulated by James Hansen, i.e., that we know global warming is happening and ought to take steps to curb climate change sooner rather than later. Though several climate skeptics (including Richard Lindzen, S. Fred Singer, and Pat Michaels) became well known in climate policy circles in the 1990s, none of these scientists testified in Congress on climate change before 1989 (table 3.3). In view of the fact that none of the climate skeptics appears in congressional hearings before 1989, it is possible that James Hansen's forceful testimony prompted climate skeptics to enter the public debate in order to articulate a counter-viewpoint.

These data do not suggest that there was no debate about climate change in hearings before 1989, but they do suggest that the picture in the first two instances of congressional attention was dominated by

Table 3.3
Appearances by contrarian scientists in climate-change hearings, 1975–1999.
Source: LexisNexis Congressional Publication.

	Appearances	Time span
Michaels, Patrick	9	1989–1999
Lindzen, Richard	6	1991–1997
Singer, S. Fred	4	1989–1998
Baliunas, Sallie	3	1994–1997
Christy, John	3	1996–1998
Balling, Robert	1	1996

actors in Congress who used the hearings to advocate a particular position on climate change. Moreover, these actors did not meet significant resistance for a period of 8 years, perhaps the amount of time it took policy entrepreneurs in Congress to generate interest in the issue. One mark of the success of these efforts is the fact that other members of Congress eventually responded and offered their own framings of the climate change issue.

Debate in Congress about climate change has focused on a number of issues. At the most basic level, scientists debated whether significant increases in global average temperature were likely (SCENR 1994: 25–31). Some scientists argued that there was scant evidence of warming and cited discrepancies between temperature observations made at the Earth's surface versus those gathered using satellites (HCR 2003: 48–49).[35] For scientists who agreed that human-induced climate change was occurring, some argued that its consequences would not be severe (SCENR 1996: 41) or might be beneficial (SCFR 1989: 256). A second line of debate centered on the issue of whether the observed increase in global average temperature was driven by human activity (e.g., emissions of "greenhouse gases") or by natural causes (e.g., changes in solar activity) (SCENR 1994: 25–31; SCENR 1996: 40). A third topic debated during the hearings was the reliability of climate models (SCENR 1996: 53). Another line of debate questioned whether scientific research had provided sufficiently reliable insights about climate change to warrant policy action (HCEC 1989: 78, 81; SCFR 1989: 264–265; SCENR 1996: 41).

Stakeholders participating in legislative debate took predictable positions on the issue that paralleled those of their counterparts in the acid rain debate. Representatives of various interest groups mounted a number of attacks on the causal story that members of Congress and witnesses had established during hearings held in the 1980s. In addition, a number of scientists participated in hearings as early as 1989, articulating several arguments against the idea that climate change was occurring and would have negative consequences. These arguments followed a number of lines of reasoning, including (1) that there was no scientific consensus on global warming (SCENR 1992) or that significant scientific uncertainties precluded action (HCS 1997; SCCST 1991b), (2) that climate models were flawed in their predictions (HCS 1995b, 1996), (3) that no significant warming had been detected, especially by satellite measurements (HCS 1997), (4) that any observed warming was due to natural causes and could not be addressed through policy action (SCENR 1994, 1996), and (5) that global warming would produce no significant negative consequences (HCS 1995b; HCGR 1999; SCCST 2001). A slightly different approach taken by critics of the causal story was to avoid the nature of the problem altogether and to argue that the costs of action far outweighed any of the benefits (HCS 1997). The Kyoto Treaty, in particular, drew this type of criticism (HCGR 1998a,b; HCSB 1998a,b, 1999; HCR 2003).[36]

Environmentalists, as one would expect, took opposing positions. They argued that the costs of not taking immediate action to curb global warming were exceedingly high in that the effects of climate change would be irreversible. They advanced the idea that there was significant consensus among scientists about the expected warming, its causes, and consequences, often referring to reports issued by the Intergovernmental Panel on Climate Change to back this claim. Further, environmentalists routinely publicized the warmest years on record. During the 1980s, they were able to cite several years, including 1981, 1986, and 1987—years that still remain on the list of the 25 warmest. Environmentalists made use of the fact that the list was continually updated as new years made it onto the list. For example, in 2008, researchers reported that the eight warmest years on record have all occurred since 1998 (Science Daily 2008).

Several members of Congress were instrumental in advancing the congressional debate on climate change. In the early part of the congressional debate on climate change, Senator Albert Gore Jr. took the lead in drawing attention to the issue and even appeared as a witness in early hearings (SCEPW 1985b, 1986a). Gore's election as vice president in

1992 prompted a number of efforts by senators and representatives to prevent the White House from implementing measures of the Kyoto Protocol without adoption of the treaty by the Senate.[37] Senator John Chafee, on the other hand, introduced two bills designed to provide credit for those undertaking voluntary actions to reduce emissions of greenhouse gases.[38] After a lull in congressional attention, Senators John McCain and Joseph Lieberman held hearings and introduced a series of bills and amendments that, had they been adopted, would have created a market for tradable allowances of greenhouse gases.[39]

Events outside of Congress in 2006 and 2007 led to a notable shift in public discussions of climate change. First, climate change received substantial media and public attention after the release of Al Gore's film *An Inconvenient Truth* on August 31, 2006. This film was in theaters a month later when Governor Arnold Schwarzenegger of California signed into law the nation's first cap on greenhouse-gas emissions (Martin 2006). Schwarzenegger's signing of the bill was carefully staged to highlight the importance of California, the world's eighth-largest economy, on the international stage. Notably, Schwarzenegger invited the heads of state of the United Kingdom and Japan to the signing. Then, early in 2007, the Intergovernmental Panel on Climate Change published its Fourth Assessment Report. This report calls global warming "unequivocal" (IPCC 2007: 5) and argues that the bulk of the warming observed in the last century can be attributed to human activities with a 90 percent level of confidence (ibid.: 10). In addition, the US Supreme Court ruled on April 2, 2007 that the US Environmental Protection Agency was required under the Clean Air Act to regulate CO_2 as a pollutant (Barnes and Eilperin 2007). In October 2007, Gore and the IPCC were jointly awarded the Nobel Peace Prize for their work on climate change.

Taken together, these events increased the willingness of the media to portray climate change as if it is no longer a matter of serious scientific debate. Members of Congress also responded to the shift in tone and began to give the issue top billing. Speaker of the House Nancy Pelosi, for example, created a Select Committee on Energy Independence and Global Warming to head up House efforts to draw up a bill that would limit emissions of greenhouse gases in the United States (*Washington Post* 2007) and called for a bill to address climate change by July 2007.[40] In addition, between January and May of 2007, Congress held 39 hearings on climate change. Although Congress has not created a regulatory framework for addressing climate change—a policy change that climate change policy entrepreneurs have sought—the issue has stayed on the formal agenda, to a greater or lesser degree, for more than 30 years.

This overview for both cases provides broad brushstrokes for understanding the context for scientists' participation. Table 3.4 summarizes the major questions that dominated the debate for each issue. Comparing legislative debate for the two issues, one is struck by the shift between distributive and regulatory politics in each case (Lowi 1964, 1972). When members of Congress are only considering allocating federal dollars for research, witnesses tend not to enter into debates over the science or the policy questions that come up during the hearings. This changes dramatically when members of Congress and stakeholders begin to see the respective issues in terms of regulatory politics. Given Lowi's insight that distributive politics does not create oppositional politics while regulatory politics clearly does, this pattern in the hearings is not surprising. At the same time, the consideration of regulation creates a dynamic that runs counter to the way in which participants in policy debates often construe the role of science in policy making—that is, that science will present an increasingly clear and uncontested picture of the phenomenon in question.[41] The pattern in congressional debates of the two issues is almost the reverse. Each issue is initially presented in fairly stable terms, only to be followed by a period of heated debate that might look like eroding consensus.

Another way to compare distributive versus regulatory politics is the length of time it takes Congress to act. Acid rain arrived on the congressional agenda in 1975. By 1980, Congress had passed legislation to create a federally funded research program to address the issue. The period of regulatory debate took ten additional years. For climate change, the initial request for federal money came in 1956, and Congress responded by allocating funds to support the International Geophysical Year (1957–58). The National Climate Program Act of 1976 followed quickly from the reemergence of climate change on the congressional agenda in 1973. The period of regulatory debate about climate change, on the other hand, has now lasted more than 30 years.

Returning to the respective science narratives for each issue, one can see that the science narratives contain distributive as well as regulatory aspects. This suggests that Congress, as an institution, is unlikely to seriously debate the idea of creating federal research programs to learn more

Table 3.4
Issues dominating congressional debates on acid rain and climate change.

Acid rain		Climate change	
Is there really a problem?	Where are acid pollutants coming from?	Is there really a problem?	Is there scientific consensus?
Do the costs of policy action outweigh the benefits?	Is there scientific consensus on acid rain?	Do the costs of policy action outweigh the benefits?	Is there actually any warming?
Do we know enough to act?	Is acid precipitation damaging forests, soils, and surface waters?	Do we know enough to act?	If there is warming, it is caused by humans?
Should we conduct more research?	Does acid rain cause damage to crops?	Should we conduct more research?	Is the expected warming likely to have significant negative effects?
If we don't act now, will the problem advance past our ability to respond?	What is the buffering capacity of lakes and soils?	If we don't act now, will the problem advance past our ability to respond?	Will there be more extreme weather events (droughts, storms, flooding)?
How can we address acid rain with the least cost to industry and to high sulfur coal producers?	Is the damage of acidification reversible?	What are the best strategies to limit climate change? Are there no-regrets policies that have benefits beyond climate change mitigation?	Is the damage irreversible? Will ecosystems be able to adapt?
How should we respond to Canada's concerns as the recipient of long-range pollutants from the US?	What are the effects of acid rain on visibility, buildings and monuments, and human health?	Should the US participate in an international agreement to limit greenhouse gas emissions?	Could there be major shifts in climate such as a change in patterns of deep ocean circulation?

about these issues. The speed at which each issue travels from initial congressional notice to the appropriation of federal research dollars is dizzying. Institutionalization of the respective issues occurred with remarkably little fanfare; each has been with us ever since.

Scientists as Witnesses

Because little has been written about scientists' role in congressional settings, one reads the hearings with little guidance as to what to look for. In this section, I present data from the hearings that illustrate common exchanges between policy makers and scientists and provide statistical analysis of witness testimony to support the qualitative findings. Analysis of the hearings demonstrates that members of Congress actively seek two things from scientists who participate in the hearings: (1) credible statements about the current scientific knowledge with respect to the issue at hand and (2) scientists' policy preferences. Scientists, for their part, adopt a number of different strategies in attempting to negotiate the legislative policy terrain.

Establishing Credibility

Both members of Congress and scientists drew attention to the idea of scientific objectivity during hearings. This suggests that one reason for including scientists in hearings is to attempt to establish the credibility of the information discussed at the hearing. These efforts are clear examples of boundary work in which members of Congress and scientists attempt to draw meaningful distinctions between that which is scientific, and that which falls outside of the realm of science (Gieryn 1983, 1995, 1999). A number of examples illustrate typical efforts to invoke "objective science." Members often refer to witnesses' scientific credentials or to the scientific status of studies being reviewed by the hearing. Representative Henry Waxman's introduction of a panel of scientists testifying about acid rain is typical: "This morning we will hear from a very distinguished panel of scientists who can inform us about the causes and effects of acid rain." (HCEC 1981a: 227) Senator John Chafee, in a hearing he chaired on climate change, begins his opening statement with an overview of important scientific discoveries with respect to climate change from 1986 to the present. His statement includes mentions of the work of the Nobel Prize-winning scientist Svante Arrhenius in the nineteenth century, a 1990 appeal signed by 49 Nobel Prize winners and 700 members of the National Academy of Sciences, and the 1995 report from the IPCC ("representing thousands of climate scientists") that argued that the balance of evidence linked human activity to climate change (SCEPW 1997: 2). Members also highlight the status of science in policy making by convening hearings in which the preponderance of witness panels are made up of scientists holding PhD degrees.[42]

Scientists also call attention to the credibility of scientific research to underscore the reliability of the information they present. There are numerous examples. For instance, Daniel Albritton, a scientist representing the National Oceanic and Atmospheric Administration, takes pains to point out the scientific credibility of the first report of the Intergovernmental Panel on Climate Change (Houghton 1990). "First of all," Albritton argues, "it is a scientific statement. It is a scientific statement done by the world's best scientists. Over 250 scientists worldwide prepared this report in a time period of a little over a year. . . . The point that I wanted to underscore in this regard is that it is a scientific document. It was peer reviewed by over 300 of the world's scientists for scientific accuracy and for consistency, just as our own scientific publications are peer reviewed." (SCEPW 1991: 6)

In another hearing on climate change, Alan D. Hecht, in testimony about a report published by the Intergovernmental Panel on Climate Change, notes that the report considers negative as well as positive effects of global warming. By pointing this out, Hecht suggests that the report provides a balanced account of the expected effects associated with climate change rather than downplaying aspects of climate change that might undermine momentum for political action to curb emissions of greenhouse gases (SCCST 1990). Here, Hecht makes a case for the neutrality of the IPCC report with respect to the political controversy over climate change.

Scientists who testify on acid rain also take pains to establish the objectivity of the science they are presenting. One example comes from scientists' testimony regarding an embattled report released by the government's National Acid Precipitation Assessment Program (HCSST 1988). Scientists attending this hearing draw a sharp distinction between the body of the report, which contains peer-reviewed chapters, and the executive summary which was included in the report without peer reviews. Gene E. Likens, for example, argues as follows in his written statement: "I am particularly critical of the Executive Summary, which badly misrepresents the general scientific understanding about air pollution and acid deposition, and either ignores or discounts out-of-hand the thousands of scientific articles published in high quality journals that show serious ecological damage caused by air pollution and acid deposition." (ibid.: 55)

Making Policy Statements

For scientists, defending the credibility of scientific work is second nature. Faith in the scientific method and in the capacity of peer review to separate good research from bad is deep-seated.[43] Scientists are in less familiar terrain, however, when members of Congress ask them to reveal their policy preferences during a hearing. The hearings in which scientists are asked to weigh in on policy options are numerous, and the coaching that often comes with such questions suggests that members anticipate the difficulty scientists have, or pretend to have, in revealing their policy preferences in the legislative setting. For example, in a hearing on the IPCC Third Assessment Report, Senator McCain prefaced his effort to get scientists on record with policy positions with the following comments:

I would like to ask one more question of the panel, and this is something which I am sure will not be an easy one or a comfortable one for you to respond to. I want you to for a moment put yourself in the shoes of the legislator. We have now received numerous reports. We now have cumulative evidence that there is climate change. We have had some disagreements on what should be done, if anything, and so I would like to begin with you, Dr. Lindzen, and ask you, as a legislator, what policies or what legislation would you propose to attempt to address these issues, if any? (SCCST 2001: 60–61)

On the other hand, scientists are also berated for not acquiescing to members' demands. For example, in a 1983 hearing, Representative James Scheuer closed the day's hearing with these comments: "I must say that I was disappointed in the testimony. . . . Maybe on some other occasion you'll [referring to a panel of scientists who testified that day] speak a little bit more directly and without so much circumlocution and backing and filling and hedging and you'll give us a little more guidance that we've been able to get out of you this morning." (HCSST 1983: 106) The extent to which members ask, push, cajole, prod, and shame scientists into making policy statements demonstrates that objective information is not the only thing members want from scientists.

One is struck by the extent to which scientists' prepared statements conform to the idealized model of science in decision making. Scientists' written statements typically include information about what is known, the major uncertainties that remain, and the time frame in which those uncertainties might be resolved. The subtext of the prepared statements is that scientists participate in congressional hearings in order to report to decision makers the state of the discipline—that is, to say "Here is what scientists know about the problem you are considering."

Perhaps more revealing than the prepared statements are the exchanges between members of Congress and scientists. The prepared statements represent scientists' expectations about what members, or maybe society at large, want from them when they come to testify. The questions scientists receive from members once they have delivered their prepared statements illustrate the gaps between what members want and what scientists, left to their own devices, will provide.

When members of Congress press scientists to take policy positions, scientists can be separated into three categories on the basis of their responses. *Unapologetic boundary crossers* reveal their policy preferences with little or no fanfare about the boundary between science and policy. *Apologetic boundary crossers* respond to questions about their policy positions by shifting roles and answer such questions as private citizens rather than as scientists.[44] *Boundary observers* are adamant in refusing to answer policy questions. The unapologetic boundary crossers exhibit similar behavior to their counterparts in agenda setting who merge objective science and policy commitments easily. The apologetic boundary crossers and the boundary observers demonstrate that boundary negotiations, at least for some scientists, are explicit in the legislative setting. The following examples illustrate the three cases.

Unapologetic Boundary Crossing

• Jay Hair, Executive Vice President of the National Wildlife Foundation, presents a letter with signatures from 35 scientists who support the view that the scientific consensus is sufficient to justify immediate legislative steps to curb acid rain. (SCEPW 1981b: 718–721)[45]

• Edward Haase of the Phelps Dodge Corporation argues that two extreme responses to acid rain are possible. One is to take no action; the other is to "[enact] a massive emission reduction program without responding to ongoing research and cost effectiveness" (SCENR 1984:

560). Haase advises supporting more scientific research, only incremental adoption of emissions reductions requirements guided by cost effectiveness, and flexible permits that would allow industry to achieve reductions in the most cost-effective manner (ibid.: 561).

• James Gibson of Colorado State University is asked whether we know enough to act. He responds that there is enough known about the effects of sulfur emissions on lake acidity to warrant controls (SCEPW 1986b: 10).[46]

Apologetic Boundary Crossing

• Barry Huebert, a professor of chemistry at Colorado College, when asked by Representative Henry Waxman if the government was doing enough to find out the effects of acid rain, prefaces his response thus: "This is purely a personal opinion. I don't think they are doing enough. . . ." (HCEC 1981a: 106–107)

• Frank Press, president of the National Academy of Sciences, is asked by Senator Gore whether a 10–15-year research program doesn't delay action too long. Press responds: "I have to be careful about going beyond my own organization's studies and recommendations. But I am sure that you do expect me to give you some of my own views on these issues, and with care I will do that." (SCCST 1987: 18) Press goes on to recommend policies creating research on alternative energy sources (SCCST 1987: 18–19).[47]

Boundary Observance

• Representative Charles Whitely asks Paul Ringold, the associate director of the National Acid Precipitation Assessment Program, to give the committee his policy recommendations. When Ringold refuses, Whitely reads language to him from NAPAP's originating legislation to point out to Ringold that NAPAP is required to base its policy recommendations on its scientific findings. Ringold again refuses to answer and only promises that NAPAP will be ready to make recommendations in 2–3 years (HCA 1986).

• Jerry Mahlman of the National Oceanic and Atmospheric Administration's Geophysical Fluid Dynamics Laboratory, prefaces his comments during congressional testimony this way: "Because I speak with the credentials as a physical scientist, I do not offer personal opinions on what society should do about these predicted climate changes. Societal actions in response to greenhouse warming involve value judgments that are beyond the realm of climate science." (HCS 1995b: 12)

• The following exchange between Senator Max Baucus and Daniel Albritton of NOAA is quoted at length to illustrate the contortions that sensitivity to the science/policy boundary can produce among scientists who participate in legislative settings[48]: Albritton mentions that he had worked on ozone depletion and has a strong sense of déjà vu in terms of the uncertainty about taking action. He says that signatories to the Montreal Protocol signed on the strength of the theory rather than waiting for confirmation through direct observation. Albritton says we should keep that in mind. Baucus responds with a question:

Baucus: Is it fair for me therefore to infer from what you just said that even though we are here now discussing this matter today and not five years from today, that based upon the probabilities and your predictions we should not wait but we should act now?

Albritton: The answer to that is not purely a scientific question.

Baucus: No, it's not a scientific question. It is your recommendation. It is your best recommendation based upon your experience.

Albritton: Well, my experience has been describing the science—the pros and cons and the knowns and unknowns—so that an informed decision could be made. I only cite that in terms of the ozone protection decision-makers took a course of action based on their strength of conviction in a theory knowing that action sooner would be easier than action later in that regard, and there are many analogies for the greenhouse effect.

Baucus: I'm not trying to put words in your mouth, but I'm just asking you as a private citizen, whether in your judgment it makes sense to therefore act now.

Albritton: Well, I can describe that as a private citizen.

Baucus: You can?

Albritton: Namely, I take out insurance against an event that I actually work hard to prevent happening, namely, my death. I view that I can safely invest a fraction of my income in taking out insurance so that something would not happen.

Baucus: I'll take that as a positive response. (SCEPW 1991: 20–21).

A special subcategory of the boundary observers are those who try to avoid being asked for their policy positions by carefully laying out, at the opening of their testimonies, the kinds of information they are willing to offer. Scientists who do this must offer their own definition of how a line between science and policy should be drawn. The following statement, in which Christopher Bernabo, Executive Director of NAPAP, offers an elaborate explanation of the division between science and policy, provides an example:

Addressing the acid rain issue effectively requires both research and appropriate environmental policies. Objective scientific information is only one input, albeit an important one, to developing environmental policies. Policymakers, not researchers, must decide when there is adequate information for them to make a given decision. The scientists can define at any point in time what is known, with what level of uncertainty, and what isn't yet known.

Questions policymakers must also address require making a host of subjective judgments for which scientists have no special expertise. For example, scientists have the task of relating the response of ecosystems to the amount of acid deposition they receive; but it is the role of policymakers to determine whether the deposition should be limited, and by how much considering the societal costs and benefits of prescribed actions. Although one major goal of the National Program is to quantify such costs and benefits, often costs and especially benefits cannot be quantified reliably, and subjective value judgments are needed to supplement scientific analyses. Science does not provide a basis for making such value judgments—those judgments are the role of the policymaker. However, the confidence in selecting the most effective actions to yield the desired environmental results can be improved greatly by enhanced scientific understanding. (SCENR 1984: 351)

Bernabo's effort at boundary work here is an attempt to manage policy makers' expectations about the role of science in policy making. Bernabo clearly is arguing that scientific research can help policy deliberations but will stop well short of actively engaging in them.

Taken together, the above examples demonstrate that scientists have a number of options in deciding how to respond to policy questions during congressional hearings. Scientists exhibit one of three responses when pressed to make policy statements during the hearings, demonstrating that negotiations of the science/policy boundary are a prominent, visible part of scientists' participation in legislative hearings.

Boundary Work in the Hearings

In evaluating the boundary work conducted by scientists at this stage, institutional affiliation surfaces as a potential explanatory variable. Three categories of institutional affiliation appear to be relevant to the boundary work in evidence during the hearings. Analytically speaking, these categories are not very robust. For example, the categories are not necessarily mutually exclusive. Any scientist may carry one or more of these institutional affiliations. However, each category serves to highlight a specific aspect of scientific work that, at some point during the time period in question, is usefully distinguished from a universal category of "scientist."

The first category—academic or university scientists—is a general one and refers broadly to the scientific community that is actively publishing in peer-reviewed scientific journals on the subjects of acid rain or climate change.[49] Second are research scientists who work for interested organizations such as energy utilities or environmental NGOs. Because these scientists' parent organizations are likely to be active lobbyists during legislative debate, their participation is shaped by the involvement of their parent institutions. The third category includes scientists who work directly for the agencies administering federally funded research on acid rain or climate change. This category is most important in the acid rain case in that scientists involved in NAPAP are often called to testify at hearings in which NAPAP reports are the subject of discussion.[50] In these instances, it is the scientists who are directly employed by the federal government to run NAPAP who testify as NAPAP scientists.[51] Though this group of scientists is small relative to the larger community conducting research on acid precipitation, they are disproportionately visible in the congressional setting.

NAPAP scientists are not the only ones who refuse to make policy statements during congressional testimony. However, they stand out in their consistency as a group in their approach, or rather their lack of approach, to the science/policy boundary. The data show that all scientists representing NAPAP who are asked to make policy statements refuse.[52] As the example of boundary work cited above demonstrates, NAPAP scientists are conscious of the boundary even when they have not been prompted by others in the hearings to approach the science/policy boundary. In the case of climate change, some scientists who work for agencies funded through the United States Global Change Research Program take care not to cross into policy territory in their testimonies. This is the case, for example, with Albritton and Mahlman (see above), though Mahlman, it appears, was less tempted than Albritton.[53] However, there is at least one notable exception. James Hansen, a NASA scientist, stepped into obvious policy territory when he published his recommendation that policy toward climate change should focus not on CO_2 but on other greenhouse gases that would be easier to reduce (Hansen et al. 2000).[54]

The explanation for the reticence of the NAPAP scientists has two likely sources. First, NAPAP began its research in 1982 under the Reagan administration, and Reagan was known to be against acid rain controls. This may have limited the willingness of NAPAP scientists to state their policy preferences, given that they were, according to one of the directors of NAPAP, "proponents or concerned observers" of the acid rain problem (HCSST 1988).[55] Second, NAPAP scientists are in close proximity to decision-making power, which increases the likelihood (a) that NAPAP research will be perceived as politicized and/or (b) that NAPAP research will become politicized.[56] That some government scientists in the climate change case exhibit similar reticence during a period of administration support of the climate change issue gives weight to the structural explanation.

Whereas the NAPAP scientists were uniformly resistant to stating their policy preferences during congressional hearings, we see a bit more variation in boundary work among agency scientists who testify in climate hearings. One reason why some scientists connected with the USGCRP may not have exhibited the same reluctance in discussing policy alternatives is that the first assessment of climate change produced by the USGCRP was released in November 2000 (NAST 2000). To date, no hearings have been held on this assessment. If the argument about proximity to power is correct, we would expect USGCRP scientists to exhibit similar reticence as their NAPAP counterparts in making policy statements in the event they are called to testify at hearings reviewing the USGCRP's work.

Another difference between the acid rain case and the climate change case is the fact that climate scientists working in government settings are somewhat insulated from the political negotiations around climate change controls given that those discussions were, at least during the 1990s, primarily taking place at the international level.[57] Another factor that may allow USGCRP scientists to make policy statements is the presence and stature of the IPCC reports on climate change. Whereas the USGCRP is not supposed to make policy recommendations, the IPCC is specifically organized to make links between the scientific understanding of climate change and policy options in responding to climate change.

Once the IPCC has made such links, scientists may feel more comfortable discussing policy options under the aegis of the peer-reviewed work of the IPCC.

One notable trend among all scientists across both cases and the entire period under study is the willingness to call for more scientific research. Typically, after scientists have discussed uncertainties in their knowledge, they raise the need for more research. On occasion, calls for research and (of course) for research funding are made much more pointedly. For example, Frank Press makes the following case for continued support for climate research: "A research effort of the complexity and magnitude I have outlined requires stable funding over a relatively long period. Staying the course has not always been the hallmark of federal research support." (SCCST 1987: 14) Though the endorsement of federal resources to support continued research is a policy recommendation, it never produces the kind of agonizing gymnastics that some of the scientists engage in when pressed to discuss the question of whether we know enough to act or what those actions might be. That is, scientists who discuss levels of federal funding for acid rain or climate research are all unapologetic boundary crossers.

The qualitative analysis suggests that scientists working directly for government research programs are the least likely to make policy statements. Academic scientists appear to go either way; scientists representing NGOs appear to be the most likely to take policy positions. To analyze this pattern more robustly, acid rain hearings from 1979 to 1990 and climate change hearings from 1975 to 1992 were coded to capture witness education, organizational affiliation, and policy position with respect to regulatory controls.[58] Twelve hundred and nine witnesses testified at the acid rain hearings held between 1975 and 1990. The climate change data include 508 witnesses who testified between 1975 and 1992.[59] Witnesses were divided into six education categories: (1) natural science PhD, (2) medical doctorate (MD), (3) engineering PhD, (4) social science PhD, (5) master's degree or any mention of graduate training in the sciences, and (6) no advanced degree or training in the sciences. In addition, witnesses were categorized according to organizational affiliation. For acid rain, the coded categories were (1) interest group, (2) business, (3) government, (4) academic, (5) think tank, and (6) self. For climate change, because there were witnesses representing countries other than the United States, a seventh category was added and coded as "other." Table 3.5 gives summary statistics for witness characteristics for acid rain; tables 3.6 and 3.7 provide summary statistics for witnesses testifying in climate change hearings.

The witnesses are coded in order to make it possible to study, in particular, how scientists interact with members of Congress during hearings on the two issues. Given that the label "scientist" might be contested in this setting, the coding scheme attempts to be agnostic with respect to who is considered a "scientist." Rather than starting with a definition of "scientist," the study examines those actors who present themselves or are presented as experts either in the science of acid rain or in climate change. The study tracks education level and distinguishes among natural science, social science, engineering, and medical training. In reviewing the data, the overwhelming majority of witnesses who introduce themselves or who are introduced as experts in the science of climate change mention having a PhD in the natural sciences.[60] Although it may be that there are many alternate ways to be an expert in the science of acid rain or of climate change, it is clear from the data that a PhD in the natural sciences is a convenient shorthand used by members of Congress and their staff to portray such expertise during congressional hearings.[61]

Table 3.5
Summary statistics on acid rain witnesses ($N = 1,210$).

	Number of witnesses	Percentage of witnesses
Education levels		
Natural science PhD	266	22.00
Medical doctorate (MD)	24	2.00
Engineering PhD	26	2.10
Social science PhD	13	1.10
Master's in sciences	22	1.80
No graduate training in sciences	859	71.00
Organization affiliations		
Interest group	457	37.80
Business	162	13.40
Government	452	37.40
Academic	111	9.10
Think tank	5	0.40
Self	23	1.90

Table 3.6
Summary statistics on climate change witnesses, 1975–1989 (*N* = 348).

	Number of witnesses	Percentage of witnesses
Education levels		
Natural science PhD	225	64.70
Medical doctorate (MD)	1	0.30
Engineering PhD	7	2
Social science PhD	9	2.60
Master's in sciences	6	1.70
No graduate training in sciences	100	28.70
Organization affiliations		
Interest group	66	19
Business	21	6
Government	141	40.50
Academic	90	25.90
Think tank	24	6.90
Self	4	1.10
Other	2	0.60

Table 3.7
Summary statistics on climate change witnesses, 1990–1992 (*N* = 159). These data are from a random sample of 50 percent of the hearings held on climate change during these years.

	Number of witnesses	Percentage of witnesses
Education levels		
Natural science PhD	99	62.30
Medical doctorate (MD)	1	0.60
Engineering PhD	0	0
Social science PhD	5	3.20
Master's in science	4	2.50
No graduate training in sciences	50	31.40
Organization affiliations		
Interest group	28	17.60
Business	7	4.40
Government	68	42.80
Academic	46	28.90
Think tank	8	5
Self	0	0
Other	2	1.30

Finally, witnesses were coded according to the policy position they took on acid rain and on climate change regulations, respectively. This coding proved to be the most difficult in that witnesses do not always state their policy positions clearly and/or they articulate different positions at different stages of their testimony. To capture the nuance in witness articulation of policy positions, several categories were created to capture the different ways that witnesses would present their policy positions. Tables 3.8 and 3.9 list the categories of policy positions found in the acid rain and climate change hearings, respectively. Both tables indicate how these coding schemes are simplified to capture categories of witnesses who broadly support regulatory action in the two cases versus those who, by and large, argue against regulations. This more simplified approach to the data also maintains a category for witnesses whose positions with respect to policy change are ambiguous.

The coding of witnesses did not prejudge which witnesses might introduce themselves as scientists or be introduced as scientists. That is, a witness who did not hold an advanced degree in a relevant field could claim the title of scientist or be given that title by the members of Congress organizing a hearing. It turns out that that happens very rarely. In the large majority of cases, if a witness is presented or presents him or herself as an expert in the sciences related to acid rain or climate change, that witness holds a PhD in the natural sciences.[62] It is, however, not surprising that witnesses who labeled scientists by themselves or others are, overwhelmingly individuals who hold PhDs in the natural sciences. Witnesses may be invited to testify before Congress for any number of reasons. Yet, in the acid rain and climate change hearings studied here, members relied overwhelmingly on individuals holding PhDs in the natural sciences when they wanted to have "scientific expertise" represented in the hearing. This suggests that, in spite of the ability for individuals to disagree on what it means to be a "scientist," this particular definition is one that participants relied upon that did not create controversy.

The coded data substantiate several patterns that emerged in the qualitative analysis of the hearings. First, these data show that scientists are more likely to avoid taking a policy position than their non-science-trained counterparts. When separating witnesses holding PhDs in the natural sciences from all other witnesses, this relationship is statistically significant for both the acid rain hearings and for the climate

Table 3.8
Acid rain witnesses' positions.

	Number of witnesses	Percentage of witnesses	Ambiguous policy position	Support for acid rain controls	No support for acid rain controls
Witness discusses acid rain but takes no policy position	267	22.00	X		
No support for acid rain controls of any kind	198	16.40			X
Controls OK in theory, but not in my state or applied to my industry[a]	185	15.30			X
Controls OK in theory, but witness argues against a specific detail of a bill in question	92	7.60	X		
Support for acid rain controls	379	31.30		X	
Argues for stronger controls than those being considered	36	3.00		X	
No mention of acid rain in witness testimony	53	4.40	X		

a. Witnesses who said that acid rain controls were acceptable, but not when applied to their industry or in their state are understood as arguing against controls given that they don't want to participate in the costs of controlling acid rain. These witnesses are basically arguing for no controls that would affect them. These witnesses differed from the witnesses who said that they supported controls, but felt like some feature of a bill was problematic. This latter category is hard to interpret as weakly supporting or being against acid rain controls given that some in this category may have honestly wanted to see regulations, but wanted to see improvements in the regulations proposed, while others used this as a rhetorical tactic to undermine support for any bill under consideration.

Table 3.9
Climate change witnesses' positions, 1975–1992. These data include a random sample of 50 percent of the hearings held between 1990 and 1992. Thus, the witness totals do not represent an accurate count of witnesses who testified during the period 1990–1992. At the same time, the random sample should provide an unbiased estimate of the percentages of witnesses taking a given policy position during this period.

	Number of witnesses	Percentage of witnesses	Ambiguous policy position	Support for acid rain controls	No support for acid rain controls
Witness discusses climate change, but takes no policy position	151	29.80	X		
Witness argues against climate change controls of any kind	8	1.60			X
Witness says controls are OK in theory, but argues against having them applied to witness's state/industry	31	6.10			X
Witness says controls are OK in theory, but argues against a specific detail of a bill in question	2	0.40	X		
Witness advocates for no-regrets policies	74	14.60		X	
Witness argues for climate change controls	101	19.90		X	
Witness argues for stronger controls than those being considered	6	1.20		X	
Witness does not mention climate change in testimony	134	26.40	X		

hearings (table 3.10). For the acid rain hearings, the relationship remains statistically significant when comparing *all* witnesses who mention advanced degrees with witnesses who claim no advanced training. Looking at the climate change hearings, we see the same relationship. Specifically, those with advanced training appear more likely than those without to refrain from stating a policy position, but the relationship narrowly misses statistical significance at the 95 percent confidence level.[63]

Turning to the organizational affiliation of this group, we also find the qualitative analysis substantiated. When we compare the natural science PhDs who take no policy position with the natural science PhDs who take any policy position, what stands out is the significant percentage non-position takers who are government scientists. In fact, the likelihood of taking no policy position increases if a natural science PhD works for the government. This relationship is statistically significant for both the acid rain and the climate change cases (table 3.11).[64] In contrast, looking specifically at witnesses who hold natural science PhDs and academic positions, they are equally divided among those who take policy positions and those who do not. Moreover, there is no statistically significant difference between academic PhDs and non-academic PhDs in the likelihood of taking a policy position in the hearings. This is true for both the acid rain and climate change hearings (table 3.12).

Table 3.10
Witnesses' positions by education level.

	Takes no policy position	Takes any position	
	N (%)	N (%)	p value
Acid rain hearings			
PhD, MD, or master's	136 (42.0)	188 (58.0)	0.000
No advanced education	103 (12.9)	697 (87.1)	
Natural science PhD	118 (47.6)	130 (52.4)	0.000
Any other education	121 (13.8)	755 (86.2)	
Climate change hearings			
PhD, MD, or master's	119 (43.3)	156 (56.7)	0.066
No advanced education	32 (32.7)	66 (67.3)	
Natural science PhD	114 (45.4)	137 (54.6)	0.005
Any other education	37 (30.3)	85 (69.7)	

Table 3.11
Witnesses' positions by education and government affiliation.

	Takes no policy position	Takes any position	
	N (%)	N (%)	p value
Acid rain hearings			
Natural science PhDs employed by government	61 (70.1)	26 (29.9)	0.000
All other natural science PhDs	57 (35.4)	104 (64.6)	
Climate change hearings			
Natural science PhDs employed by government	50 (62.5)	30 (37.5)	0.000
All other natural science PhDs	64 (37.4)	107 (62.6)	

Table 3.12
Witnesses' positions by education and academic affiliation.

	Takes no policy position	Takes any position	
	N (%)	N (%)	p value
Acid rain hearings			
Natural science PhDs with academic affiliations	45 (50)	45 (50)	0.565
All other natural science PhDs	73 (46.2)	85 (53.8)	
Climate change hearings			
Natural science PhDs with academic affiliations	46 (44.7)	57 (55.3)	0.841
All other natural science PhDs	68 (46)	80 (54)	

These data suggest that government scientists are less likely to take policy positions than their counterparts in academia or those who represent interest groups. This may, of course, be selection bias—scientists attracted to government jobs may be more likely to feel that it is important to maintain their objectivity. On its face, this argument, however, seems counter-intuitive. Scientists who most value objectivity seem like they would stay in academia and avoid the potential of advising policy makers altogether. A more likely explanation is that scientists who work for the federal government feel that their credibility as objective scientists is much more fragile than their academic counterparts feel that theirs is. Using the same logic, scientists who are employed by interest groups may feel that their organizational affiliation, by itself, casts them as interested scientists, leaving them little to lose if they express policy positions before legislators.[65]

Analysis

The empirical evidence presented here reinforces expected patterns of congressional policy making. Supporting the findings of Talbert, Jones, and Baumgartner (1995), early congressional hearings are held by proponents of a policy issue who wish to see that issue advanced on the formal congressional agenda. These hearings are biased toward the committee chair's preferred view, as expected. In addition, however, these data show that these early hearings match closely the science narratives established during agenda setting and offer little opportunity for dissenting views. Moreover, scientists are very heavily represented in these early hearings. Thus, one finds a period in congressional policy making during which debate is limited and science narratives are prominently displayed in the legislative setting.

At the same time, this chapter raises several interesting questions about scientists' role in policy making: Why do scientists become more visibly aware of a boundary between science and policy in the legislative stage of the process when they display no such sensitivity during agenda setting? Why do members of Congress push scientists to make policy statements in the first place? Can we predict which scientists will observe the science/policy boundary in legislative settings? The section addresses these questions and explores several notable differences across the two cases in patterns' of scientists' participation.

What Is So Special about Congress?

If, as this study claims, scientists' behavior is systematically different in each stage of the policy-making process, context might be driving how scientists view their roles in each setting. The question, then, is What happens in the congressional setting that makes scientists more aware of or concerned about a boundary between science and policy? A related question is Why would the expectation of neutral participation not apply evenly across the policy-making process?

There are three factors that might explain scientists' tendency to show explicit concern about the science/policy boundary during congressional hearings. The first is that scientists may have less control of their message during congressional hearings. During agenda setting, scientists rely on publications intended for non-science audiences, editorials, press conferences, and interviews with the media to get their message out. Some of these outlets allow scientists to directly control the information they wish to convey. On the other hand, media coverage of scientific research relies on journalists and editors as intermediaries between scientists and the public. Although journalists may mischaracterize scientific findings, professional norms in journalism dictate that journalists suppress their own political views in order to accurately reflect "both sides" in a debate. A journalist working under this norm will try to convey as accurately as possible the story the scientist wants to tell—that is, to let the scientist represent that "side" of the issue. Members of Congress are under no such obligation. To the contrary, members of Congress very often push scientists to say what the *members* want them to say and steer scientists away from the comfortable terrain of prepared statements during a hearing. Coming up against such clear role expectations may put scientists on guard and make them more concerned about how their statements will be interpreted.

Adding to that is the problem of proximity to decision-making power. When concrete policy action is under consideration, scientists may feel pressure to say only things that are likely to be backed by the larger scientific community. The immediate goal of agenda setting, on the other hand, is to hold up an idea for debate and deliberation. A restrained account of scientific certainties and uncertainties regarding an emerging environmental policy issue might be insufficient to generate interest outside of scientific circles. If scientists feel like the agenda-setting stage does not carry with it specific political commitments, it may be easier for them to justify straying from the strict scientific record. The fact that the stakes clearly are higher in the congressional setting once an issue has reached the formal agenda may, in and of itself, alter scientists' conduct.

Another explanation for the change in behavior is that scientists themselves may view the process of agenda setting as apolitical or "prepolitical." Scientists' own conceptions of their social role may include alerting the public to potential problems in the environment. Such action may not alter their view of themselves as objective experts. Participating in debates about choices among policy alternatives, however, falls squarely in political territory. Attention to the science/policy boundary may arise in the legislative stage of decision making because it is here that scientists recognize, definitely, that they have entered the political fray. Though such a boundary between what is scientific and what is political does not stand up under strict scrutiny, it still may function as a marker that is meaningful for scientists.

Finally, scientists who are not active during agenda setting sometimes appear in legislative hearings. In such cases, the setting selects for type of scientist. Those willing to make policy statements appear both in agenda setting and in legislative debates. Those scientists who are wary of being viewed as biased, on the other hand, might be less likely to be active in the agenda-setting stage, where scientists, almost by definition, have to make a political case for why their issue merits attention. If setting selects for type of scientist, then the differences we see when comparing agenda setting and legislation may be explained by the fact that more "types" of scientists are participating in legislative debates, including those who are very wary of making policy statements.[66]

Who Cares What Scientists Think about Policy Options?

Evidently, members of Congress care about scientists' views of policy choices related to acid rain and climate change. The frequency with which scientists are asked their policy preferences suggests that members of Congress value such statements from scientists. Efforts to engage scientists in discussions of policy options are clearly at odds with what some scientists see as their role, i.e., providing objective information and letting policy experts draw implications from that information. It is curious that members of Congress who seem to draw on scientists' credibility also put them in a position that might erode that credibility. In fact, there is evidence that members of Congress become less interested in scientists who are viewed as having an obvious policy bent.[67] By pushing scientists to make policy statements, members of Congress rely on scientists as a resource in congressional hearings, but are also willing to erode the future usefulness of that resource by encouraging scientists to go on record with policy commitments.

Certainly, members of Congress want to be able to claim that their own policy positions are supported by objective science. If it is true that objective science leads to obvious policy choices, then there is no contradiction between seeking objective scientific inputs and showing that scientists are behind a member's preferred policy position. The practical problem is that numerous and even contradictory policy positions can be supported by legitimate interpretations of the scientific record.[68] This is not purely a function of the wiggle room that scientific uncertainty affords. Because objective scientific information does not point to incontrovertible policy choices, members of Congress are, in fact, placing scientists in an awkward position by asking them to make policy commitments. In saying "Given the scientific evidence you have seen, what would you do?" members ask scientists to provide political interpretations of the existing scientific record. Though asking for this type of boundary crossing may not contradict the fundamentals of scientific practice in society, it certainly does counter the rhetorically invoked role for scientists in policy making, i.e., that of neutral experts.

One reason that members of Congress might press scientists for their policy views is to gauge the confidence that the scientists have in the findings they are reporting.[69] This assumes, of course, that scientists will not recommend action until major scientific uncertainties are resolved, an assumption that may not be warranted.[70] Another reason that members of Congress might press scientists to make policy claims is that scientists' statements appear to garner a great deal of media attention. One way to see this is to compare the media coverage that Al Gore (then a senator) and James Hansen (a NASA scientist) received during the 1980s. Both men, arguably, have been important agenda setters for climate change. Although this comparison may only tell us something about Hansen's skills versus Gore's, the literature on agenda setting leads us to expect that a senator would have an enormous advantage over an agency scientist in capturing media attention (Kingdon 1984). The outcome is quite the reverse in the case of these two individuals. Between 1980 and 1989, the years in which climate change gained prominence as national policy issue, Gore is mentioned in 29 media stories related to climate change; Hansen is mentioned in 41 stories.[71] Another noteworthy aspect of the comparison is that, although the majority of the stories about both individuals were written in 1989 (a particularly good year for media coverage of climate change), there are only two stories about Gore before 1989; there are 17 stories about Hansen in that period. This comparison suggests that Gore became a major spokesperson for climate change only *after* the issue had risen to prominence as a national policy issue.[72] Given that both Gore and Hansen are participants in the early climate change hearings, the fact that Hansen received more media attention points to a willingness on the part of journalists and editors to portray scientists as spokespersons for environmental policy issues. Members of Congress may push scientists to take policy positions during hearings because they perceive scientists to carry more weight with the public than non-scientists, at least when addressing environmental policy issues. That Gore was well schooled in the science of climate change adds further emphasis this point. That is, a prominent elected official who was particularly knowledgeable about the issue proved to be less effective in grabbing media attention than an agency scientist.

Lacking definitive data on why members of Congress are so insistent that scientists make policy recommendations, the frequency with which such exchanges occur suggests that members perceive such statements to be valuable. Thus, we see members of Congress seeking to portray scientists as objective advisors—remaining within the boundary that legitimizes their participation—and, at the same time, coaxing them to cross that boundary and enter into political discussions about possible courses of action. During agenda setting, the science/policy boundary is transgressed with little fanfare or even recognition. During legislation, however, scientists appear much more self-conscious about the boundary in that discussion of the boundary and explicit boundary work are much more likely during legislative debate. This observation does not exclude the possibility that scientists are equally aware of the boundary earlier in the policy process, but it does demonstrate that explicit attention to the boundary occurs more often in legislative policy making than in agenda setting.

The Science Narrative at the Legislative Stage

Returning to the comparison between the agenda-setting and legislative stages of the policy process, we find that the science narrative stays largely intact for both acid rain and climate change.[73] This is especially true during early hearings in each case, when there is little visible opposition. However, even after serious debate ensues on each issue, early institutionalization of the respective issues provides a stabilizing force that bolsters the science narrative in the face of counter-narratives that do eventually emerge. This stability does not imply that the respective narratives do not evolve over the course of legislative debate; they do. Rather, the major features of each science narrative persist throughout this period of congressional debate.

In the case of acid rain, the science narrative was supported by the continuous research effort—from 1982 to the mid 1990s—conducted by NAPAP. In addition, members of Congress who chaired the Senate Committee on Environment and Public Works pursued the issue throughout the 1980s, even during the period of Republican control of the Senate. NAPAP's role in stabilizing the acid rain science narrative, however, is complex and must be carefully explained.

NAPAP's symbolic role is important in sustaining the science narrative. The fact that the government supported and engaged in scientific research into the problem gave the issue legitimacy as a problem worthy of public attention.[74] The resources given to the program also created an interest group in favor of scientific research. This group was not limited to the scientists receiving research support, but included the program administrators who were likely to defend the program as a way to protect their turf in an environment of relatively scarce resources.

A second factor in the stability of the science narrative was Reagan's support of NAPAP. Admittedly, Reagan allied himself with NAPAP as a way to insulate himself from pressure to take action on acid rain; Reagan used NAPAP as a way to dodge a more serious policy commitment to addressing acid rain. Given that research is an integral part of the science narrative for acid rain, this turns out to be a poor strategy for someone who wants the issue to go away. By supporting acid rain research, Reagan contributed to the legitimacy of the science narrative that, ultimately, outlasted his administration.

NAPAP's substantive contribution to the science narrative is much more tenuous. First, NAPAP was criticized as not being able to provide timely or relevant information to policy making (Roberts 1991; Rubin, Morgan, and Lave 1991). This lacuna between science and policy is not predicted by the acid rain science narrative that closely links scientific research and decision making. Perhaps more surprising is that NAPAP findings actually revise *downward* the predictions for ill effects from acid rain.[75] This revision might be expected to alter the science narrative by giving a valuable resource to opponents of acid rain controls in their arguments that the costs of controls outweigh the benefits. Opponents of regulation, however, never relied on NAPAP data to bolster their arguments. In fact, during the period that NAPAP's revisions were released, members of Congress who had previously opposed acid rain controls began to join forces with those advocating for a regulatory program. While a few actors in Congress (particularly Representative John Dingell and Senator Robert Byrd, who were protecting specific industries in their districts) were able to stall legislation consistently in the 1980s, the overall trend in Congress was toward a greater acceptance of the idea of acid rain controls. This trend parallels public opinion during the time, which was increasingly supportive of congressional action to limit acid rain.[76]

This general trend also appears in the hearings. A number of the members who initially worked to protect industry from regulation shifted their tactic to pursuing the most flexible regulatory scheme possible. Byrd, for example was on record against acid rain controls in 1981 (SCENR 1984). In a 1987 hearing on clean coal technologies, however, Byrd made a case for adopting a flexible compliance scheme for industry (SCEPW 1987b).[77] This change reflects the growing awareness that the Clean Air Act Amendments were imminent and arguments against acid rain controls were no longer politically legitimate.

Certainly NAPAP's findings, overall, remained consistent with the science narrative in that NAPAP reports contained evidence that acid rain was occurring and was causing damage to vulnerable ecosystems. In this sense, the policy outcome should not be viewed as out of step with NAPAP findings. It remains curious, however, that those opposed to acid rain controls did not try to play up NAPAP's more nuanced story about the effects of acid rain. NAPAP, as an institution, appears to have supported the original science narrative in spite of findings it reported that created a more moderate picture than that originally depicted by the science narrative.

In the case of climate change, scientists and climate change research programs (the USGCRP and the IPCC) appear to have similarly stabilized the science narrative.[78] New reports and assessments produced by these research efforts reiterate the concern about climate change and disseminate research findings that claim to improve our understanding of the problem (Houghton et al. 1990, 1992, 1996, 2001; NAST 2000;

IPCC 2007). The IPCC's 1996 report garnered major media attention by arguing that "the balance of evidence . . . suggests a discernible human influence on global climate" (Houghton et al. 1996: 5). These measured words were replaced in the 2007 report by language calling climate change "unequivocal" and citing human influence with 90 percent confidence (IPCC 2007: 5). Both media attention and congressional attention to these reports reinforce these messages.[79]

What is most surprising about the case of climate change is the resilience of the science narrative in the face of both congressional and presidential attempts to stall any policy response that would commit the United States to reducing its emissions of greenhouse gases, particularly the Kyoto Treaty. During the Clinton administration, Congress held hearings (HCS 1995b; HCGR 1998b) and included language in appropriations bills calling for "no premature implementation of Kyoto" (Morrissey 1999). The Senate also passed a measure rejecting the Kyoto Treaty on the ground that developing countries were not included in emissions reductions. Surprisingly, during this same period, agency staff seemed to feel that a regulatory program on climate change was inevitable and reported that there was active competition among agencies and departments over who would implement the presumed, yet nonexistent, carbon emissions trading program.[80] In addition, the EPA testified in a hearing before Congress that it had the regulatory authority to regulate CO_2 as a global warming pollutant (SCENR 1999), a contention supported by a recent Supreme Court decision that rebuked the G. W. Bush administration for declining to regulate CO_2 as a pollutant.[81] More recently, Senators John McCain and Joseph Lieberman sponsored a bill to reduce emissions of greenhouse gases to 2000 levels by 2010. In spite of the fact that the Senate rejected the bill, McCain signaled his intention to keep the issue on the agenda (Pianin 2003). The combination of the election of a Democratic Congress in 2006 with feverish media attention to climate change in 2007 ended a period of intermittent attention to climate change by placing the issue squarely in the public spotlight.

Conclusion

The analysis of scientists' participation in the legislative hearings process reveals two crucial issues for science in policy making. First, the effect of the visibility of scientists' role increases with proximity to policy-making power. Because the hearings are public and are recorded, scientists who participate go on record as experts. This ensures a measure of scrutiny that scientists do not experience when they become involved in agenda setting. Going on record in policy settings may be similar in some respects to going on record in the scientific literature. However, peer review of scientific research does not focus on the political ramifications or leanings of scientific research, though ideally it should unearth these to the extent that they affect research methods and results. When science is introduced into policy making, on the other hand, attention is focused specifically on the political aspects of scientists' work. Because of the difficulty that non-scientists have in assessing the quality of the scientific information presented, scientists' credibility is based on the consistency of their behavior with the legitimate role of scientists in decision making, i.e., the expectation that they will participate objectively. This draws attention to the science/policy boundary.

The fact of public scrutiny drives the second issue—the attention given by both scientists and policy makers to the science/policy boundary. Scientists' responses to the boundary vary. Some scientists express their awareness through careful negotiation of the boundary by shifting from the role of scientist to the role of citizen when making explicit links between scientific information and policy options. Other scientists are careful not to make policy recommendations in order to stay within their role as scientific expert. In addition, there are scientists who, by making both science-based and policy-relevant statements in hearings, display a lack of awareness of the boundary. Finally, there are scientists who, in order to avoid any association with policy issues, never accept invitations to Congress.[82] Scientists' behavior in the legislative setting is orchestrated by a combination of professional community norms, the dictates of institutional affiliation, and scientists' personal choices about the role or roles they play as scientific experts.

Equally, we see members of Congress negotiating the science/policy boundary in pursuit of their legislative goals. Members invoke scientists' objectivity at the same time that they threaten that objectivity by asking scientists to give political interpretations of the evidence they present. Some members, in the way they coax and coach scientists across the boundary, demonstrate that they are aware of the difficulties the latter move poses. To the extent that both scientific objectivity and scientists' statements in support of policy positions add to the credibility of members' preferred policy positions, we can expect to see members continue to press scientists into these two contradictory roles. The awareness and negotiation of the science/policy boundary that emerges during legislation is given full expression during policy implementation. In the next chapter, we will see how the formalization of the science/policy boundary increases the salience of the boundary for scientists and decision makers alike.

4

Scientists and Implementation

Today I phoned the "Good Science" Research Labs to follow up my letter requesting an interview. This lab conducts scientific research in support of regulatory decision-making. I spoke with my contact at the lab who told me he had received my letter and circulated it among his colleagues to see if any one was interested. He explained, however, that it seemed like I was really interested in politics, not science. Consequently, he argued, his research lab was an inappropriate site for my study. Kindly, he offered to put me in touch with his counterparts on the policy side of regulatory decision-making. I pursued my case by explaining that I was interested in the information produced through scientific research and the transfer of this information to political decision-makers. This clarification did nothing for my case. My contact refused a second time, yet on quite different grounds. He said that his lab had provided research support for a recent visible and highly controversial regulatory decision. The politics surrounding the ruling made the scientists at the lab feel uncomfortable about discussing their role in the setting of the regulatory standard.
—field notes, July 1, 1998

Scientists have a central role in environmental policy making both in indicating to the public the existence of environmental problems and lending their expertise to the development of policy solutions (Yearly 1991). The ability to fulfill these roles without also appearing to act politically, however, is crucial in order for scientists to maintain their legitimacy as participants in policy deliberation. During the implementation stage of decision making, explicit negotiation of the science/policy boundary becomes a substantial component of the work that scientists do. In addition to conducting research and providing the results of their research, they must defend their ability to carry out this task neutrally and objectively. During the agenda-setting and legislative stages of decision making, the belief in scientists' objectivity is invoked rhetorically.

In the agenda-setting stage, scientists are assumed to be constrained by the larger scientific community so that their claims about the policy implications of their research are taken as objective. During legislation, the repeated invocation of a boundary between science and policy produces, among many scientists, a reluctance to cross the boundary without at least some negotiation of their role as scientists. During implementation, the science/policy boundary exists both rhetorically and materially through structures designed to produce boundary-respecting behavior among scientists who participate in this policy setting.

In the example from my field notes cited above, I was not able to interview anyone from the office in question.[1] Because of this, I can only speculate about the reason that a controversial political decision would make scientists wary about discussing the research they submitted to decision makers—something scientists were willing to do in both of the earlier stages of decision making. What I can say about the interaction is that it indicates the prominence of the science/policy boundary in the worldview of scientists participating in policy implementation. Rather than actively claiming their authority and expertise, the group of scientists sought cover in the laboratory—an arena that is generally viewed as being outside of the political fray.

In order to understand scientists' role in policy implementation and how that role differs from the earlier stages of decision making, I analyze the formally expressed role expectations that shape scientists approach to the science/policy boundary. During implementation, scientists find themselves in a heavily formalized and procedurally driven policy setting. Formal structure—a characterizing feature of the implementation stage of decision making—provides a basis against which to judge the legitimacy of policy decisions. Included in this formalization is a particular understanding of the role of science in decision making—an understanding that provides legitimacy for scientists insofar as they adhere to the formal definition of their role. The constraints applied through formal organizational structures produce two effects. One is a visible increase in efforts to demonstrate proper, legitimizing conduct. This task, one that is largely symbolic, is undertaken *in addition to* the research that scientists conduct in the service of policy making.[2] The second effect of these constraints is that they can limit scientists' access to policy deliberations. This allows for the emergence of competing narratives that challenge scientists' ability to influence the policy-making process.

During implementation, the evolution of acid rain and climate change policies is significantly shaped by the governmental programs created to address each issue. The National Acid Precipitation Assessment Program and the Acid Rain Program are the two implementation efforts associated with acid rain, and the United State Global Change Research Program is the government's current programmatic commitment to climate change. While the USGCRP is carrying out climate change research in keeping with the original science narrative, the acid rain issue has been fundamentally redefined through the Acid Rain Program enacted as part of the Clean Air Act Amendments of 1990.

By focusing on the implementation of research programs as well as on regulations, this chapter includes two types of implementation environments. Though they fit into the category of policy implementation equally well, they present distinct characteristics.[3] Theodore Lowi's typology, which emphasizes the politics that accompany a specific type of policy program, highlights several differences one would expect to see when comparing research programs—distributive policies—versus regulatory programs. Lowi (1964, 1972) argues that distributive policies subdivide federal resources according to the number of groups pressing for those resources and that, owing to the committee structure in Congress and the size of federal largesse, such groups rarely see themselves as in competition with one another. When such programs are implemented, agencies work closely with organized groups that support the agencies' missions and face few organized opponents. This low-conflict environment is sustained because the costs of distributive policies are distributed broadly across society (Lowi 1964, 1972; Wilson 1989). The National Institutes of Health is an example of an agency whose policies are largely distributive and whose environment is, comparatively speaking, supportive of its mission. Regulatory programs, on the other hand, create politics where there are real winners and losers. As a consequence, regulatory agencies face organized and hostile interests (Lowi 1964, 1972; Wilson 1989). Regulatory programs, in comparison with distributive ones, are both harder to pass legislatively and more contentious to implement. At the same time, agencies having jurisdiction over distributive programs are no less involved in policy implementation than their counterparts are in implementing regulatory programs.[4]

I begin this chapter with a discussion of formal structures in organizational design, especially those that emerge during policy implementation.

Next, drawing from a number of examples from my field work, I examine the formal apparatus that guides scientists who are involved in implementation and analyze how this apparatus shapes scientists' participation. In particular, I study the types of boundary negotiation that emerge to allow for the legitimate application of science in policy making. This section draws on Thomas Gieryn's concept of boundary work (1983, 1995, 1999). In the next section, I discuss the application of a particular version of the science/policy boundary with respect to NAPAP and the USGCRP. That is followed by an analysis of scientists' status in implementation settings. Finally I discuss how the science/policy boundary, as it is expressed in implementation settings, limits scientists' participation in policy deliberations and erodes their authorship over policy narratives. My analysis in this chapter is informed by empirical evidence from the implementation of acid rain and climate change policy programs and by more general evidence from agencies that routinely employ scientists.

Formalization and Legitimacy

The implementation stage of decision making is characterized by formal rules that are established to reduce uncertainty and to produce legitimate policy outcomes.[5] Formal organizational design expresses expectations about policy outcomes. In addition to its formal features, an organization inevitably has informal components that are equally important in supporting the organization's ability to achieve its goals. However, the formally elaborated structures and procedures of an organization are created and applied in pursuit of organizational control and predictability. Formal organizational design sets up specialized units within the organization and specifies their tasks, designates relationships among units, defines roles for members of the organization, and specifies ways of engaging with the organizational environment. In addition, formal structures and procedures are used to communicate an organization's intentions and priorities to external audiences who are concerned with the organization's performance (Meyer and Rowan 1991).

Early work in organization theory, the "rationalist" approach, focused exclusively on formal organization.[6] This approach has been revised by a more realistic view of the organization—the natural systems approach—that accounts for informal features of the organization that are not explained by or even anticipated in the formal organizational design.[7] In spite of this move in organization theory, formal structures continue to be an important subject of research, especially when the subject of research are organizations created to implement public policy.

Regulatory agencies, in particular, are characterized by political battles fought over the structural elements that will shape their performance.[8] Specifically, regulatory agencies participate in policy making through the process of rule making, which involves setting specific standards and guidelines to fulfill legislative mandates. Rule making itself is conducted according to procedures. These procedures can be reformulated, yet even the reformulation is formalized and is conducted according to rules that agencies, Congress, the Executive Branch, and interest groups are aware of and often agree on.[9] An important component of the formalization of policy implementation is a written record of procedures and of all rule-making processes. Formal procedures, though they can be heavily contested when initially set, act as a stable referent for policy makers and stakeholders alike. Procedures become scripts for policy action. Moreover, they create a track record for policy decisions in that they increase transparency and empower stakeholders to examine the exercise of power.[10]

Although formal procedure is a general characteristic of bureaucratic organizations, a number of important changes in administrative decision making that occurred during the 1970s have increased Executive Branch agencies' reliance on formalized policy making.[11] Increased standing in Executive Branch decision making and a more open and transparent decision-making process—attributable to the Freedom of Information Act and the Federal Advisory Committee Act—have encouraged interested actors to check the use of political power in the Executive Branch.[12] The most common form of check is litigation. Judicial review of agency decisions often turns on the agency's adherence to formal rule-making procedures.[13] Legitimacy cannot be defined solely in terms of the absence of litigation or, in cases in which litigation does occur, by an agency's successful defense of its rule. Yet the connection between formal procedure and legitimacy that is often made in the context of litigation is one that operates broadly in administrative decision making and informs administrative practice.

Reliance on formal procedure in establishing the legitimacy of policy decisions is an attempt to link political power to public accountability.[14]

From the point of view of the decision maker, formalization acts both as a constraint and as a protection. The constraints are straightforward: decisions must not be made arbitrarily. On the other hand, formalization protects policy makers in that it reduces their uncertainty about what will be accepted by stakeholders and by the courts as legitimate policy. The existence of formal procedures establishes routine paths that can be followed in demonstrating legitimate policy practice. From the point of view of those for whom power is exercised (citizens and stakeholders), formal procedure is a guide that can be used to judge the appropriate use of power.

Linking power and accountability is especially important in policy domains that rely heavily on scientific input.[15] For policy programs that require scientific expertise, organizational design often includes a formally specified role for scientists. This role assumes scientific objectivity and seeks to maintain it in the policy process.[16] Because scientists' legitimacy as participants in the policy process is based on this idealized view, scientists have an incentive to limit their action or to appear to limit their action to that which is formally defined for them.[17] This incentive increases as a function of scientists' proximity, in organizational terms, to the exercise of public decision-making power.

Boundary Work during Implementation

The most prominent organizing image for formally structuring science into regulatory decision making is the "assessment/management" framework that defines distinct domains for scientists and policy makers in the process of setting regulations. This demarcation is an expression of the science/policy boundary and is institutionalized throughout regulatory agencies that implement environmental and health policies. The assessment/management distinction comes from the articulation of two stages of the process known as *risk analysis*. *Risk assessment* is the scientist-dominated, fact-gathering stage of the process that is ideally insulated from subjective views about policy outcomes and should precede policy considerations. *Risk management*, on the other hand, marks the end of scientists' involvement and is conducted by policy makers who incorporate scientific findings in a normative consideration of policy alternatives. The assessment/management distinction attempts to create a clear role for scientists that draws on their special knowledge yet keeps them from overstepping their bounds. Ideally, it allows scientists to participate in decision making without compromising the basis of their legitimate participation—their objectivity.

An examination of the arguments for separating science from policy reveals contradictory understandings of science in decision-making settings. The first argument for separate science and policy domains is an anti-technocracy argument. Because expertise is not a democratically distributed resource, democracy is preserved in a political system that relies on scientists only if scientists are prevented from exercising decision-making power. Concerns about technocracy, however, reject a deeply embedded notion about what scientists do. According to the Enlightenment view of science, we understand nature or reality through scientific discovery of that reality. If scientists represent nature in policy making, they are constrained by ontological truths that are not subject to political debate. Given this, fear of the abuse of power by scientists is not consistent with the Enlightenment view of science. Rather, the argument for separate domains, from an Enlightenment perspective, is to preserve the integrity of science.

In spite of the inconsistent views of science embedded in the anti-technocratic and the Enlightenment models, the assessment/management framework addresses them both. Keeping scientists out of the arena of decision making alleviates concerns about technocracy. Equally, separate domains for science and policy uphold the Enlightenment ideal in that science is protected from political bias so that its natural (i.e., objective) state is preserved. The ability to speak to both of these models of science in decision making may account, in part, for the prevalence of the assessment/management framework in regulatory settings.[18]

Though the assessment/management distinction was evident in agencies' attempts to conduct risk analyses during the 1970s, it was first formally articulated in a 1983 report by the National Research Council. The NRC produced this report in response to a congressional request for a review of the regulatory process used for estimating environmental risks to public health. This report argues for the procedural separation of risk assessment from risk management.[19] Further, the report breaks down the risk-assessment process into four clearly delineated steps: hazard identification, dose-response relationship, exposure assessment, and risk characterization. The steps involved in risk management are less clearly defined but include the consideration of political, social, economic, and engineering factors along with the risk-related information generated during risk assessment. This information is then used to compare and decide among regulatory options in addressing potential public health issues.

The NRC report does acknowledge the difficulty of separating science and policy making in evaluating risks to human health (NRC 1983b: 33).[20] Still, the report maintains the status of science over policy when both come into play in risk assessment. That is, the report argues that policy considerations are necessary for deciding how to make inferences when scientific information is incomplete. On these occasions, however, the report argues that policy should follow the dictates of science (ibid.: 37). The demarcation set out by this report, a classic example of boundary work that seeks to establish the position of science by comparing it to non-science (Gieryn 1983), is now deeply embedded in federal regulatory procedure.[21]

The assessment/management structure developed in the 1983 NRC report was originally conceived of as a way to identify human health risks (1983b). In spite of this focus, the structure was rapidly taken up not only by agencies studying human health effects, but also agencies studying risks to the environment or to ecosystems. The list of agencies and departments who rely on the assessment/management paradigm includes both health and environmentally oriented organizations. For example, the Department of Health and Human Services—which houses the National Institutes of Health, the Centers for Disease Control and Prevention, and the Food and Drug Administration; the Environmental Protection Agency; the Occupational Health and Safety Administration; Department of the Interior; Department of Transportation; and Department of Energy all use the assessment/management distinction to organize their approach to risk assessment.[22]

Additional evidence of the centrality of the NRC report in setting up the assessment/management distinction is the report's currency in discussion of environmental and health regulations. So common is the NRC report to these discussions that it is referred to primarily by its well-known nickname, "the red book." On occasion, one of my interviewees would mention "the red book" and then, in consideration of my status as an outsider, would make sure that I understood the reference. More often, however, my interviewees referred to the report by its nickname with no additional specification, demonstrating how deeply embedded in their practice and lexicon the report is.[23]

Congress's commitment to the importance of science in risk analysis reinforces the assessment/management distinction in agencies' decision making. For example, in an attempt to ensure reliance on scientific information in regulatory rule making, legislation adopted in 1994 required that all proposed rules in the USDA with a cost of more than $100 million be subject to risk assessment and to cost-benefit analysis. This legislation created the Office of Risk Assessment and Cost-Benefit Analysis (ORACBA), whose purpose was to ensure that USDA regulations would be "based on sound scientific, technical and economic analysis."[24] The office, in setting up its risk-analysis program, sought guidance from both the Environmental Protection Agency and the Food and Drug Administration (interview, September 23, 1998). Such coordination among agencies ensures that the of the assessment/management distinction set out in the NRC report is maintained across Executive Branch agencies.

The assessment/management distinction is deeply embedded in the structures and language that guide the use of science in policy making in implementation settings. At the same time, such institutionalization does not create a stable boundary between science and policy making. Scholarship treating the science/policy boundary repeatedly calls out this aspect of science in policy settings (Jasanoff 1990; Gieryn 1995; Guston 2000). For example, Guston argues that some organizations are set up to internalize the science/policy boundary so that the organization can conduct carry that boundary internally. Such arrangements are helpful in policy settings in that the uncertainty around the boundary is managed by a single organization. Negotiations of the boundary under such conditions may be less visible, but they are no less constant.

Gieryn equally emphasizes the fluidity of the science/policy boundary in implementation settings in his discussion of "protection" boundary work.[25] Gieryn draws on Jasanoff's study of science advisors in regulatory policy making to exemplify the problem of science in implementation settings. For Gieryn, the goal of boundary work is to keep science close enough to policy activity so that science is pertinent for policy making but distant enough for science maintain its autonomy from political authority (1995: 434–435).

Price (1965) addresses just this problem in setting out a normative framework for applying science to policy. Price offers four "estates," each of which offers a different mix of autonomy and relevance. Scientists with complete autonomy and no authority are at the opposite end of the spectrum from policy makers, who have little autonomy—constrained as they are by democratic structures and norms—but have significant authority through their decision-making capacity. In between these two extremes are professionals and administrators, who mediate between the scientific and policy estates.

Unlike Price, Gieryn does not expect that participants will agree on a stable division of labor between science and policy making. Instead, he argues that boundaries between science and policy making are constantly under negotiation. Jasanoff, in her 1990 analysis of science advisory bodies, demonstrates the accuracy of Gieryn's observation. Jasanoff shows that none of the mechanisms for drawing science into regulatory decision making that she studies comes to a stable equilibrium. Instead, each decision requires a new negotiation about what counts as science and what counts as policy. In addition, Jasanoff shows that scientists are not alone in negotiating the boundary. Policy makers and stakeholders are equally active in trying to assert distinctions between science and policy that will produce outcomes that will serve their respective aims.

In this chapter, I highlight specific instances of boundary work in implementation settings. All of these fall into the category that Gieryn labels "protection" boundary work. For my analysis, I specify the tools scientists use to maintain their status in these settings and emphasize the fact that scientists are not alone in negotiating science/policy boundaries. Scientists who participate in policy implementation face intense scrutiny when compared with their counterparts who participate during agenda setting and legislation. This raises the salience of boundary work in this setting and creates a dynamic in which scientists devote considerable energy to defending themselves as scientists. This sets them apart from their counterparts in other settings in that their counterparts have to attend publicly to the science/policy boundary only periodically if at all. Also notable during this stage of policy making is the fact that scientists tend to rely heavily on the assessment/management framework in order to defend their credibility in spite of the availability of other schemas that might shore up their participation in policy making; the boundary is fluid, but the repertoire of available tools to draw the boundary in legitimizing ways appears to be limited.

Three distinct solutions to the problem of setting up an appropriate proximity between science and policy emerge in implementation settings. The first—asserting a clean separation between science and policy— comes from advocates who adhere to the assessment/management framework and draw on the language provided by that framework to argue that objective science can be produced and handed off to policy makers, who will incorporate science into their policy decisions. The second type of boundary work—linking strategies—draws on the idea of science and policy as distinct, but relies on indicators established in the scientific community as the metric for good science. In this case, scientists in policy settings who publish and receive awards from the science community work to establish their membership within the scientific community in spite of their proximity to policy making by linking their behavior to that of academic scientists. The third type of boundary work—regulatory science—creates a separate category of science for policy making that does not try to replicate the standards articulated for academic science (Weinberg 1982; Salter 1988). This distinction suggests that the assessment/management framework does not or cannot provide adequate separation between science and policy making in regulatory settings. At the same time, it carves out a space for scientists to address policy-relevant questions without undermining the notion of an objective science existing outside the political area.

The three types of boundary work are presented below.

Boundary Work I: Clean Separation

There are a number of examples of boundary efforts that seek to reinforce the separation of science and policy.[26] For example, the National Institute for Environmental Health Sciences (NIEHS), a research organization within the Department of Health and Human Services, engages in a number of boundary efforts to assert its distance from policy making. First, the public relations literature on the NIEHS clearly points out that the institute has no regulatory power (US Department of Health and Human Services 1990: 1). Rather, the NIEHS emphasizes that it exists to conduct basic research and to award grants for non-governmental research. A second expression of the organizational distance from decision-making power is the geographical setting of the NIEHS: Research Triangle Park, in North Carolina. This distances the organization and its research efforts considerably from its parent organization, the Department of Health and Human Services, which is located in Washington.

This general reinforcement of the assessment/management distinction is further articulated through the NIEHS's more conservative interpretation of the National Research Council's formulation of the assessment stage of risk analysis. One interview contact working in the NIEHS characterized the scientists in the organization as participating in only the first two steps of risk assessment—hazard identification and dose-response relationship—and, from time to time, the third step—exposure assessment (interview, June 1, 1998). The official argued that any scientist who went further than that did so as a matter of personal choice and not as a member of the research organization. Further, the official expressed doubt about the ability of scientists to participate in risk characterization, the fourth stage of risk assessment, while maintaining the objectivity that is a necessary component of scientists' legitimate role in policy making.[27] The credibility of the research conducted at the NIEHS is articulated and reinforced through boundary efforts that are consistent with the assessment/management notion of science and policy domains.

Similar boundary efforts drawing on the assessment/management distinction are conducted by Environmental Protection Agency's research arm, the Office of Research and Development. The ORD, like the NIEHS, works to secure its legitimacy—and the legitimacy of science at the EPA more generally—by demonstrating its independence from regulatory considerations. Unlike the NIEHS, the ORD is housed within the EPA, a regulatory agency. This creates additional pressures on the scientists who work in this setting. One interview contact referred to "high walls" separating scientific research and policy at the EPA (interview, July 16, 1998). For example, the ORD consults the EPA's "program" offices—the offices within the agency that refine and implement regulatory policy—in order to set the research agenda for the agency. The consultation is important in that the program offices can signal to the ORD gaps in the scientific record that, if filled, might support regulatory decision making. Once research projects have been selected, however, the ORD operates without input from the program offices. This separation is also maintained for extramural research or research that is conducted for the agency by independent researchers. Contact between any EPA official and researchers working under an EPA grant is strictly prohibited (interview, July 16, 1998). Finally, scientists working for the EPA's Science Advisory Board also characterize their work as separate from that of the agency (interview, September 19, 1998). One member argued that SAB scientists are "in the agency, but not of the agency," emphasizing their distance from policy makers in the organization (interview, November 10, 1998).

Boundary Work II: Linking Science Performed in Policy Settings to Academic Science

A second set of boundary efforts consistent with the assessment/management formulation argues for the legitimacy of scientists in policy making by making links between scientists working within the policy arena and those working in more traditional research settings, i.e., linking strategies. This demarcation is established not through the articulation of differences between scientists and non-scientists, but by emphasizing similarities among scientists working in different professional settings. Links between agency scientists and academic scientists are both a check on the behavior of agency scientists and evidence that agency scientists are part of the academic science community.[28] This type of boundary work seeks to establish that scientists who participate in decision making bring with them the norms of the academic science community—norms that can protect scientists working in policy settings from political bias.

There are a number of strategies that agency staff use to make links to academic research settings. The most widely used link is the practice of peer review, in which an agency submits its own research or its use of research conducted outside the agency to evaluation by non-government scientists (i.e., university and perhaps industry scientists).[29] Peer review is intended to protect against policy-oriented biases by removing the determination of credibility from the institutional settings in which the information is to be used.[30] Information that is deemed acceptable by independent scientists is more likely to avoid or withstand charges of policy bias.

Another typical linking effort is the attempt to establish the credibility of scientists working in regulatory settings among their counterparts in universities. Examples of such efforts are publishing research findings in peer-reviewed science journals, maintaining membership in professional science associations, and attending and presenting work at professional conferences. If agency scientists are accepted among their peers, they can argue that they are able to maintain science norms successfully in policy settings. As an alternative to using the norms of professional science to evaluate agency scientists, a more direct linking mechanism is for regulatory agencies simply to set up research contracts with university scientists.

Returning to our earlier examples, the National Institute for Environmental Health Sciences and the EPA's Office of Research and

Development, we can see these linking efforts in action. The NIEHS creates a strong link with the non-governmental science community by filtering the products of its research through publication in peer-reviewed science journals.[31] Both internally conducted research and contracted research must go through the publication process in order for research results to be made public. The NIEHS sponsored scientific journal *Environmental Health Perspectives* is one avenue for publication of research results. The process of publishing an article in this journal is similar to that of publishing one in a non-government journal, with a professional editorial board and anonymous peer reviewers.[32] The NIEHS sees the government, scientists, the health care community, labor organizations, and the public as its audience. All these groups gain access to NIEHS-supported research through published reports.[33]

The EPA's Office of Research and Development similarly makes use of linking strategies. Peer review makes up a large portion of the ORD's and, more generally, of the EPA's linking strategies.[34] Both the research agenda and the products of ORD research are peer reviewed by independent science committees (US EPA 1997: 21). Extramural research also goes through two stages of peer review. First, proposals received by the ORD are sent to reviewers to be ranked. When ORD-funded extramural projects are completed, independent scientists review the results. The ORD also attempts to bolster its research findings by sending them to non-governmental researchers for replication (interview, July 16, 1998).

Another linking effort on the part of the ORD is its reliance on standards established by the scientific community. The ORD actively seeks to have its scientists' performance measured according to standards established outside governmental settings. ORD researchers are expected to publish in peer-reviewed scientific journals. In addition, the ORD tracks the scientific citations of its research. It also pursues external recognition of ORD scientists (interview, July 16, 1998). Scientists on the EPA's Science Advisory Board also say that they use linking strategies to establish their credibility. Specifically, one member of the Science Advisory Board reports that the board makes an effort to recruit scientists outside of the agency in order to create a network of scientists that can serve on SAB boards and act as consultants (interview, November 10, 1998).

Boundary Work III: Separating Regulatory Science and Academic Science

Both the clean-separation type of boundary work and the linking type are consistent with organizational structures and procedures designed to maintain the assessment/management distinction in that they are intended to demonstrate that science is insulated from the polluting influence of politics. A third type of boundary work present in regulatory settings, however, suggests the inadequacy of the assessment/management distinction in protecting scientists from political bias. This type of boundary work capitalizes on a distinction between science conducted for policy and science carried out in traditional, academic settings. The assertion of a difference between "regulatory science" and "academic science" suggests that the proximity of policy considerations substantially alters the conduct of science. Specifically, science in policy making is asked to be predictive and to answer questions quickly under conditions of high uncertainty (Weinberg 1982). This makes regulatory science unlike academic science in that the latter is not required to produce results under such relentless conditions. With this demarcation, regulatory science, because it is set apart from academic science, can operate under standards that differ from those normally used in academic settings.[35]

The distinction between regulatory science and academic science supports the legitimacy of science by allowing for a type of science that is affected by policy interests but is ultimately not a reflection on academic practice. Under these conditions, the merit of regulatory science is the balance that it strikes between the necessity of providing timely information to policy makers and the adherence to academic scientific standards.[36] Academic science, then, stands apart from regulatory science in the rigor of its method and in the independence of its inquiry.[37] Notably, the scrutiny and potential criticism that regulatory science invites does not threaten academic practice if the two types of science are distinct.

Once the two domains are established, scientists can argue that regulatory science is a legitimate approach that allows scientists to be responsive to policy makers without producing unreliable, biased results. This move might reduce the frequency with which science produced for decision making is attacked as substandard. However, there is little evidence that scientists who participate in policy making make use of this third type of boundary work. Much more common are attempts to show that scientists have maintained a proper distance between science and policy and that scientists who work in policy settings really belong to scientific communities and adhere to the same professional norms that guide those communities.

In addition, boundary work seeking to protect the status of academic science relative to science conducted in policy settings poses a direct challenge to the ORD's boundary efforts. Unlike the NIEHS, which has been relatively successful at portraying its science as part of the community of academic researchers, the ORD must conduct boundary work in an effort to contradict a general perception of EPA science as second rate.[38] One ORD staff member argued that the perception of science at the EPA as something less than academic science might result in a severely diminished budget for science research at the EPA in favor of supporting the EPA's program offices (interview, July 10, 1998). Furthermore, the same staff member decried the dismissal of high-quality work conducted by the ORD by the larger science community under the assumption that the ORD cannot produce "good" science.[39]

Research on the science/policy boundary, particularly in regulatory policy settings, suggests that the concept of "regulatory science" might provide a practical solution to the problem of science and decision making. Jasanoff, in particular, finds that efforts by scientists and policy makers to blur the boundary between science and politics were often more successful in legitimizing policy outcomes than efforts to shore up the boundary (1990: 208–228). Though regulatory science might provide a defensible way forward in regulatory settings, the formal procedures that guide scientists' participation in decision making and the rhetorical repertoire used to invoke the boundary rely much more heavily on the first two models presented here.

The implementation setting presents an environment in which scientists must repeatedly demonstrate their scientific credentials and practices. The lack of stability of the science/policy boundary in these settings means that the boundary must be established anew in each instance of policy making in which science is invoked. Training and professional affiliation are, in this setting, insufficient cues to convince stakeholders of the quality of work produced. The decline in presumptive credibility acts as a constraint on scientists in this setting in that they must expend time and energy defending their role and their work. The status of the profession and the spoils that status brings do not extend very far into the implementation setting. To combat the idea that it is difficult to produce good science in implementation settings, scientists and policy makers involved in policy implementation rely heavily on the first two models of the assessment/management framework and forgo other available constructs and symbols that might lead them to a different type of boundary negotiation.

Government-Sponsored Research: Accepting the Assessment/ Management Framework in NAPAP and the USGCRP

The two federal research programs created to study acid rain and climate change, NAPAP and the USGCRP, are administered in keeping with the assessment/management distinction. That is, they are insulated organizationally from political decision making. NAPAP's organizing legislation actually includes language that requires NAPAP to make recommendations on the basis of its research findings. This language, because of its lack of adherence to the science/policy boundary, became a point of contention between NAPAP's leaders and members of Congress. The scope of NAPAP research encompasses emissions contributing to acid deposition, effects from emissions, and comparisons of the effectiveness of various control technologies.[40] NAPAP reports have covered each of these topics. At the same time, NAPAP's leaders have consistently resisted delving into policy recommendations, even when pressed by members of Congress to do so.[41] NAPAP's insistence on keeping to the science side of the science/policy boundary is reflected in the language of its reports, appears when NAPAP leadership's testifies before Congress, and has been noted by outside observers of the program (Roberts 1991).

One concession to the requirement for recommendations comes when a NAPAP scientist, pressed during congressional testimony to overcome his reluctance to make policy recommendations, falls back on promising recommendations in future reports (HCA 1986). In a second concession to the requirement for recommendations, NAPAP, in its 1991 assessment, acknowledges the call for recommendations while attempting to preserve the science/policy boundary:

Policy decisions on acid rain will be most effective and efficient when based on a compilation of the best available scientific, technological and economic information relevant to the issue. The National Acid Precipitation Assessment Program (NAPAP) is responsible for providing credible, well-reviewed technical findings and *recommendations* to inform the public decision process. NAPAP is not responsible for establishing control policy; *policy decisions must remain the responsibility of public officials*, who ultimately make those decisions on the basis of technical information, social values, political considerations and other aspects of the public interest. (NAPAP 1991: i, emphasis added)

NAPAP's attempt to distinguish "recommendations" from "policy decisions" by linking social and political considerations to the latter is notable.

NAPAP's negotiation of the science/policy boundary—one that emphasizes NAPAP's involvement in assessment rather than management—demonstrates an acceptance of the assessment/management distinction. In addition, NAPAP employs linking efforts—mainly through extramural research—to support the credibility of the science it produces. Through extramural research, NAPAP is able to rely on the work of the academic research community. This linkage is prominently displayed in its 1991 assessment, for example, in the list of contributors for each chapter, a collection of government scientists, academic scientists, and scientists from the national laboratories (1991: iv–vi).

In spite of the controversy over the policy relevance of NAPAP's assessment, the United States Global Change Research Program (USGCRP) is formally required to adhere to the science-policy norm practiced by NAPAP. While NAPAP leadership sought to insulate its research from potentially corrosive policy considerations, the USGCRP was instructed to adhere to this boundary by its organizing legislation. The USGCRP is specifically prohibited from recommending policies on global change, participating in energy technology R&D, or conducting research on mitigation strategies (USGCRP 1997: 110). The purpose of this proscription may be to protect the credibility of the USGCRP as an independent and objective research program. Alternatively, it may be to keep the USGCRP from becoming influential in policy development regarding climate change.[42] Either way, it leaves the research program vulnerable to criticisms similar to those leveled at NAPAP (Roberts 1991; Rubin, Lave, and Morgan 1991).[43]

Like NAPAP, the USGCRP employs a number of linking strategies to ensure the quality of its research. First, each agency and each department working in coordination with the USGCRP sponsors extramural (i.e., academic or industry) research to fulfill its program goals. These links with researchers outside government contribute to the credibility of the research program. In addition, all USGCRP research programs undergo "external peer review" (USGCRP 1997: 110). By passing muster with the larger scientific community, the USGCRP protects its credibility in spite of its location within the government. A final linking strategy employed by the USGCRP is to coordinate and carry out its research in conjunction with a number of reputable scientific organizations, namely the Intergovernmental Panel on Climate Change, the International Geosphere-Biosphere Program, and the National Academy of Sciences (USGCRP 1997: 111–112). To the extent that the USGCRP can maintain equal footing with these high-status science organizations, it can resist charges of politicization that might arise as a consequence of its association with any specific presidential administration.

Preserving Status: Extra-Scientific Work during Implementation

The use of formal structure to maintain the science/policy boundary and, in so doing, to maintain the legitimacy of science produces two effects we do not see in earlier stages of policy making. The first is an increase in the amount of time scientists must devote to public demonstrations that they are adhering to the assessment/management distinction and should be judged as objective participants. The second effect, addressed in the following section, is a marginalized role in articulating the policy narrative as it evolves during policy implementation.

During agenda setting and legislation, a scientist who enters policy making from the academic community routinely needs do little more than state his or her credentials for the status of "scientist" to be conferred. For scientists participating in implementation, credibility must be demonstrated repeatedly. The structures that define scientists' role in this stage of decision making encourage proactive attempts to demonstrate credibility. This extra-scientific work is, of course, can also be found outside the policy implementation setting. As such, it is a *general* method scientists use to distinguish themselves from non-scientists (Gieryn 1983). However, this practice becomes a part of the standard routine for scientists involved in implementation and often has formal expression in agency procedures. This codification of boundary work is specific to the implementation stage of decision making and makes boundary work more visible than it is during agenda setting and legislation.

The presence of this extra-scientific component of scientists' role is a function of scientists' formal incorporation into the policy process. During both innovation and legislation, scientists can deliver science narratives to policy makers without formally entering the policy process. During implementation, many scientists leave their academic setting and join regulatory agencies as permanent employees.[44] Proximity to regulatory decision-making power is directly correlated with this increase in symbolic action to defend scientists' status.

A comparison between the NIEHS and the ORD demonstrates the correlation between proximity to regulatory decision making and the need for such status-defending acts to support scientists' participation. The organizations have a number of comparable features.[45] Each focuses on environmental health issues,[46] and each implement research programs that include in-house research and grants to outside researchers. In addition, both operate within larger policy-making organizations yet lack power to make regulatory policy themselves.

In spite of their similarities, the NIEHS and the ORD differ with respect to their proximities to decision-making power. The NIEHS is one part of the larger research organization, the National Institutes of Health, which is located within the Department of Health and Human Services but which has no regulatory decision-making power.[47] The ORD is located within the Environmental Protection Agency and works directly with program offices involved in regulatory decision making. Because of this difference, there is considerable variation in the boundary efforts that the two organizations mobilize in order to support the status of science conducted under their auspices.

The NIEHS obviously benefits from its organizational and actual distance from centers of decision making. Because it functions within a larger research institution (the National Institutes of Health), and because of its geographic location (away from Washington),[48] the NIEHS is credible in arguing that it is well insulated from the policy-making process. In addition, the procedural mechanism used to establish the currency of NIEHS science in the larger scientific community—i.e., that results of NIEHS research are available only in articles published in peer-reviewed scientific journals—is fairly straightforward and does not require scientists working with the NIEHS to engage in efforts to establish the credibility of their work above and beyond what they would do in a university setting.

In attempting to establish the credibility of science at the EPA, the ORD engages in boundary efforts both more elaborate and numerous than those of the NIEHS. The proximity of science and policy within the EPA makes it difficult for scientists to demonstrate adherence to the assessment/management distinction, something that becomes essential once that distinction has been articulated as the proper way to produce credible science in policy settings. The ORD's boundary efforts work against a common perception that science at the EPA is affected by the EPA's larger regulatory goals.

A portion of the research organized by the ORD is conducted to answer specific questions posed by the EPA's program offices. Because of the specificity of these research projects and the need to produce rapid results, the ORD cannot implement the NIEHS solution of filtering all research through professional journals. Instead, the ORD uses a multi-layer peer-review process that relies on independent scientists to review its research agenda, its programs, and its research results. In addition, the ORD takes the precaution of having its research results replicated outside the agency. The organization's enumeration of relevant academic science standards as its measure of success signals its rejection of the "regulatory science" label. These efforts may have the effect of improving the quality of science at the EPA. Because of the difficulty of measuring such an improvement, these efforts act symbolically to demonstrate the appropriateness of the procedures set up to protect science at the EPA from distorting political considerations.

Linking efforts are one way for the ORD to show that it engages in "good" science practice. Another way the ORD tries to defend its credibility is by renegotiating the assessment/management distinction in terms that are favorable to its organizational position. While the NIEHS occupies safe ground in its conservative approach to the role of science in risk assessment, the ORD argues for the legitimate participation of scientists in the management stage of risk analysis. ORD, in its 1997 update to its strategic plan, highlights technical elements of risk management, making an argument for a role for science in risk management that others have overlooked: "[The ORD] expands on the Risk Management Options portion of the NAS paradigm[49] to show the many scientific and technical activities, in addition to risk assessment, that are part of risk management." (US EPA 1998: 2) According to the ORD, scientists can evaluate the feasibility of different response options, can develop compliance models or methods once options have been selected, and can provide data that is needed to monitor compliance (ibid.: 5). While the NIEHS can comfortably defend its position as well within the science side of the assessment/management divide, the ORD must try to negotiate its legitimacy as it interacts with offices in the EPA that are making regulatory decisions. Calling attention to highly technical aspects of risk management, the ORD argues that the risk-analysis process can be enhanced by extending the reach of objective information. In turn, this extension of science into the management stage of risk analysis supports the idea that good research can be done at the boundary between science and policy.

The comparison between the NIEHS and the ORD brings the differences between distributive policy arenas and regulatory ones to the foreground. While both organizations may be trying to monopolize boundary work that affects their organizational goals, the NIEHS appears to be more successful. This suggests that the success of efforts to internalize boundary work within an organization—that is, to create a boundary organization—may depend, in part, on that organization's environment.[50]

The Status of Science in NAPAP and in the USGCRP

Like the ORD, NAPAP and the USGCRP have both experienced challenges to the credibility of their research. This produces in both organizations efforts to defend their propriety as scientific research organizations. NAPAP's 1987 report, in particular, was challenged both by members of Congress and by scientists. Members of Congress who were in favor of controls on acid rain objected to the report's "non-action political agenda"; academic scientists argued that the report's executive summary did not faithfully represent the science contained in the report itself (HCSST 1988). NAPAP's preemptive stance against making political statements was unsuccessful, in this instance, in protecting the organization from the charge of politicization. In response to the charges that the executive summary was politically biased in presenting the scientific evidence, NAPAP's director, James Mahoney, proposed to include a "summary of science" section in the next report that would be different from a section that included findings and recommendations (ibid.: 15). Mahoney hoped that a "summary of science" section would allow researchers to discuss findings and uncertainties without having to worry that their discussion would be taken as policy recommendations (ibid.: 15).[51]

The science of the USGCRP, like that of NAPAP, has come under attack, although its critics have largely been those who oppose climate change regulations. For example, the USGCRP was indirectly implicated in a review of the modeling efforts of climate change scientists by the House Science Committee through a congressional hearing seeking to expose the tendency of scientists to overstate the certainty of their conclusions in order to secure continued funding from the government (HCS 1995b).[52] In spite of these criticisms, external scientists have reviewed the science of the USGCRP favorably (Reichhardt 1995). This allows the USGCRP to retain its credibility and to characterize the criticisms as politically motivated rather than scientifically based.

Furthermore, the USGCRP shied away from endorsing controversial policies in its first published assessment on climate change. The cover page of the assessment contains the following two statements:

Humanity's influence on the global climate will grow in the coming century. Increasingly, there will be significant climate-related changes that will affect each one of us. (NAST 2000)

We must begin now to consider our responses, as the actions taken today will affect the quality of life for us and future generations (National Assessment Synthesis Team. (ibid.)

The first statement takes no risks in that the Intergovernmental Panel on Climate Change, in its 1995 report, linked human activity to an increase in global average temperature (Houghton et al. 1996). The second statement, which suggests action, is tempered by the fact that the recommendations in the body of the report all call for more research (NAST 2000: 124–133). The purpose of the research, however, is linked to the ability to "provide more effective guidance for responding to the challenges posed by climate change" (ibid.: 122). Giving an official account of climate science might have been an occasion for the USGCRP to come under fire, but this report received relatively little public attention.[53]

Erosion of the Science Narrative for Acid Rain

The second difference in scientists' role that appears during implementation is a diminished ability to shape the narratives that frame environmental policy issues. There are at least two factors that limit scientists' role in setting policy narratives. First, the formalization of separate domains for science and policy and the use of boundary work to reinforce that demarcation proscribes scientists from engaging in the normative practice of defining policy issues in terms of blame and likely policy solutions. A second issue is the expansion of organizations involved in policy implementation that can host competing policy narratives. In the case of acid rain policy, the competing narrative arises from the need to demonstrate the legitimacy of the policy program to its supporters and critics. In the case of acid rain, this need is met by linking those programs to improvements in public health, an ever-popular policy goal.

The Acid Rain Program, originally conceived as a way to protect lakes and forests, is currently being characterized as a program for improving the health of vulnerable human populations from the pollutants that cause acid rain. This shift in emphasis has diminished the role of environmental scientists in shaping the evolution of the Acid Rain Program. This has affected NAPAP, but it has also implicated the ORD (owing to the placement of the Acid Rain Program within the EPA). Both NAPAP (the organizational center of the environmental science approach to acid rain) and the ORD (the office within the EPA that oversees the agency's research agenda) have resisted this change in focus. NAPAP continues to prioritize ecological effects. In it's publications, human health effects are consistently listed and treated after information about ecological effects is presented.[54] This shows a framing—consistent with the original science narrative—of acid rain as primarily an ecological issue. The ORD, for its part, has argued that toxicological data are needed to demonstrate a causal mechanism linking acid rain pollutants to human health effects. The Acid Rain Program relies, instead, on epidemiological evidence to show a link between pollutants and health effects (interview, October 29, 1998). The ORD's concern with toxicological data suggests that scientists within the EPA are attempting to reassert their role in defining the scientific terms of the Acid Rain Program.

As a consequence of this shift, the prominence of NAPAP, and the acid rain narrative it supports, has been dramatically eroded. It is important to note, however, that the shift is not a shift away from *science*, merely a shift among scientific disciplines, albeit one that limits the role of those scientists who were initially involved in placing acid rain on the political agenda. One reason for this shift may be that NAPAP has largely fulfilled its purpose by conducting science in support of a regulatory program that, now up and running, needs less scientific input. NAPAP, however, continues to have a role in assessing the effectiveness of the acid rain program. What is striking is how marginal its role has become *in spite of* scientific evidence that the current emissions caps are not sufficiently tight to produce significant improvement in lakes and forests.[55]

Two factors, both arising from the need to demonstrate legitimate policy activities, act to reduce the centrality of NAPAP in guiding the evolution of acid rain policy.

The first of these is the attempt to formally construct separate domains for science and policy. The efforts from within NAPAP to work within the boundaries of what is considered objective and "scientific" did protect the body of NAPAP reports from charges of political bias.[56] At the same time, this boundary work prevented NAPAP scientists from articulating a complete policy narrative about acid rain. That some links between scientific research and policy were expected was demonstrated by the criticism that NAPAP drew for the distance it maintained between science and policy. Although scientists had engaged in normative constructions of the acid rain issue during the agenda-setting and legislative stages of policy making, scientists' organizational position during implementation restricts their ability to articulate their findings through a science narrative which makes implicit links between research and policy choices.

A second factor that diminishes scientists' role in setting the acid rain policy narrative is the emergence of an alternative, organizationally supported narrative. This narrative arises from the need to demonstrate the legitimacy of the existing regulatory program. Those involved in implementing the Acid Rain Program must demonstrate the program's effectiveness to its supporters and to its detractors.[57] In order to prove that money spent on mitigating acid rain is well spent, program administrators must show that the benefits outweigh the costs. The method that Acid Rain Program administrators have used to make this case is to construct acid rain policy as a matter of pollution and human health effects.

The argument that reductions in the pollutants that cause acid rain will improve the health of sensitive human populations was made intermittently during initial debate about the issue.[58] However, the human health focus has not been a major feature of the science narrative on acid rain. In part, this may have to do with the extent of expertise of the scientists who initially brought the acid rain issue to light. The scientists originally involved in naming acid rain as a policy problem came from, among other disciplines, atmospheric chemistry, lake ecology, forest ecology, and soil ecology. These scientists did not have appropriate expertise to conduct research on human health effects from acid pollutants. The inclusion of the human health aspect of the acid rain issue shifts the policy issue away from their area of expertise.

For its part, the Acid Rain Program at the EPA has two incentives to focus on improvements in human health to justify the program. First, protecting humans from adverse environmental conditions is central to the EPA's mission. Second, from an organizational standpoint, the ability to show an improvement in human health is procedurally simpler than demonstrating ecological improvements. This has to do with the kinds of data available to EPA staff. Both epidemiological evidence and toxicological data are used to link respiratory ailments and sulfate aerosols in the atmosphere (US EPA 1995, chapter 4: 1–11). Using this information, EPA staff can estimate the incidence of health effects associated with increased pollution concentrations and estimate their costs (ibid., chapters 4 and 5). Though there are difficulties in determining the incidence of health-related effects of sulfur emissions and in estimating the costs of these health effects, it is substantially more difficult to determine the extent of impacts and the costs associated with damaged lakes and forests.[59] Given this, it is not surprising that EPA staffers have placed emphasis on human health effects associated with sulfur and nitrous oxide emissions. The ability to show human health benefits from regulatory actions is a reliable method for defending the Acid Rain Program's cost effectiveness.[60] The general worthiness of human health as a regulatory goal makes it easier for EPA staff to successfully defend their program.

As a result of this shift in focus, NAPAP scientists have been less involved in the implementation of the Acid Rain Program than they might have been if cost-effectiveness evaluations were focused on ecological effects. This does not mean that NAPAP no longer plays a role in the Acid Rain Program. Rather, other actors who have stakes in the evolution of the policy narrative framing acid rain join NAPAP scientists in trying to articulate and maintain that narrative. Because the separation of science and policy is embedded in NAPAP's organizational culture, NAPAP scientists lack either the experience or the inclination to engage normative arguments that would reassert the policy goals articulated in the original science narrative about acid rain. The need to demonstrate the legitimacy of the policy program has led to an alternative policy narrative for acid rain that has its own organizational base. From that base, the new narrative challenges the exclusively ecology-centered science narrative embodied in NAPAP.[61]

Though there is no federal regulatory program to address climate change, there are at least glimmers of similar challenges arising for climate change scientists. For example, the USGCRP's proscription from engaging in policy considerations—similar to NAPAP's self-imposed, science-only research focus—sets it apart from other organizations studying climate change. For example, the Intergovernmental Panel on Climate Change, the preeminent climate change science organization, includes as part of its mission the consideration of policy alternatives. Further, the USGCRP's restriction represents a departure from the agenda-setting context in which scientists' public statements about climate change have explicit policy implications.[62]

A second similarity between the evolution of acid rain policy and that of climate change policy is resistance to the incorporation of human health issues into the science narrative. One interviewee reported a specific reluctance to engage in conversations about the human health effects of climate change within the USGCRP (interview, June 1, 1998). Though it remains to be seen whether a human health focus will be incorporated into the broader policy narrative framing climate change, the current organizational monopoly that the USGCRP has on government-supported climate change research suggests that human health issues will continue to have secondary status to ecological effects.

Conclusion

Scientists who participate in the policy process during implementation operate under a number of constraints. These constraints arise from the attempt to formalize scientists' participation according to a prescribed and defensible role that supports their legitimacy in the policy process. This role is based on a specific model of scientific practice: the assessment/management framework, which seeks to eradicate or protect against normative commitments among scientists. When comparing scientists who participate in implementation settings with those who participate in legislation, one sees more freedom to express policy preferences and positions among the scientists in legislative settings. Consistent with the findings in this chapter, however, government scientists rarely express policy positions when they participate in hearings. Another distinction to make in comparing the constraints that exist in each setting is that boundary work is formalized at the organizational level during policy implementation such that scientists working for the ORD operate under one model of the science/policy boundary while those employed by the NIEHS operate under a different model. Scientists participating in legislative politics often are put in the position of explicitly negotiating the science/policy boundary, but their solutions are individual. The exceptions among government scientists —those, including James Hansen, who do articulate policy positions in legislative settings— underscore this point. Constraints scientists face in implementation settings are more elaborated, more institutionalized, and more likely to quell explicit policy discussion on the part of scientists than those scientists face in agenda setting or legislation.

As a consequence, scientists who participate in implementation are measured against the expectations set out in the assessment/management framework. Scientists, in attempting to uphold the science/policy boundary elaborated through formal structures in the implementation setting, spend a larger percentage of their time defending their credibility as scientists than their counterparts in earlier stages do. In addition, they are limited in their capacity to discuss the policy implications of the research results they bring to decision making. Because of this, scientists have less capacity to articulate policy narratives and begin to rapidly lose ground to actors working from other organizational bases who advance competing narratives.

An idealized model of science in decision making sees scientists as contributing substantively to policy decisions by providing reliable, objective information that will help policy makers reach publicly articulated goals. This model, which fails to acknowledge decades of interested and even activist involvement by scientists in policy making, persists in implementation settings.[63] The need to demonstrate the legitimacy of the policy process and the way that need is expressed through formalization pressures scientists to engage in symbolic behavior as a way to defend their status in environmental policy making. From an analytical standpoint, the symbolic behavior of scientists, intimately linked with their status and, as a consequence, with their level of influence, must be studied in its own right. It is not immediately clear that scientists' symbolic acts should be suspect. All actors involved in the political process must engage in some legitimacy-producing behavior. Though we might believe that scientists should be judged solely on their substantive contributions to policy making, most actors in the political process lack the expertise necessary to evaluate the substantive contributions of scientists. At the same time, if the symbolic acts scientists use to establish their credibility are divorced from the substantive information they provide, our acceptance of scientists as legitimate actors in the policy process may be manipulated. Concerns about scientists' misuse of power may be connected to evaluations of the appropriateness of symbolic action as a part of scientists' role in policy making.

A second theme of this chapter is the difficulty of relating "objective" scientific information to policy decisions. We see conflicting outcomes when we compare the controversy over the publication of NAPAP's first integrated assessment and the experience of the ORD within its regulatory setting, the EPA. Scientists involved in NAPAP were careful to conduct their research and to present its results in a way that demonstrated their distance from policy considerations. NAPAP was then criticized for providing information that was too technical to be of much use in constructing policy. The ORD, which operates more closely with policy makers in an attempt to provide them with information that is timely and relevant, suffers from the image that its science is biased by organizational commitments to environmental protection. These two examples suggest that striking an appropriate balance is difficult at best; scientists can fail by being overly insulated from policy makers and they can lose their credibility when they are perceived as being too close to policy making power. The contradiction in these two outcomes demonstrates the limits of science in resolving political conflict. Science, at its most objective and most legitimate, does not necessarily answer political questions about distribution of costs and benefits or about the links between political action and public consequence. Science that is more intimately linked to policy questions loses its objective status and, therefore, its legitimacy.

The problem of the tradeoff between relevance and objectivity has been addressed in the analytical literature and in policy circles. Several organizational solutions have been advanced that are intended to situate scientists in proximity to policy in a way that allows for their relevance and preserves their objectivity.[64] It may be that a comparative study of these organizational solutions and an evaluation of their relative rates of success might indicate more and less effective ways of mediating between science and policy. This is a practical approach, however, that leaves aside the normative implications of portraying through organizational or procedural means an image of science as objective and relevant. Once science becomes a resource in policy making, it is a political resource with political consequences. The need for scientists to defend their status in policy making is, itself, extraneous to the substantive information they bring to the process. The literature on scientists' use of boundary work is helpful here in that it explains how scientists establish their authority relative to non-scientists and in that it highlights the social underpinnings of such boundary-setting practices.

Structures and procedures erected in the implementation stage of policy making seek to limit scientists to their most neutral and objective roles. These structures are legitimizing, and yet they do not produce the substance-driven, objective participation they intend. A precarious tension arises out of the need for legitimacy in policy making and the understanding that that legitimacy is based on a false conception of scientific practice. A central question for future research and analysis is whether a more accurate picture of science can be incorporated into decision making in a way that will allow for policy decisions relying on science to be accepted as legitimate.

Conclusion

Studies of science in policy making have struggled over the question of whether scientists have significant influence in the policy-making process. This comparison, both across cases and across time, suggests that scientists' potential for influence changes with the policy setting in which they participate. More specifically, this research finds that scientists' participation is least contested during agenda setting. At this stage of the policy process, scientists are influential participants in establishing environmental issues as important policy problems. The success of the respective science narratives for acid rain and climate change is exemplified by the rapid institutionalization of each in the form of national research programs created to provide science advice to policy makers as they weigh their options in responding to each problem. That the respective science narratives contained oversimplified understandings of how science informs policy making had little effect on the widespread support for creating national research programs.

My research points to procedural constraints that become increasingly important as the policy process evolves. For scientists, these constraints are designed to restrict scientists' participation to that of neutral advisor. Though the constraints are unlikely to affect scientists' putative objectivity, they do ensure that scientists who participate in more formal policy settings spend a good deal of their time engaging in explicit discussions of the science/policy boundary and working to demonstrate that they have remained neutral.

My research also contributes to current understandings of the policy-making process by suggesting an alternate view of scientists in the policy process than that offered by Kingdon. Where Kingdon argues that experts play almost no role in agenda setting, my analysis demonstrates that scientists are important actors in setting environmental policy agendas.

In addition, my research takes a relatively unexplored insight of Gieryn's about the potential for "obduracy" in debates about the boundaries of science and demonstrates an arena in which such obduracy may, in fact, exist. Specifically, there is relatively little debate surrounding the role that scientists take in policy agenda setting and a surprising willingness accept scientists' definition of the most important environmental policy problems. Before exploring the implications of the research, I will discuss several competing explanations that might explain the changes we see over the course of policy making for the two issues.

Competing Explanations

The central argument—that formal constraints restrict scientists' participation such that their potential for influence declines as the policy process evolves—fits well with the details of the acid rain and climate change cases. Still, a number of competing explanations might also explain the variation we see over time. For example, as the policy process evolves, so does the scientific understanding of both acid rain and climate change. One might expect that scientists' influence is linked to the level of certainty surrounding the scientific record at issue in the policy debate.

A closer look at the trends in scientific understandings of the two issues shows that that scientists' influence cannot be easily predicted by assessing the strength of the scientific record that supports their arguments. In general, one would expect that, as scientific uncertainties are resolved, scientists would have less difficulty maintaining their credibility. My analysis shows the opposite. As the policy process unfolds, scientists are placed under increasing scrutiny with respect to the credibility of the advice they offer, even as scientific uncertainties are reduced.

The relationship between scientists' credibility and the resolution of scientific uncertainties, however, may be somewhat complicated by the fact that increased scientific understanding of a problem may show that scientists' original claims about the problem were either overstated or incorrect. It may be that scientists' credibility only increases in the course of the policy process when scientific uncertainties are resolved in ways that support rather than weaken scientists' original claims. This was the case for climate change in that improved scientific knowledge has bolstered scientists' original claims about global warming. The resolution of uncertainties for acid rain, however, went in the opposite direction. Though continued research supported the broad argument about acid rain, i.e., that certain pollutants released into the atmosphere are transported over long distances and lead to acid precipitation, it also showed that scientists' original predictions about the *effects* of acid rain were overstated. Scientists may have lost some credibility as a result of a perception that they could not correctly predict the impacts of acid rain. Such a loss of credibility may also have diminished scientists' ability to control the terms of their participation in the policy process. If this were the explanation for scientists' loss of autonomy in the acid rain case, we would expect climate scientists not to have experienced a similar loss of autonomy, but they did. Moreover, even as scientific research was revising downward the expected impacts of acid rain, legislative momentum was picking up. Therefore, scientists do not seem to have experienced any loss of credibility at the time in the policy process when the expected effects of acid rain were revised. Scientists' loss of influence in shaping the acid rain narrative came later in the policy process, when the Acid Rain Program was being implemented. Comparison of the strength of the scientific record to scientists' credibility yields, at best, a complicated picture. Moreover, it is difficult to come up with a relationship between strength of the science and scientific credibility that can account for both the acid rain case and the climate change case.

Another possible reason for the change in scientists' level of influence in the policy process might be interest-group activity. When problems of environmental policy are transferred from scientific circles into the public domain, interest groups, both those supporting and opposing early scientific framings, are likely to give standard responses to the suggested policy implications.[1] Industry interest groups reliably argue that regulations are inefficient and that supporters of regulation are engaging in scare tactics. Environmental groups, on the other hand, are likely to emphasize that irreversible environmental damage is close at hand and that swift action is called for. As the policy process matures, interest groups usually develop more detailed arguments to support these standard positions.

Invariably, opponents of suggested regulations call attention to uncertainties in the scientific record. This puts scientists on the defensive in policy settings, in that they must be able to account for their predictions in light of uncertainties in the science. It makes sense that, under these conditions, scientists would be more circumspect in the kinds of statements they are willing to make and might retreat into a more "objective" role.

The interest-group explanation, however, is not very successful in distinguishing scientists' experiences in legislative settings from their experiences in implementation settings. Interest-group pressure is intense during legislative debates—a stage in the policy process when industry has a chance of defeating a proposed regulatory program. Although industry groups continue to pursue their interests in implementation settings, the passage of legislation reduces the scope of what is open for debate. In particular, successful legislation settles the question of whether the scientific record is sufficiently clear to warrant policy action. If interest-group scrutiny were the crucial factor in shaping scientists behavior, scientists would look more constrained in legislative settings than in implementation settings, rather than the reverse. That said, interest-group pressure is probably one of the reasons why role expectations affect scientists' behavior. Role expectations are more powerful if there are actors who will call attention to deviations from expected roles.

The explanation that ties the change in scientists' behavior to the constraints that come with formalized procedures present in later stages of policy making fits the two cases better than either the scientific-uncertainty explanation or the interest-group explanation. An important consideration when one is discussing the change in scientists' behavior is whether the individual scientists changed or whether the setting affects scientists' behavior in policy making by selecting which scientists appear during which stages. In the latter case, scientists can remain constant in their approach to policy making while the "public face of science" changes, as each policy stage attracts only a subsection of the larger scientific community. The fact that there are relatively few scientists involved in the implementation of the acid rain program who were present during the first two stages suggests that selection bias might be at work. Adding to this is the fact that the scientists who participate in the implementation of research programs for acid rain appear to be the scientists who are least likely to make policy statements during legislative hearings. These scientists were, notably, not involved in agenda setting for acid rain. On the other hand, the legislative setting in both the acid rain case and the climate change case allows for scientists to take one of three approaches.

This demonstrates that scientists who are participating in the same stage of the policy process do not necessarily behave uniformly. Various *types* of scientists appear during legislative debate, and the choices they make about how to negotiate the science/policy boundary are apparent. Although the cross-sectional and longitudinal analyses do not settle the question of whether setting shapes behavior more than it selects for a particular type of scientist, the insight that scientists' potential for influence changes across settings is robust in either case, because both pathways ultimately lead to a distinct "public face of science" in each setting.

Implications of the Research Findings

The issue of changing constraints across the policy-making process may be analytically interesting in its own right, but it is important from the standpoint of science in decision making only if scientists' responses to those constraints produce outcomes that have the potential to undermine democratic decision making. From Sheila Jasanoff we learn that even in implementation settings—the settings that, I argue, are characterized by the greatest constraints—scientists are able to present findings, under the authority of science, that merge political judgments with scientific information. Jasanoff's research (1990) suggests that the constraints are, at best, imperfect in preventing scientists from crossing the science/policy boundary as articulated in these settings.

Still, the presence of role expectations that call for scientists to act objectively increases the potential for deviations from the norm to be noticed by other policy participants. This, in turn, creates more opportunities for participants to actively debate where the line between science and policy should be drawn. Such debate promises to democratize the incorporation of science into politics. During agenda setting, scientists' persuasive efforts attract less critical attention. The lack of critical attention here is counter-intuitive because, at this stage, scientists have the potential to exercise considerable influence.[2] Persuasion is a central currency of political debate (Majone 1989), and scientists, with their insight into the state of the environment, have an advantage in environmental policy debates over other actors in advancing persuasive positions. First, scientists are likely to be the actors who initially sound the alarm. This means that they introduce a policy frame in the absence of other, targeted counter-frames. Second, policy frames that make use of the status of science and scientists tend to be more persuasive than those expressed in non-scientific terms (Stone 1989). Lack of constraint does not, in and of itself, translate into influence for scientists. Equally, scientists may attempt to be persuasive without actually succeeding. However, there is strong evidence from the cases presented here that scientists' framings were convincing. In addition, there is evidence that, as the policy process evolves, scientists' framing efforts were challenged by others.

Framing is important because successful frames are likely to be institutionalized in the policy process. For example, congressional committees can adopt a specific frame and reinforce that frame through committee hearings and bills voted out of committee. Policy, communities and interests groups, following congressional activity, might then organize their activities around that frame. Finally, in some cases, legislation will be successful and give legal expression to a successful frame that will then guide agency implementation or even create a new organization that is structured in terms of that frame. Once a particular frame has taken hold, actors tend to see that frame as the only way to think about the problem and are likely discount or even overlook competing arguments.[3]

Baumgartner and Jones (1993: 83–102) highlight the particular dynamics of policy making during periods of "Downsian mobilization" in which policy entrepreneurs create institutions around a policy problem during a wave of public enthusiasm that creates particularly favorable conditions for institution building. The early stages of policy formation for acid rain and climate change illustrate this process and exemplify periods in which a lack of debate about the dominant policy narrative is particularly noteworthy. Baumgartner and Jones, in presenting their theory of Downsian mobilization (ibid.: 88), observe that Anthony Downs, in his own discussion of policy dynamics, overlooks the staying power of institutions set up during such waves of enthusiasm. Downs (1972) predicts that decline in public enthusiasm undermines any forward progress related to the initial program. Baumgartner and Jones, to the contrary, argue that institutions can support a given approach to a policy problem such that that approach remains stable over long periods of time (1993: 89).

This view of a period of enthusiastic institution building dovetails nicely with Thomas Gieryn's argument about the relative obduracy of some science/policy boundary settlements. Gieryn argues that although most attempts to advance science as a force in society are accompanied by vigorous debate about what constitutes science, there are spaces in which such debate does not occur (1995: 407). We see this in the early stages of acid rain and climate change policy making, in which the framing of each is one-sided. Once members of Congress begin to argue for remedial action, participants in the policy debate are likely to offer alternative framings. The perspectives offered by Baumgartner and Jones and by Gieryn offer some insights into why studies of science in policy making have differed about scientists' influence in the policy process. If, as we see in this research, scientists' behavior changes predictably over the course of the policy-making process, then generalizations based on an examination of scientists in a single policy stage will not be able to account for their activities in another stage.

Institutionalized science narratives are important in the policy process because they treat as settled—and, therefore, they take out of contention—a number of factors bound up in addressing issues such as acid rain and climate change.[4] If the normative aspects of scientists' stories about acid rain and climate change are debated and subjected to democratic processes, we can be confident that their institutionalization is democratically supported. If, on the other hand, scientists' normative commitments are understood as scientific rather than political, their institutionalization raises some concern. As a practical matter, allowing scientists to set to the terms of debate can narrow the scope of policy innovation, since most scientists have limited experience, at best, in designing policy.[5] More sobering is the potential for scientists' role as agenda setters to produce technocratic outcomes.

Turning to the legislative stage of decision making, we see scientists in a different role. Scientists continue to enjoy a special status during the legislative process in that, for environmental policy issues, scientists are often called before congressional hearings as witnesses. Scientists are given a voice in the legislative stage of the policy process. The pressures of the legislative process, however, ensure that scientists are not the only voice in policy debate. Members of Congress, in order to be successful in pursuing their policy goals, must ensure that they consider a number of different views in shaping legislation.[6] This is especially true when members of Congress are proposing concerted policy action to address a problem. In spite of the fact that multiple groups are present in legislative policy making, scientists who act as witnesses are typically accorded a certain amount of respect. In addition, scientists enter into a policy process that has been framed according to a science narrative established by themselves or their colleagues. So, while scientists are not the only actors involved in legislative decision making, they do have a particular status in the process owing to their expertise. Their heavy representation among witnesses demonstrates the extent to which members of Congress view scientists as integral to their congressional goals, at least in the arena of environmental policy.

Given this, what do we learn about scientists in the legislative stage of policy making? First, the legislative arena offers the first glimpse into the tension between the idealized image of scientists that emphasizes the universality and objectivity of science and the wish for scientists to offer clear links between scientific findings and policy options, a process that is neither universal nor objective. In many scientists who participate in legislative decision making, this tension produces a visible effort to negotiate the boundary between science and policy. Through such negotiation, scientists attempt to retain their status as neutral experts and to provide relevant information to policy makers. But the ability to fulfill one of these roles almost precludes the ability to satisfy the other. In spite of this, scientists are repeatedly called upon to play both roles when they participate in congressional hearings. The variety of tactics employed in confronting the science/policy boundary refutes any notion of scientists behaving as a unified group when they enter the arena of policy making.

An interesting point to make about scientists in legislative decision making is that this is an arena in which scientists' interests are very likely to be exposed or "deconstructed." Sociologists do not precede policy makers in seeking to uncover politically relevant agendas that are being packaged in universal terms.[7] In environmental policy making, efforts to deconstruct participants' claims seek to expose both pro-environmental and anti-environmental positions. This means that other types of policy commitments can pass through the policy process with little examination. At the same time, scientists' status does not guarantee them more influence than non-scientists. In legislative settings, some scientists are careful to articulate how they understand the science/policy boundary. This is something we do not see among scientists engaged in agenda setting.

Turning to the question of improving the way scientists are drawn into legislative decision making, we must consider the appropriateness of relying on an image of science that, while lending scientists status, is descriptively inaccurate. However, because members of Congress use myriad rhetorical devices in an effort to mobilize support for their favored policy positions, it is unlikely that they will cease to rely on objective expertise as one of these devices. It is also hard to see how this effort, so easily countered by an opponent who also claims to have expertise on his or her side, subverts democratic decision making.

In implementation, the last stage of decision making, we see scientists working actively to demonstrate and maintain a status that was presumed during agenda setting and was even somewhat in evidence during legislation. Implementation is the most formally elaborated stage of the policy-making process. The procedures and structures found in this stage of decision making are designed around an idealized notion of science. As a consequence, scientists are much more preoccupied with upholding this ideal during implementation than during agenda setting or during legislation (when the ideal is invoked rhetorically). During implementation, the ideal is enacted through numerous procedures set up to demonstrate links between agency scientists and their university counterparts and through efforts to show either that the boundary between science and policy is being maintained or, where that cannot be shown, that the boundary has been incorrectly placed. Efforts to justify and maintain a boundary between science and policy account for much of what scientists do during implementation.

The question of influence during implementation is difficult. Science still retains its status as a rational tool to use in policy making that can reduce or resolve political controversies. Intractable policy decisions are often handed to science advisory committees that attempt to repackage political debates in calmer, technical terms that will settle conflicts over outcomes (Jasanoff 1990). At the same time, we see in the acid rain case that scientists face serious challenges to their previously exclusive role as the authors of the science narrative framing the approach to acid rain. Political pressures to defend the acid rain program actually reduce the influence of the scientists who first articulated the policy issue. It is difficult to generalize from this single case, but the experience of examining scientists in each of the three stages of acid rain policy suggests that the science narrative, initially a significant influence on the course of acid rain policy, is challenged and altered by political actors who face a different set of pressures and constraints in pursuing their policy-making goals.

In general, during implementation, scientists' status is repeatedly challenged by the ease with which science, so proximate to political power, can be politicized. Scientists must work hard to maintain their status as "objective" participants. Because the types of scientific claims whose credibility can be readily demonstrated are often less useful in answering policy questions, scientists can risk their relevance by defending their credibility.[8] Alternatively, scientists who preserve their relevance do so at the risk of their credibility.[9] Implementation offers countless opportunities for scientists to strike this balance incorrectly and, therefore, limit their influence in shaping policy outcomes. This finding is important when reviewing the literature on science in policy making. The notion of "translation" advanced by Latour (1985, 1988) and Callon (1985) places scientists in an authoritative role through their ability to bring non-scientists into their way of seeing the world and recasting non-scientists' problems in scientific terms. This ensures that non-scientists will turn to scientists in attempting to achieve their goals. Translation allows scientists to maintain a position of authority over non-scientists in approaching problems newly "translated" into scientific terms. Several scholars counter this view of scientists and society and argue instead that the process of defining roles for scientists and non-scientists involves multiple actors (Star and Griesemer 1989; Jasanoff 2004a; Jasanoff and Wynne 1998; Miller 2004a; Shackley and Wynne 1995, 1996). From this perspective, scientists do not necessarily have more authority than non-scientists in influencing the way common social problems are defined. By comparing scientists who participate in agenda setting with those who are active in policy implementation, we see evidence for both perspectives and at least the suggestion that the two patterns of scientific involvement occur predictably in the policy-making process.

The co-production approach privileges neither science nor non-science in analyzing how science and policy are understood. Instead, the co-production approach argues that science and policy are formed together through a process of mutual negotiation (Jasanoff 2004a; Jasanoff and Wynne 1998; Miller 2004a). The evidence here suggests that scientists operate under fewer constraints during agenda setting. However, it does not suggest that scientists are somehow insulated from larger political and social forces that shape their own representations of environmental policy problems. The shift between the 1950s framing of climate change and the 1970s framing is a prominent example of co-production.

Generalizability of the Findings

It is important to consider the applicability of the findings of this research beyond the cases of acid rain and global warming. First, we want to know whether these cases are representative of environmental policy making in general. The two cases were selected specifically for their characteristics that are typical of environmental policy making. However, there is some evidence that both the scientists and the policy makers involved in global warming policy learned from the acid rain case. This suggests that the cases are not entirely independent. Evidence for learning comes from the fact that Two individuals, Bert Bolin and Dennis Tirpak, were involved in acid rain and in climate change policy. Their participation in both policy debates provides support for the idea that climate change policy was influenced by experience gleaned from the acid rain case. evidence that learning did occur from acid rain to climate change.[10] Furthermore, some policy makers involved in implementing the Acid Rain Program were also involved in climate change negotiations (interview, September 14, 1998). The issue of emissions trading meant that those involved with the Acid Rain Program had relevant expertise in setting up a climate change treaty that would use the concept of emissions trading.

On the other hand, evidence that counters the idea of learning between the two cases can be found in early congressional hearings on global warming. Before 1990, when the emissions trading program at EPA that links acid rain and global warming was created, the referent that was used in congressional hearings for guidance in thinking about global warming policy was ozone depletion (SCEPW 1989: 12, 1991: 20, 1997: 33, 36, 42, 211, 221). Because the evidence is mixed, it is difficult to tell whether or not the cases are independent. To the extent that they are not, the issue of learning may mean that the findings of these cases do not extend to other issues of environmental policy. On the other hand, if learning occurred from acid rain to global warming or from ozone depletion to global warming, it may be that learning will spread throughout the general policy community working on environmental policy issues.

The applicability of the findings to other issue areas should also be addressed. Kingdon's 1984 work on health policy suggests that professionals have a slightly different role in the stages of policy making than the scientists in my two cases. Kingdon finds that professionals involved in health policy (he does not study scientists specifically) have influence in suggesting possible solutions for policy problems, but are not especially important in placing those problems on the agenda. My research finds that scientists have more influence during agenda setting than during later stages of policy making.

Certainly, part of the discrepancy in findings might be due to the fact that Kingdon does not try to trace the issues he studies from their origins. In fact, he argues that, given the issues he studies, he could not find an indisputable starting point. My research, on the other hand, allows for insight about how issues move from scientific circles into the public eye. My evidence supports the argument that scientists were very effective in placing issues previously confined to scientific communities on the public policy agenda. One might argue that this is due to selection on the dependent variable; after all, my study focuses on issues that are known to be on the policy agenda. However, the question is not whether the issues reach the policy agenda, but which actors are instrumental in getting issues on the public agenda. The differences in the types of policy issues treated by my study and by Kingdon's call for more cross-sectional analyses that might further elaborate where actors are most likely to wield power in the policy process.

Equally, in moving beyond regulatory policy to domains in which scientists are involved in producing technology, we may find further additional types of boundary work. For example, in non-regulatory agencies such as the National Aeronautics and Space Administration or the Army Corps of Engineers, science is applied in a less contested political environment than it is in regulatory settings. In political science terms, these are arenas of distributive rather than redistributive policy. Scientists are routinely included in discussions about how and where federal dollars should be spent to further science and technology objectives. Operating in these environments may produce less boundary work than we see in the later stages of policy making for acid rain and climate change. It would be interesting, then, to set out as a hypothesis that the science/policy boundary is less salient for scientists involved in distributive policy.[11]

Research comparing national styles of applying science in decision making (Brickman, Jasanoff, and Ilgen,1985; Vogel 1986; Jasanoff 1993, 2004b; Hajer 1995; Daemmrich 2004; Parthasarathy 2004) and research on civic epistemology (Jasanoff 2005a) demonstrates that the role of science and scientists is shaped by context and culture. This cautions against assuming that these findings will apply outside the United States. The case material treated here—the debates about acid rain and climate change in the United States—elucidates environmental policy making in the American political system. Degree of formalization, in particular, may not extend beyond the American case; the emphasis on legal procedures in American policy, which encourages formalization, is not found in other countries (Kagan 2001). In countries where policy making, overall, tends to be more collegial than legalistic, scientists may not be subject to a similar set of formally elaborated role expectations. Though the findings here are not expected to be relevant in other countries, it is possible that a hypothesis regarding the level of formality of policy-making processes could guide expectations about how and where to expect explicit contests over the science/policy boundary in other settings.

A New Role for Scientists?

In studying the role of science in environmental policy making, the tension between the ideal for science in decision making (i.e., that scientists should provide objective information) and the actual practice of using science in policy makes the persistence of the ideal intriguing. If the ideal image is hard to sustain, why is it so durable? The preponderance of my interviewees made some mention of the tension. They argued that, in practice, the role of science is only one of many factors that shape policy outcomes. The ideal, however, drives a symbolic reliance on science that calls for a record of scientific research to support policy decisions. Ample evidence of this can be found both in the records of committee hearings and in the *Federal Register* (where much of the information recorded for environmental policy decisions is scientific or technical).[12] This demonstrates the extent to which policy decisions are defended in scientific terms.

Some scholars have argued that the gap between practice and ideal should be closed by simply allowing scientists to express their policy preferences (Primack and von Hippel 1974; Collingridge and Reeve 1986; Salter 1988). This would allow both scientists and policy makers to be open about the ways they link scientific evidence to policy decisions without having to assert that this is done according to objective criteria. This might work particularly well in the legislative setting, where members of Congress are already inclined to press scientists to make policy-relevant statements. The fact that members of Congress seek out this information suggests that it is relevant to policy making even if it does not carry with it the consensus and the credibility associated with "good science."

There are, however, a number of pressures that work against this move. First of all, both scientists and policy makers benefit from the idealized image of scientists as objective actors offering universal information. Explaining political action in scientific terms presents those acts as technical rather than political and, when it works, can be a powerful political strategy for reducing controversy. Jasanoff articulates a related concern. To the extent that scientific authority legitimizes regulatory decisions, anything that undermines that authority might also slow down the decision-making process. Jasanoff argues this with reference to the flaws in the system of peer review that make it a poor mechanism for filtering out bad science. Jasanoff worries that if this were common knowledge, and if science were understood to be less rigorous that the science ideal suggests, regulatory decision making might lose a powerful legitimizing tool (1990: 82). Jasanoff seems to be concerned about the built-in conservatism of the US decision-making system. Since the system is more likely to produce no outcome than to produce new policy, anyone who supports environmental regulation might be worried about the removal of a force that legitimizes policy decisions. If we undermine the status of science that is linked to the idealized image of scientific practice, we may buy more controversy.

Dorothy Nelkin's analysis of technical controversy makes a similar point. In evaluating the sources of controversy in technical decision making, Nelkin argues that a technical decision becomes controversial when a group of challengers claim that the decision is actually political rather than technical. Nelkin says that the challengers, like the original decision makers, use technical knowledge. However, the challengers use technical information *tactically* (Nelkin 1979: 17). Nelkin overlooks the political power exercised by the original group of decision makers in deciding that a decision is technical. She therefore privileges those with agenda-setting power over those who come later to decisions and attempt to recast those decisions in terms that ensure their access to decision making. Nelkin wishes to constrain technical controversy for much the same reasons that Jasanoff worries about the loss of scientists' status that might come with exposing the weaknesses of the peer-review process. That is, decision making under these conditions is time consuming and complicated and is often stalemated.[13] These perspectives suggest that environmental policy making in the United States will be further fragmented if we remove from the process the putatively authoritative voice of science.

Nelkin's push for ways to limit controversy, in addition to her view that scientists and technical experts are subject to politicization but have no role in politicizing technical decisions, suggests that she accepts the ideal image of science in policy making—i.e. that objective, universal information limits political controversy. Jasanoff, on the other hand, views the ideal image as inaccurate but argues that decision making would be much more difficult if the ideal were not in place. These evaluations of the importance of scientific authority in policy making raise the question of whether scientists can be relevant *and* credible in policy making without invoking the science ideal.

The push to improve the use of science in decision making arises from two distinct goals. One is the rationalist goal of ensuring that decisions correctly link means and ends. The other is the democratic goal of ensuring broad participation, which relies on a different set of criteria for evaluating good decision making and places less emphasis on finding the "correct" solution. A third perspective, which does not fit in with either the rationalist goal or the democratic goal, is to see the use of science in policy making as symbolic. Throughout this book, we have seen that the use of science in decision making is characterized by reference to an ideal of science that is normative rather than descriptive. In spite of the fact that the ideal does not provide an accurate account of how science is incorporated in decision making, the ideal serves a symbolic role in that it demonstrates the *attempt* to use science in a way that is rational and that upholds democratic norms of decision making. This effort is symbolic to the extent that the attempt rather than the actual achievement of rational and democratic decision making is rewarded.[14] The persistence of this ideal in informing the use of science in decision making suggests that the attempt itself carries weight in policy settings. In this way, decision makers communicate to interest groups and to the public their good will in attempting to find solutions to complex environmental problems.

Using science symbolically is an affront to the rationalist perspective in that it relaxes the goal of making better policy decisions. Likewise, a symbolic role for scientists in policy making can undermine democratic decision-making goals when the symbolism that surrounds scientists in policy making places them in a privileged position with regard to non-scientists in decision making. Because of the extent to which the ideal image of science is used to justify scientists' role in policy making, the symbolic element of their participation must be considered in evaluating the acceptability of relying on scientists in making environmental policy decisions. From the standpoint of policy practice, subjecting scientists' arguments about environmental issues that merit public attention to more open debate and discussion could go a long way toward balancing democratic ideals against the crucial information scientists bring to the policy-making process.

Appendix A

A Primer on the Roots of a Constructivist View of Science in Society

A number of scholars have contributed to a constructivist understanding of science in society through a methodical critique of work in the philosophy and history of science that attempts to isolate the particular characteristics of science that sustain its unique cultural authority. Karl Popper (1963) pursued this question in trying to isolate the characteristics of quantum physics that made it different from other contemporary theories about the way the world works. These included history, psychoanalysis, and individual psychology. Popper settled on falsifiability as the characteristic that made science unique in producing reliable knowledge. For Popper, verification through an inductive approach of observation and experimentation—i.e., an empirical approach—was insufficient in that the next observation might prove a theory wrong. Moreover, many of the theories that Popper considered pseudo-science claimed empirical verification. According to Popper, pseudo-science managed this by stating theories so vaguely that their empirical confirmation was guaranteed. What distinguished real science from pseudo-science, Popper argued, was the interplay between conjecture and criticism that takes place in real science. Scientists, by stating theoretical expectations so that they might be criticized and ultimately falsified, contribute to the advancement of science in that only robust theories survive attempts to tear them down.

Popper's explanation of how scientific theories come to be falsified, however, depended on experimentation. Tests of the physical world must be conducted in order to falsify scientists' claims. For Popper, this process of experimentation was straightforward; either an experiment falsifies or validates a scientific claim. Harry Collins (1981) questioned this picture of experimentation and argued that the results of an experiment are open to interpretations that are often based on non-scientific judgments.

Collins, relying on his study of debates about gravitational radiation, points out that, in areas of science where results are established, one knows an experiment has been performed correctly when the experimenter gets the correct answer. But when experimenters are entering novel territory, debates about whether or not the results are reliable or whether the experiment was performed correctly can and do arise. Collins explains the dilemma this way: "Usually, successful practice of an experimental skill is evident in a successful outcome to an experiment, but where detection of a novel phenomenon is in question, it is not clear what one should count as a 'successful outcome'—detection or non-detection of the phenomenon." (1981: 34) From the scientific standpoint, replication of a new experiment can show whether or not the outcome is valid. Collins, however, argues that efforts at replication often result in disputes among scientists whether the replication was a faithful recreation of the first experiment.

In his study of debates about the detection of gravitational radiation, Collins finds that none of the six attempts at replication, all of which showed negative results, produced consensus among participants in the debate that it was, in fact, a good replication of the original study.[1] Each of the scientists who were critical of the original experimental results was also critical of at least one of the attempted replications (Collins 1981: 44). Moreover, Collins notes that most of the scientists involved had formed opinions about the original work before the results of the negative experiments were in, which suggests that their interpretation of the quality of experiments was influenced by their previous theoretical commitments. Collins (1985: 2) coined the term "experimenter's regress" to capture the dynamic that can ensue in attempts to validate or refute an experiment. Collins's work raised the question of how, in cases of novel scientific experiment, a community of scientists form a consensus about whether an experiment is reliable. Collins's work points to the potential for non-scientific factors to play a role in what scientists ultimately consider valid science. This raises a question about the extent to which the cultural authority of science comes from its unique ability to represent reality.

Additional research contributes to the idea that social interactions rather than verifiable correspondence with reality serves as the basis for what separates good science from bad science or science from non-science. For example, Robert Merton, himself a defender of the idea that intrinsic properties of science contribute to its objective account of reality, pointed out another non-scientific dynamic in scientific practice: the "Matthew Effect" (1968).[2] The Matthew Effect occurs when scientists who have established reputations get disproportional credit for comparable work than lesser-known scientists (1968: 57). In addition, the Matthew Effect occurs in communications about science any time that announcements made by scientists with strong reputations get more publicity than announcements made by scientists who have yet to establish themselves (ibid.: 58). Similar patterns show up in peer review. One study of peer review found that reviewers are more likely to review positively studies whose findings agree with reviewers' expectations (Mahoney 1977). This runs counter to the expectation that peer review will separate good science from bad by judging a study on its individual merits. In another study of the peer-review process, researchers compared the rankings given by two independent review panels to the same set of grant proposals. This comparison showed a high rate of disagreement between the two panels (Cole, Cole, and Simon 1981). Moreover this disagreement was not concentrated around those proposals that received a ranking that was on the border between grants that would receive funding and those that would not. The disagreement about proposal quality existed across the rankings given. This suggests that it is even difficult for reviewers to agree about the best and worst proposals in a group.

If falsifiability is socially negotiated rather than verified through reference to objective criteria, then the status of science as an accurate reflection of reality is open to question. Adding to this contingency is Thomas Kuhn's account of the function of paradigms in scientific research (1970).[3] According to Kuhn, paradigms create a coherent framework for scientific work by articulating interesting questions, defining accepted methods and procedures, and creating the promise of theoretically expected empirical outcomes. Kuhn argues that unexpected findings often lead to redefinition of a paradigm. In fact, because anomalous findings can overturn a paradigm, scientists who are committed to a certain paradigm will sometimes discount the implications of their findings in order to maintain the coherence of the framework that the paradigm offers.

Kuhn created enormous controversy by arguing that the replacement of one paradigm by another should not be viewed as scientific progress. He argues that scientific progress can only be judged within the context of a specific paradigm and that competing paradigms cannot be meaningfully compared as superior or inferior. This implies that, when a new paradigm replaces an existing paradigm, one cannot conclude that scientific progress has occurred.

Kuhn's view of science challenges the notion of linear scientific progress. He argues that replacement of one paradigm by another is not a function of which paradigm is more ontologically successful. Instead, a paradigm becomes dominant by being able to answer questions that scientists value at the time. Here, Kuhn suggests, what is in vogue in a discipline or a subdiscipline provides a better explanation for the success of a new paradigm than any correspondence that paradigm has to reality. Kuhn argues, further, that one cannot compare the ontological status of paradigms, insofar as paradigms represent incompatible ways of viewing nature. As a consequence of this incomparability, Kuhn writes, "We may . . . have to relinquish the notion . . . that changes of paradigm carry scientists and those who learn from them closer and closer to the truth." (1970: 170)

At the same time that Kuhn rejects the idea of paradigm shifts representing progress in science, he also argues that normal science—science conducted under the guidance of a particular paradigm—can produce facts that are consonant with the theory laid out by the paradigm. Normal science, as it is carried out within the context of a paradigm, can produce scientific progress. The social element of Kuhn's articulation of science comes into play primarily in the process of scientists making judgments about which paradigm to adopt during periods in which competing paradigms are available.

Bruno Latour and Steve Woolgar offer a more thoroughly social view of science through their argument that scientific facts are, ultimately, the products of social negotiations. For Latour and Woolgar, the process of constructing scientific facts begins in the laboratory when a scientist makes a tentative claim to have found a new fact. Other scientists, doubting the "factness" of the new claim, will typically meet the new claim with their own counter-arguments. During this stage, while scientists debate the status of a factual claim, the "fact" goes through a circular process of gaining and losing its standing as a fact. One cannot tell during the debate whether a claim will eventually achieve the status of fact among debaters, or whether the debate will be resolved in the other direction. Akin to the findings in other studies, Latour and Woolgar argue that social processes are at work in settling controversies about which claims should have the status of fact.

Latour and Woolgar argue that their account is not an attack on whether facts are, in fact, facts: "We do not wish to say that facts do not exist, nor that there is no such thing as reality. In this simple sense, our position is not relativist." (1986: 180) They explain their view of the social underpinnings of facts as follows: "It is *because* the controversy settles, [*sic*] that a statement splits into an entity [i.e., reality] and a statement about an entity [i.e., a factual claim]; such a split never precedes the resolution of the controversy." (ibid.: 180) In this way, they argue that a claim about what is "out there" does not begin to look unique—i.e., like a fact—until a network of actors has accepted a specific claim as a true representation of reality. Up until the point of agreement among scientists involved in a controversy, a claim has no *a priori* power to explain reality. Many claims that are advanced as facts never achieve the status of fact. Therefore, the reality they claim to represent is never acknowledged. From an epistemological standpoint, the implication of Latour and Woolgar's argument is that, even if reality exists "out there," its status, or its availability as reality, is entirely contingent up to the moment when antagonists come to agreement about the existence of that reality. A crucial aspect of Latour and Woolgar's argument is that the status of a fact depends on the social networks that support it.[4] For Latour and Woolgar, the more elaborate the network of actors are who accept a claim as factual, the more factual status the claim has.

Upon first reading, constructivist arguments about the social underpinnings of science can be unsettling. If (as the constructivists suggest) consonance with reality is socially negotiated rather than verified through some objective process, this opens the door to relativism. If there are not empirical or natural-world constraints on this process, then, one might argue, there are few reliable guides for identifying good science. Under such circumstances, social trends or ideology might dictate what stands for science.

Most scholars who argue for the social underpinnings of science do not endorse relativism.[5] Instead, the constructivists point to social processes involved in stabilizing the boundary between science and nonscience and argue that such mechanisms are sufficient to maintain the cultural authority of science as producing reliable, verifiable knowledge. The constructivist approach does not dispense with reality. It dispenses with the idea that determining what counts as reality requires objective means.

Appendix B

Methodology for Analyzing Scientists' Participation in Legislative Settings

The data collected for the analysis in chapter 3, which covers scientists in legislative settings, are drawn from congressional hearings on acid rain and climate change. Lists of hearings for each case were drawn from the LexisNexis Congressional Information Service database.

Data on Acid Rain Hearings

For acid rain, the time period studied was 1975–1990. The first congressional mention of acid rain occurred in a hearing held in 1975. In 1990 Congress passed the Clean Air Act Amendments containing a program for controlling acid rain. In order to find a list of hearings that focused on acid rain, I searched the Congressional Information Service, Inc. index for hearings with the terms "acid rain," "acid deposition," and "acid precipitation" anywhere in the summary. This produced a list of 172 hearings. From this list, I discarded those in which acid rain was mentioned only once or was not otherwise a substantial focus of the hearing. This produced a list of 73 hearings. From this list of hearings that focused substantially or entirely on acid rain, I selected 24 hearings and subjected them to close, qualitative analysis. The hearings selected for close analysis were selected to include hearings across the relevant time period. Hearings were also selected so that the range committees involved would be included in the analysis. Finally, hearings in which scientists were significant participants were analyzed. For a list of these hearings, see appendix C.

In addition, I conducted a quantitative analysis of the list of 90 hearings that focused on particularly or substantially on acid rain. The data set classifies the hearings by name, committee, and date and tracks whether the hearing was legislative or non-legislative. The database also includes the name, education level, organizational affiliation and policy position of every witness who testified at one of these 90 hearings, for a total of 1,209 witnesses. This number includes witnesses who testified on more than one occasion, so the database may include a single person multiple times. Questions raised in the qualitative analysis of the hearings can be tested across the entire list of hearings by querying this larger data set.[1]

Data on Climate Change Hearings

I selected a sample of climate change hearings for qualitative analysis in a similar fashion. Using the CIS index and the search string "global warming" OR "climate change" AND NOT "appropriations" produced a list of 196 hearings.[2] Excluding hearings whose summaries included only single mentions of climate change produced a list of 143 hearings. This list is longer than that for acid rain because legislative debate about climate change is ongoing.[3] From this list, I analyzed 41 hearings. The list includes (a) hearings that spanned the period 1956–2002, (b) hearings from the committees most heavily involved in the issue, and (c) hearings where scientists dominated the witness list. These hearings are listed in appendix D.

The data collection for quantitative analysis of the hearings held on climate change follows the same format as that for the acid rain hearings. The data set classifies the hearings by name, committee, and date and tracks whether the hearing is legislative or non-legislative. The database also includes the name, educational level, organizational affiliation, and policy position of every witness who testified. However, there are notable differences between the two databases. First, in the absence of a federal program to regulate emissions of greenhouse gases, debate concerning climate change has been ongoing since the mid 1970s. The open-ended nature of the legislative debate means both that many more hearings have been held on climate change than on acid rain and that there is no obvious endpoint to congressional debate. As a consequence of the open-ended nature of the climate change debate, not all of the hearings held have been coded. Instead, all the hearings that treat climate change between 1976 and 1989 have been coded. During the late 1980s, there was a significant increase in the annual number of hearings held on climate change. This increase signals a gain in the issue's salience in Congress. To capture this stage of congressional attention, a random sample of 50 percent of the hearings held in 1990, 1991, and 1992 were coded. This limits the workload associated with coding hearings, which is significant, while ensuring that an unbiased picture of the trends in these three years is captured. Still, it is important to note that data for the climate change hearings from 1990 to 1992 are estimated from the randomly sampled hearings. Full count data exist only for the years 1976–1989.[4]

Appendix C
Acid Rain Hearings Included in Qualitative Analysis

HCA (House Committee on Agriculture). 1986. Effects of Acid Deposition and Air Pollutants on Forest Productivity: Hearing before the Subcommittee on Forests, Family Farms, and Energy of the House Committee on Agriculture. 99th Congress, 2nd Session. Government Printing Office (May 13).

HCA. 1987. *Forest Ecosystems and Atmospheric Pollution Research Act of 1987: Hearing before the Subcommittee on Forests, Family Farms, and Energy of the House Committee on Agriculture.* 100th Congress, 1st Session. Government Printing Office (June 9).

HCEC (House Committee on Energy and Commerce). 1981a. *Acid Precipitation (Part 1): Hearings before the Subcommittee on Heath and the Environment of the House Committee on Energy and Commerce.* 97th Congress, 1st Session. Government Printing Office (October 1, 2, and 6).

HCEC. 1981b. *Acid Precipitation (Part 2): Hearings before the Subcommittee on Heath and the Environment of the House Committee on Energy and Commerce.* 97th Congress, 1st Session. Government Printing Office (October 20).

HCFA (House Committee on Foreign Affairs). 1981. *United States-Canadian Relations and Acid Rain: Hearing before the Subcommittee on Human Rights and International Organizations and on Inter-American Affairs of the House Committee on Foreign Affairs.* 97th Congress, 1st Session. Government Printing Office (May 20).

HCIFC. 1980. *Acid Rain: Hearing before the Subcommittee on Oversight and Investigations of the House Committee on Interstate and Foreign Commerce.* 96th Congress, 2nd Session. Government Printing Office (February 26–27).

HCIIA (House Committee on Interior and Insular Affairs). 1984. *Effects of Air Pollution and Acid Rain on Forest Decline: Hearing Before the Subcommittee on Mining, Forest Management, and Bonneville Power Administration of House Committee on Interior and Insular Affairs.* 98th Congress, 2nd Session. Government Printing Office (June 7).

HCSST (House Committee on Science, Space and Technology). 1975a. *Research and Development Related to Sulphates in the Atmosphere: Hearings before the Subcommittee on the Environment and the Atmosphere of the House Committee on Science, Space, and Technology.* 94th Congress, 1st Session. Government Printing Office (July 8, 9, 11, 14).

HCSST. 1983. *Acid Rain: Implications for Fossil Fuel R&D. Hearings before the Subcommittee on Energy Development and Applications and the Subcommittee on Natural Resources, Agriculture Research, and Environment of the House Committee on Science, Space, and Technology.* 98th Congress, 1st Session. Washington, D.C.: Government Printing Office (September 13, 20).

HCSST. 1985. *Acid Rain Research: Hearing before the Subcommittee on Natural Resources, Agricultural Research and Environment of the House Committee on Science, Space, and Technology.*

HCSST. 1988. *National Acid Precipitation Assessment Program: Hearing before the Subcommittee on Natural Resources, Agriculture Research and Environment of the House Committee on Science, Space and Technology.* 100th Congress, 2nd Session. Government Printing Office (April 27).

HCSST. 1989. *Air Pollution Research and Development Needs: Hearing before the Subcommittee on Natural Resources, Agriculture Research and Environment of the House Committee on Science, Space and Technology.* 101st Congress, 1st Session. Government Printing Office (November 16).

HSCA (House Select Committee on Aging). 1983. *Alzheimer's Disease: Is There an Acid Rain Connection? Hearing before the Subcommittee on Human Services of the House Select Committee on Aging.* 98th Congress, 1st Session. Government Printing Office (August 8).

SCENR. 1984. *Implementation of the Acid Precipitation Act of 1980: Hearing before the Senate Committee on Energy and Natural Resources.* 98th Congress, 2nd Session. Government Printing Office (April 30).

SCEPW (Senate Committee on Environment and Public Works). 1981. *Acid Rain: Hearing before the Senate Committee on Environment and Public Works.* 97th Congress, 1st Session. Government Printing Office (October 29).

SCEPW. 1983. *Environmental Research and Development, Part 2. Hearing before the Senate Committee on Environment and Public Work.,* 98th Congress, 1st Session. Government Printing Office (October 17).

SCEPW. 1986a. *Acid Deposition and Related Air Pollution Issues: Hearing before the Committee on Environment and Public Works, United States Senate.* 99th Congress, 2nd Session. Government Printing Office (June 26).

SCEPW. 1986b. *Review of the Federal Government's Research Program on the Causes and Effects of Acid Rain: Hearing before the Committee on Environment and Public Works, United States Senate.* S. Hrg. 99–578. Government Printing Office (December 11).

SCEPW. 1987a. *Health Effects of Acid Rain Precursors: Hearing before the Subcommittee on Environmental Protection of the Senate Committee on Environment and Public Works.* 100th Congress, 1st Session. Government Printing Office (February 3).

SCEPW. 1987b. *Acid Rain Control Technologies: Existing and Emerging Acid Rain Control Technologies: Hearing before the Subcommittee on Environmental Protection of the Senate Committee on Environment and Public Works.* 100th Congress, 1st Session. Government Printing Office (March 4).

SCEPW. 1987c. *Acid Rain Control Technologies: Clean Coal and the US and Canada's Acid Rain Envoys' Report: Hearing before the Subcommittee on Environmental Protection of the Senate Committee on Environment and Public Works.* 100th Congress, 1st Session. Government Printing Office (March 11).

SCEPW. 1987d. *Acid Rain and Nonattainment Issues: Hearing before the Subcommittee on Environmental Protection of the Senate Committee on Environment and Public Works.* 100th Congress, 1st Session. Government Printing Office (April 22).

SCFR (Senate Committee on Foreign Relations). 1982. *Acid Rain: Hearing before the Subcommittee on Arms Control, Oceans,*

International Operations and Environment of the Senate Committee on Foreign Relations. 97th Congress, 2nd Session. Government Printing Office (February 10).

SSCSB (Senate Select Committee on Small Business). 1980. *Economic Impact of Acid Rain: Hearing before the Senate Select Committee on Small Business and the Senate Committee on Environment and Public Works.* 96th Congress, 2nd Session. Government Printing Office (September 23).

Appendix D
Climate Change Hearings Included in Qualitative Analysis

HCoA (House Committee on Appropriations). 1956. *Second Supplemental Appropriation Bill, 1956. Hearings before the House Committee on Appropriations.* 84th Congress, Second Session. Government Printing Office (February 6–8, 16, 23, 27, 28, March 1, 5, 6, 8).

HCoA. 1957. *National Science Foundation. Report on International Geophysical Year. Hearings before the House Committee on Appropriations.* 85th Congress, First Session. Government Printing Office (May 1).

HCoA. 1958. *National Science Foundation. Review of the First Eleven Months of the International Geophysical Year. Hearings before the House Committee on Appropriations.* 85th Congress, Second Session. Government Printing Office (June 2).

HCoA. 1959. *National Science Foundation; National Academy of Sciences. Report on the International Geophysical Year (February 1959). Hearings before the House Committee on Appropriations.* 86th Congress, First Session. Government Printing Office (February 18).

HCGR (House Committee on Government Reform). 1998a. *Kyoto Protocol: Is the Clinton-Gore Administration Selling Out Americans? Parts I-VI: Hearings before the Subcommittee on National Economic Growth, Natural Resources, and Regulatory Affairs.* 105th Congress, 2nd Session. Government Printing Office (April 23; May 19, 20; June 24; July 15; September 16).

HCGR (House Committee on Government Reform). 1998b. *Will the Administration Implement the Kyoto Protocol through the Back Door? Hearing before the Subcommittee on National Economic Growth, Natural Resources, and Regulatory Affairs of the House Committee on*

Government Reform and Oversight. 105th Congress, 2nd Session. Government Printing Office (October 9).

HCIFC (House Committee on Interstate and Foreign Commerce). 1958. *International Geophysical Year. Hearing before the House Committee on Interstate and Foreign Commerce.* 85th Congress, 2nd Session. Government Printing Office (March 26).

HCR (House Committee on Resources). 2003. *Kyoto Global Warming Treaty's Impact on Ohio's Coal-Dependent Communities.* 108th Congress, 1st Session. Government Printing Office (May 13).

HCS. 1995b. *Scientific Integrity and the Public Trust: The Science Behind Federal Policies and Mandates: Case Study 2—Climate Models and Projections of Potential Impacts of Global Climate Change: Hearings before the Subcommittee on Energy and Environment of the House Committee on Science.* 104th Congress, 1st Session. Government Printing Office (November 16).

HCSB (House Committee on Small Business). 1998a. *Oversight Hearing on the Kyoto Protocol: The Undermining of American Prosperity: Hearings before the House Committee on Small Business.* 105th Congress, Second Session. Government Printing Office (June 4).

HCSB. 1998b. *Kyoto Protocol: The Undermining of American Prosperity—The Science: Hearings before the House Committee on Small Business.* 105th Congress, Second Session. Government Printing Office (July 29).

HCSB. 1999. *Effect of the Kyoto Protocol on American Small Business: Hearings before the House Committee on Small Business.* 106th Congress, First Session. Government Printing Office (April 29).

HCSST. 1975b. *Costs and Effects of Chronic Exposure to Low-Level Pollutants in the Environment: Hearings before the Subcommittee on Environment and the Atmosphere of the House Committee on Science, Space, and Technology.* 94th Congress, 1st Session. Government Printing Office (November 7, 10–14, 17).

HCSST. 1976. *The National Climate Program Act: Hearings before the Subcommittee on the Environment and the Atmosphere of the House Committee on Science, Space, and Technology.* 94th Congress, 2nd Session. Government Printing Office (May 18–27).

HCSST. 1977. *National Climate Program: Hearings before the Subcommittee on the Environment and the Atmosphere of the House Committee on Science, Space, and Technology*. 95th Congress, 1st Session. Government Printing Office (April 4–6).

HCSST. 1979. *Implementation of the Climate Act: Hearings before the Subcommittee on Natural Resources and Environment of the House Committee on Science, Space, and Technology*. 96th Congress, 1st Session. Government Printing Office (July 10).

HCSST. 1992. *US Global Change Research Program. Hearing before the Subcommittee on Environment of the House Committee on Science, Space and Technology*. 102nd Congress, 2nd Session. Government Printing Office (May 5).

SCA (Senate Committee on Appropriations). 1956. *Second Supplemental Appropriation Bill, 1956. Hearings before the Senate Committee on Appropriations*. 84th Congress, Second Session. Government Printing Office (March 20–23, 26).

SCANF (Senate Committee on Agriculture, Nutrition and Forestry). 1973. *US and World Food Situation: Hearing before the Senate Committee on Agriculture, Nutrition and Forestry*. 93rd Congress, 1st Session. Government Printing Office (October 17, 18).

SCANF. 1989. *Global Climate Change Prevention Act of 1989—S. 1610: Hearing before the Senate Committee on Agriculture, Nutrition and Forestry*. 101st Congress, 1st Session. Government Printing Office (November 6).

SCASS (Senate Committee on Aeronautical and Space Sciences). 1975. *Stratospheric Ozone Depletion, Part 1: Hearings before the Subcommittee on the Upper Atmosphere of the Senate Committee on Aeronautical and Space Sciences*. 94th Congress, 1st Session. Government Printing Office (Sept 8, 9, 15, 17).

SCCST (Senate Committee on Commerce, Science and Transportation). 1977. *National Climate Program Act: Hearings before the Subcommittee on Science, Technology, and Space of the Senate Committee on Commerce, Science, and Transportation*. 95th Congress, 1st Session. Government Printing Office (June 8–10, July 5, 6, 8).

SCCST. 1987. *Global Environmental Change Research: Hearing before the Subcommittee on Science, Technology and Space and the National Ocean Policy Study of the Senate Committee on Commerce, Science and Transportation*. 100th Congress, 1st Session. Government Printing Office (July 16).

SCCST. 1990. *Global Climate Change: Seeking a Global Consensus: Hearing before the Senate Committee on Commerce, Science and Transportation.* 101st Congress, 2nd Session. Government Printing Office (June 14).

SCCST. 1991. *Policy Implications of Greenhouse Warming. Hearing before the Senate Committee on Commerce, Science and Transportation.* 102nd Congress, 1st Session. Government Printing Office (April 25).

SCCST. 1992. *Global Change Research: Global Warming and the Biosphere: Hearing before the Senate Committee on Commerce, Science and Transportation.* 102nd Congress, 2nd Session. Government Printing Office (April).

SCCST. 2000a. *Science Behind Global Warming. Hearings before the Senate Committee on Commerce, Science and Transportation.* 106th Congress, 2nd Session. Government Printing Office (May 17).

SCCST. 2000b. *Climate Change Impacts to the US. Hearings before the Senate Committee on Commerce, Science and Transportation.* 106th Congress, 2nd Session. Government Printing Office (July 18).

SCCST. 2000c. *Solutions to Climate Change. Hearings before the Senate Committee on Commerce, Science and Transportation.* 106th Congress, 2nd Session. Government Printing Office (September 21).

SCCST. 2001. *Intergovernmental Panel on Climate Change (IPCC) Third Assessment Report. Hearings before the Senate Committee on Commerce, Science and Transportation.* 107th Congress, 1st Session. Government Printing Office (May 1).

SCENR (Senate Committee on Energy and Natural Resources). 1980. *Effects of Carbon Dioxide Buildup in the Atmosphere: Hearings before the Senate Committee on Energy and Natural Resources.* 96th Congress, 2nd Session. Government Printing Office (April 3, 1980).

SCENR. 1988. *Greenhouse Effect and Global Climate Change, Part 2: Hearing before the Senate Committee on Energy and Natural Resources.* S. Hrg. 100–461, pt. 2 Government Printing Office (June 23).

SCENR. 1994. *Science Concerning Global Climate Change: Hearing before the Senate Committee on Energy and Natural Resources.* 103rd Congress, 2nd Session. Government Printing Office (May 24).

SCENR. 1996. *Global Climate Change: Hearing before the Senate Committee on Energy and Natural Resources.* 104th Congress, 2nd Session. Government Printing Office (September 17).

SCENR. 1999. *Global Climate Change: Hearing before the Senate Committee on Energy and Natural Resources.* 106th Congress, 1st Session. Government Printing Office (May 20).

SCEPW. 1985. *Global Warming: Hearing before the Subcommittee on Toxic Substances and Environmental Oversight of the Senate Committee on Environment and Public Works.* 99th Congress, 1st Session. Government Printing Office (December 10).

SCEPW. 1986c. *Ozone Depletion, the Greenhouse Effect, and Climate Change: Hearing before the Committee on Environment and Public Works, United States Senate.* S. Hrg. 99–723. Government Printing Office (June 10).

SCEPW. 1989. *Responding to the Problem of Global Warming: Hearing before the Subcommittee on Environmental Protection of the Senate Committee on Environment and Public Works.* 101st Congress, 1st Session. Government Printing Office (August 10).

SCEPW. 1991. *Global Warming and Other Consequences of Energy Strategies: Hearing before the Subcommittee on Environmental Protection of the Senate Committee on Environment and Public Works.* 102nd Congress, 1st Session. Government Printing Office (March, 13, 20, and April 26).

SCEPW. 1997. *Global Climate Change: Hearing before the Senate Committee on Environment and Public Works.* 105th Congress, 1st Session. Government Printing Office (July 10).

SCEPW. 2002. *Clean Air Act: Risks from Greenhouse Gas Emissions. Hearing before the Senate Committee on Environment and Public Works.* 107th Congress, 2nd Session. Government Printing Office (March 13).

Appendix E

Interviews (Dates and Organizations)

February 20, 1998, Congressional Research Service

May 12, 1998, U.S. Global Change Research Program

May 14, 1998, House Committee on Science

June 1, 1998, National Institute of Environmental Health Sciences, National Institutes of Health

June 10, 1998, National Environmental Policy Institute, Washington

June 16, 1998, U.S. Office of Science and Technology Policy, Executive Office of the President

June 30, 1998, Office of Air Quality Planning and Standards, U.S. Environmental Protection Agency

July 1, 1998, Office of Prevention, Pesticides, and Toxic Substances, U.S. Environmental Protection Agency

July 2, 1998, Resources for the Future, Washington

July 7, 1998, Office of Policy Planning and Evaluation, U.S. Environmental Protection Agency

July 10, 1998. Office of Research and Development, U.S. Environmental Protection Agency

July 16, 1998, Office of Research and Development, U.S. Environmental Protection Agency

July 22, 1998, Committee for the National Institute for the Environment, Washington

July 23, 1998, H. John Heinz III Center for Science, Washington

July 30, 1998a, Office of Pollution Prevention and Toxics, U.S. Environmental Protection Agency

July 30, 1998b, Office of Pollution Prevention and Toxics, U.S. Environmental Protection Agency

August 21, 1998, Office of Air and Radiation, U.S. Environmental Protection Agency

August 24, 1998, Climate Wise, U.S. Environmental Protection Agency

August 25, 1998, Environmental Defense Fund, Washington

August 26, 1998, Office of Pesticide Programs, U.S. Environmental Protection Agency

September 9, 1998, Climate Wise, U.S. Environmental Protection Agency

September 10, 1998, Office of Atmospheric Programs, U.S. Environmental Protection Agency

September 14, 1998, Acid Rain Division, U.S. Environmental Protection Agency

September 15, 1998, Office of Air and Radiation, U.S. Environmental Protection Agency

September 22, 1998, Office of Risk Assessment, U.S. Department of Agriculture

September 28, 1998, American Association for the Advancement of Science, Washington

September 29, 1998, Science Advisory Board, U.S. Environmental Protection Agency

October 8, 1998a, Office of Science Policy, U.S. Environmental Protection Agency

October 8, 1998b, Office of Science Policy, U.S. Environmental Protection Agency

October 28, 1998, Acid Rain Division, U.S. Environmental Protection Agency

November 10, 1988, Science Advisory Board, U.S. Environmental Protection Agency

December 2, 1998, Acid Rain Division, U.S. Environmental Protection Agency

Notes

Introduction

1. Roger Revelle added the material that is quoted here just before sending the paper off for publication. Though the findings in the paper were the joint work of Revelle and Seuss, Revelle was more active than his co-author in telegraphing the findings and their potential relevance to decision makers and to the public.

2. The US budget supporting scientific research for acid rain was over $500 million from 1982 to 1990. The research budget for climate change averaged $1.8 billion per year from fiscal year 1995 to fiscal year 1998. From fiscal year 1999 to fiscal year 2004, the budget ranged between $1.65 billion and $1.82 billion per year (USGCRP 1996, 1997, 2002; USCCSP 2004).

3. The iconic example of a scientist influencing the direction of policy is Albert Einstein's influential letter to President Roosevelt urging him not to let American research efforts fall behind those of Nazi Germany in producing an atomic weapon. The issue of scientists in natural security policy has drawn considerable scholarly attention. See, e.g., Gilpin and Wright 1964; Price 1965; Greenberg 1967; Primack and von Hippel 1974; Boffey 1975.

4. Beginning with debates regarding the wisdom of developing the hydrogen bomb, a number of political scientists did take up the question of scientists in public decision making (Gilpin 1962; Gilpin and Wright 1964; Price 1965; Greenberg 1967; Primack and von Hippel 1974; Boffey 1975). For more recent works in which political scientists specifically address science in public policy, see Bryner 1987; Haas 1990; Guston 1999, 2000; Litfin 1994; VanDeveer 2006; Zehr 1994a,b, 2005.

5. The field of STS, while agreeing on the importance of studying the role of science and technology in society, continues to debate how effective scientists are in shaping social interaction around scientific norms. Some argue that scientists are able to set themselves up in society as "obligatory points of passage" so that non-scientists come to view science as central in achieving their goals (Callon and Law 1982; Law 1987). Critics of this approach argue that scientists' role in society is negotiated among scientists and non-scientists alike such that scientists

are dependent on other actors for their status in society rather than being able to merely impose their worldview on an accepting audience (Star and Griesemer 1989; Jasanoff and Wynne 1998; Jasanoff 2004a,b; Miller 2004a).

6. For examples of studies that took up policy making outside of the halls of Congress, see Baumgartner and Jones 1993; Polsby 1984; Pressman and Wildavsky 1973.

7. For a review of scholarly work using the policy-stages approach, see deLeon 1999.

8. Polsby (1984: 2–3) divides the process into three stages: innovation, enactment and implementation. These correspond to the three stages in my study. I use the term "agenda setting" instead of "innovation" because it is more commonly used in the current literature. In addition, I use "legislation" rather than "enactment" to signal the broad range of legislative activities, including enactment, that draw on scientific expertise. Other studies divide the process into four stages (Kingdon 1984: 3) or seven (Lasswell 1956: 2).

9. "Formalization" refers to the explicit organizational structures that guide action within an organization. These include divisions or units within an organization designed to accomplish specific tasks, roles for organizational members, and procedural rules that guide action among members and set out reciprocal expectations between organizational members. For a discussion of the role of formal structure within organizations, see Schulman 1989.

10. DeGregorio (1992) presents three different leadership styles that committee chairs adopt in setting up hearings and finds that, although other actors and events can shape the agenda of a hearing, the committee's chair exerts the greatest amount of influence on its agenda.

11. Cohen (1995), however, argues that the crucial work of Congress is often carried out behind closed doors rather than in the public forums of the institution.

12. Although statutory authority is a reliable guide for predicting implementation jurisdictions, there are notable exceptions. For example, a number of entrepreneurial agencies used their existing jurisdictions as a platform for creating laws around tobacco use in the face of congressional inaction. For a cogent discussion of these policy innovations and congressional efforts to quell them, see Fritschler and Hoefler 1996.

13. Research in organization theory establishes that even the most formalized of organizations also have elaborate informal components (Selznick 1957). That the implementation stage of decision making is more formalized than agenda setting does not suggest that there are no informal aspects to policy implementation, nor does it establish the relative importance of formal and informal procedures in shaping policy outcomes during implementation.

14. For example, Talbert, Jones, and Baumgartner (1995) provide convincing evidence that non-legislative hearings (i.e., hearings that do not consider a specific bill) have a role in carving out turf and jurisdiction in the chamber.

Specifically, committees often hold hearings on a specific topic to indicate to the chamber leadership that the committee has the necessary expertise to manage future bills that touch on that topic. These activities, to be effective, have to be staged in advance of major congressional activity on a specific issue in order for the committee to be given jurisdiction over relevant bills.

15. Although there are several studies that consider the role of expertise in the US legislative process (Huitt 1954; Weiss 1989; Esterling 2004; Bimber 1996), there are almost no studies of scientists in legislation. Zehr's 2005 study of boundary work in hearings on acid rain and climate change is an exception.

16. Note that Zehr's 2005 study of boundary work among scientists involved in congressional hearings is, perhaps, the only existing study that explicitly treats scientists' role in Congress. Zehr, however, does not come to any specific conclusions about the importance of scientists' participation in influencing congressional decision making.

17. This discussion does not assume a definitive boundary between science and policy. Rather, it adopts rhetorical conventions about the proper role for science in policy making while recognizing that those conventions are contested and often in flux (Gieryn 1995; Jasanoff 1990). To the extent that such conventions shape actors expectations and behavior, they are important, even if the conventions assume a distinct boundary that does not, in fact, exist. For a more detailed discussion of boundary work, see chapter 1 of the present volume.

18. Deborah Stone develops the concept of "causal story" in her 1989 work on agenda setting. A "casual story" contains both a causal explanation of an event or a state of affairs and a persuasive account of the policy implications of that causal relationship. Here, I am concerned specifically with how scientists create causal stories, what I call "science narratives." In chapter 2, I explore this concept in light of the two cases—policy formation for acid rain and climate change.

19. Controversies among scientists around the executive summaries of reports on acid rain and on climate change demonstrate just this problem. Though scientists often agree that the content of the reports are scientifically sound, they can rarely agree on how to summarize the scientific findings for use by policy makers. See, e.g., Shabecoff's (1987) coverage of the debate about the National Acid Precipitation Assessment Program's first report. Notably, some of the scientists who were critical of the report's executive summary had participated in the preparation of the body of the report. On a similar debate that erupted after the Intergovernmental Panel on Climate Change reported a "discernable human influence on global climate" (Houghton et al. 1996), see Stevens 1996.

20. That scientists begin to openly address the idea of a science/policy boundary in legislative settings does not suggest that scientists are unaware of the boundary during agenda setting. Rather, scientists' outward performance across the two stages varies, whereas their understanding of the science/policy boundary in these two stages may be constant. On scientists' concern with how they can maintain

their status as scientists and apply their knowledge in policy settings, see Tackacs 1996; Keller 2002.

21. For a description of the tasks associated with risk assessment versus those associated with risk management, see NRC 1983b.

22. Agencies rely mainly on the so-called "Redbook" (NRC 1983b) for guidance in risk analysis. In addition, departments that are developing their own risk-analysis capabilities sometimes seek advice from more experienced agencies. The US Department of Agriculture, for example, sought help from both the Food and Drug Administration and the Environmental Protection Agency in designing its congressionally mandated Office of Risk Assessment and Cost-Benefit Analysis (interview, September 23, 1998).

23. For a discussion of organizations that attempt to codify informal practices through continuous identification of such practices and subsequent update of organizational procedures in light of those practices, see Schulman 1993.

24. Cohen, March, and Olsen (1972) point out that solutions can precede problems in decision making.

25. Jasanoff (1990) concentrates on science advisors who participate in policy implementation and finds that science advisors do, in fact, include normative judgments in the advice they provide as scientists.

26. For examples of analyses that similarly combine structure and agency in explaining outcomes, see Kingdon 1984; Baumgartner and Jones 1993. Kingdon, in his work on the policy process, explains how actors who are influential in one stage of policy making may be minor participants in a subsequent stage. In addition, Kingdon highlights the role of focusing events, which can turn latent public concern into active political pressure. Here structure and exogenous factors constrain or enable actors in the policy process. At the same time, Kingdon emphasizes the role of policy entrepreneurs (resourceful and politically savvy actors who use their skills to advance favored issues at opportune moments). Overall, Kingdon's explanation emphasizes the combined influence of structures, actors, and chance events in shaping policy outcomes. Though policy entrepreneurs are able to take advantage of fortuitous events in pursuing their goals, they are not able to remake the policy world to their liking. At the same time, outcomes cannot be predicted from structure alone. Baumgartner and Jones similarly tackle agency and structure in explaining policy change in their work on punctuated equilibria. In general, policy change is incremental and is dominated by stable actors and structures. Occasionally, however, policy entrepreneurs are able to reframe policy issues in ways that create novel venues for policy deliberation. These venues can then provide a platform for new policy ideas that can challenge existing patterns of policy making. Sometimes this leads to rapid and substantial policy change.

27. Using statistical language, this analysis points to differences in means across stages of decision making. A difference in means across cases, however, can be consistent with even substantial variation *within* cases. Means and variances are two, independent methods of summarizing a distribution of characteristics within

a population. This analysis acknowledges variation in scientists' behavior within each stage, but points to more significant differences across cases.

28. Bowker and Star (1999) show how ubiquitous classification systems are in society in general. Further, they demonstrate how important classification systems are, for example, in preserving ideologies and sensitize the reader to the social implications of any classification system.

29. Litfin (1994: 187) argues that scientists were not willing to make policy recommendations based on their research in the case she studies (ozone depletion). This leaves open the possibility that scientists who are willing to enter policy debates might themselves act as knowledge brokers.

30. For example, Takacs's study of conservation biologists demonstrates that scientists can view themselves simultaneously as objective scientists and as activists whose duty is toward the preservation of their subject matter, i.e., diverse and thriving ecosystems. In this case, the full range of professional activities that conservation biologists undertake extends beyond a traditional interpretation of the label "scientist."

31. The Acid Rain Control program is ongoing, whereas National Acid Precipitation Assessment Program research was funded only through the mid 1990s.

32. The following reports of hearings held in the 1950s give at least brief attention to climate change: HCoA 1956, 1957, 1958, 1959; SCA 1956; HCIFC 1958.

33. For a detailed discussion of media coverage of climate change, see chapter 2 of the present volume.

34. For a detailed analysis of the USGCRP's creation, see Pielke 2000a,b.

35. The exception to this is, of course, the ban on chlorofluorocarbons (CFCs). However, the ban was made in response to ozone depletion before CFCs were recognized for their significant global warming potential. The EPA ran the voluntary programs "Climate Wise" and "Energy Star" (now merged under the name "Energy Star"). These programs provide industry with information and advice about energy efficiency that reduce costs and emissions of greenhouse gases. Industry participates, obviously, on a voluntary basis. More information about the Energy Star program is available at http://www.energystar.gov.

36. Two groups of states are considering regional agreements to create cap-and-trade programs for reducing greenhouse gases. The states are Connecticut, Delaware, Maine, Massachusetts, New Hampshire, New Jersey, New York, Rhode Island, and Vermont in the Northeast and Washington, Oregon, and California on the West Coast (DePalma 2005). For a discussion of California's law, passed in September 2006, see Martin 2006.

37. A number of studies that consider scientists role in policy formation have studied environmental and environmental health policy cases (Bryner 1993; Boehmer-Christiansen 1988, 1996; Crandal and Lave 1981; Collingridge and Reeve 1986; Demerrit 1999; Ezrahi 1980; Fleagle 1994; Gould 1985; Greenwood 1984; Haas 1990, 1992; Hajer 1993; Jasanoff 1990; Landy, Roberts, and

Thomas 1994; Litfin 1994; Parson 2003; Powell 1999; Shackley et al. 1998; Shackley and Wynne 1995, 1996, 1997; VanDeveer 1998; Wagner 1995; Zehr 1994a,b).

38. Recognition of problems in these cases did not arise primarily in academic communities. Either the issue had been around for a long time, as in the cases of nationalized health care (Kingdon 1996: 6–9) and waterway user charges (ibid.: 12–14), or non-experts were able to detect problems without recourse to academic research, for example, rising health care costs (ibid.: 5–6)—something apparent in the federal budget for Medicare and Medicaid—and transportation deregulation (ibid.: 9–12) where the industry itself complained of onerous regulations. One of Kingdon's examples lends some support for the argument presented here, however. Kingdon points out that the economics literature preceded government attention to transportation deregulation and *did* impact the political agenda (ibid.: 54–55). Moreover, Kingdon gives credit to two economists, Hendrick Houthakker and Paul MacAvoy, members of the Council of Economic Advisors, for bringing the new orthodoxy in economics to bear on public policy (ibid.: 54).

39. Rowland and Molina's results were published in *Nature* (June 28, 1974). The date of the discovery is given in Molina's autobiography at http://www.nobel.se. Notably, this autobiography includes Molina's account of their decision to publicize their findings outside of the academic community owing to their political and social importance. Molina writes: "The years following the publication of our paper were hectic, as we had decided to communicate the CFC-ozone issue not only to other scientists, but also to policy makers and to the news media; we realized this was the only way to insure that society would take some measures to alleviate the problem."

Chapter 1

1. See, e.g., Ezrahi 1980; Grobstein 1981; Greenberg 1984; Mazur 1981; Nelkin 1979; Price 1965; Primack and von Hippel 1974; Weinberg 1972.

2. For a review of the basic elements required for democratic participation in a polity, see Dahl 1956.

3. An alternate view of technocracy argues that embracing a rationalist approach to decision making is, in and of itself, technocratic in that causal connections and high standards of proof are required to justify political action. This definition of technocracy requires no specific role for scientists to the extent that non-scientists can present their cases in rationalist terms. Though this does involve a barrier to entry, it is one that can be overcome (see, e.g., Brown 1992; Epstein 2000). Here, I use the term in a quite different sense. Specifically, technocratic outcomes obtain when scientists, drawing on their social status, are able to limit the participation of other actors who would normally have access to decision making. The issue here is not scientists' ability to persuade other actors of the wisdom of the policy choices they endorse; persuasion is not only fair game in

democratic decision making, it is one of the most important techniques for achieving consensus. Instead, technocracy obtains when scientists are able to convince other actors that a decision lies purely in the domain of science and, therefore, should not be subject to democratic debate. This involves persuasion of a sort, yet it limits the potential for non-scientists to articulate their own interests with respect to policy outcomes.

4. This extensive literature includes the following: Gieryn 1983, 1995, 1999; Star and Griesemer 1989; Jasanoff 1990, 2004a; Fujimura 1992; Shackley and Wynne 1996; Jasanoff and Wynne 1998; Guston 1999, 2000; Zehr 2005.

5. Much of this work comes from the field of science and technology studies. For a brief review of the early roots of this constructivist approach to science, see appendix A.

6. Reiner Grundmann notes this tendency in his analysis of ozone and climate policy making. He argues that "practitioners in many fields still subscribe to the 'speaking-truth-to-power view of science'" (2006: 74–75), in spite of the fact that this view of science in decision making has been thoroughly challenged.

7. See, e.g., Lindblom's 1959 discussion of synoptic decision making.

8. The distinction between risk assessment and risk management, which I discuss in greater detail in chapter 4, is an example of such institutionalization.

9. In fact, early writings in public administration (Taylor 1911; Gulick and Urwick 1937; Fayol 1949) even sought to apply scientific principles to bureaucratic organizations to ensure that they would operate rationally and efficiently. The idea that the bureaucracy was merely a center for neutral implementation of important decisions made elsewhere was so thoroughly accepted in the discipline that the study of public administration fell out of favor relative to studying Congress and the presidency. Pressman and Wildavsky's work on implementation revived interest in the bureaucracy as a source of policy outcomes rather than merely a receptacle for them (Pressman and Wildavsky 1973).

10. For a more detailed discussion of the institutional mechanisms that support and sustain this view of science in decision making, see chapter 4 of the present volume.

11. Lindblom (1959)) links his rejection of a rationalist approach to Herbert Simon's concept of "bounded rationality," for which Simon would be awarded the Nobel Prize in economics in 1978.

12. A number of critics have attacked Lindblom's emphasis on incremental policy change for its inherent acceptance of the status quo. For a cogent review of these criticisms, see Weiss and Woodhouse 1992. For Lindblom's own response to his critics, see Lindblom 1979.

13. Stone (1989: 294) lists several characteristics of causal stories that increase their chances for success. A causal story, she writes, is more likely to be successful if (a) its proponents are visible, have access to the media, or hold prominent positions, (b) it taps into deeply held cultural values, (c) it dovetails with the

"national mood," and (d) it implies no major redistribution of wealth or power.

14. Jasanoff (1990: 208–28) compares several institutional mechanisms for incorporating expert advice.

15. Guston's use of the term "boundary organization" draws from the work of Susan Leigh Star and James Griesemer, who developed the concept of the "boundary object" to account for how actors with different conceptions of science might find a mutually acceptable science/non-science settlement (1989).

16. In his 1991 study of how the public assesses the role of the American president, Richard Brody argues that the public focuses specifically on outcomes associated with presidential policies and is much less influenced by prospective statements presidents make about their policy goals. Results, rather than position taking, influence public opinion regarding the presidency. This offers some empirical support for Ezrahi's claim that state action is judged on the basis of a state's ability to reach its goals.

17. For the classic view of the use of analysis or expertise in Congress, see Fiorina 1989; Jones 1976; Mayhew 1974.

Chapter 2

1. In referring to scientists involved in agenda setting for acid rain and climate change, I am not seeking to portray the scientific community as united around the initial framings offered by scientists. In fact, scientists do emerge in the public discussion of each issue and argue against the early framings that appeared in the media and in Congress. The more pertinent point here is that members of a vocal subgroup of the scientific community were allowed to speak publicly about these two issues for a significant period of time before their framing was countered by others in the scientific community and by non-scientists. This allowed members of each subgroup to "speak for science" early in the process without having their authority to do so challenged.

2. I cover the periods of intense debate on the two issues in chapter 3.

3. In chapter 3, where I analyze scientists' participation in legislative decision making, I also discuss the effects of an institutionalized science narrative.

4. A long-standing debate in political science between elite and pluralist schools argues about whether one can study the ability to keep an issue off the public agenda. See Bachrach and Baratz 1962 for an overview of this debate. Baumgartner and Jones refer to the "intractability" of agenda setting and point out that, thus far, studies of agenda setting have not produced a set of indicators that can be used across cases (1993: 39). Polsby, in his study of policy innovations, describes the difficulties in delimiting the universe of cases from which one might draw samples to study (1984: 6–13).

5. Stone (1989: 283) argues that there are two elements to "causal stories" in policy making: the empirical and the moral. The first establishes causal relationships while the moral element assigns blame.

6. In history, narrative analysis suggests a methodology that is appropriate when events cannot be represented through general laws or conclusions. William Paulson elucidates this through his comparison of narrative and science, or algorithm, as occupying opposite ends of a continuum of explanation. Narrative, Paulson argues (1994), emphasizes the element of chance in events, while the use of science or algorithm implies a measure of predictability in outcomes. Used in this manner, narrative refers to the way in which an historian recounts events, as well as the underlying assumption that the only way to explain an outcome is to detail the events leading up to it rather than attempting to codify those events through some formula. For a concise review of the debate about the use of narrative analysis in history, see Rosaldo 1989: 127–143. However, the term "narrative" also refers to an analytic tool that draws attention to the organizing frameworks that guide and justify an individual or group's beliefs and actions. It is the latter sense of the term that is used here.

7. For an analysis of the consolidation of the framing of climate change as a problem of pollution, see Miller 2000.

8. By "science narrative" I mean the narrative that is established and reinforced by scientists or actors who claim membership in the larger scientific community. This distinguishes it from narratives that incorporate scientific information, a characteristic that, although expected as part of a science narrative, is not limited to it.

9. That scientists' factual claims do not translate immediately into policy imperatives is demonstrated, in part, by the existence of "knowledge brokers"—actors in the policy process who "have a flair for translating the work [of academics and other researchers], identifying the policy-relevant angles in it, and framing it in language accessible to decision makers" (Litfin 1994: 37). The boundary-spanning role played by knowledge brokers demonstrates a need for translating science as it is practiced professionally into a format more useful for policy makers. The concept of co-production equally asserts a role for non-scientists in establishing the meaning of science for society (Jasanoff and Wynne 1998; Jasanoff 2004a,b). At the same time, the suggestion that scientific findings do not necessarily have immediate meaning in policy making does not imply that the scientific community or its products are apolitical.

10. For example, Senator John Chafee, in a 1987 hearing on climate change, credited scientists for informing policy makers about global warming and the ozone hole: "The scientific community as a whole, I believe, should be congratulated for recognizing these problems and for bringing them to our attention. A significant number of scientists are telling us that these problems can no longer be treated solely as important scientific questions." (SCCST 1987: 6)

11. The climate change case is discussed later in this chapter.

12. For an overview of the history of scientific research bearing on acid rain, see Cowling 1982.

13. Cowling (1982: 111A) credits Gorham with producing "the first detailed analysis of Smith's early work."

14. For example, scientists began to organize explicitly as acid rain researchers. This new scientific identity gained formal expression in the International Directory of Acid Deposition Researchers, which attempts to list all scientists by both discipline and country who are working on some aspect of acid deposition research (North Carolina State University Acid Deposition Program for National Acid Precipitation Assessment Program 1983, 1986).

15. There are, no doubt, important social contingencies that affected scientists' understanding of acid rain as a subject of scientific research. By asserting that acid rain had relevance only within the scientific community is not to say that it existed in some "objective" state. In fact, there is evidence that scientists' understanding of acid rain was heavily influenced by social and cultural events occurring in the 1960s. Evidence from the climate change case offers a useful comparison that substantiates this point. In addition, although the term "acid rain" did, as far as records show, originate in the scientific community, it is possible that non-scientists were aware of ecosystem changes (e.g., declines in fish populations) and did not have to rely on a pronouncement from the scientific community in order to see its effects.

16. A pH of 7 is the measure for pure water. Lower scores on the pH scale indicate greater acidity.

17. Even in this spare statement, NAPAP leans toward a negative framing with the sentence "The *major concern* about the aquatic effects of acidic deposition [is toxicity] to aquatic organisms." (emphasis added) An entirely value-neutral statement about acid rain might indicate that acid rain creates conditions that do not support aquatic life without labeling that as a "major concern." Even so, this statement represents a typical causal story for acid rain.

18. Stephen Zehr's work on acid rain countered a number of analyses that portrayed scientists as relatively powerless in the acid rain debate in the US (Gould 1985; Yanerella 1985). Unlike his predecessors, Zehr takes a Latourian approach and argues that scientists were critical in shaping acid rain policy, particularly in portraying science as crucial step in finding a solution (Zehr 1994a).

19. For more examples from early publications aimed at public audiences, see Galloway 1978; NRC 1981; Cowling 1982.

20. The case of forest decline is complicated because nitrogen oxides, which form acid rain, are also a pollutant that contributes to the formation of surface ozone. In this regard, lowering emissions of nitrogen oxides could limit subsequent ozone formation. Still, this longer linked chain of causation was distinct from the initial claim that the acid deposition, itself, was harming forests. Though some species of trees did suffer from acid deposition, forests, in general, were not at risk.

21. The Atmospheric Sciences Program of Ohio State University hosted the conference and acted as a co-sponsor (USDA 1976).

22. See SCEPW 1979 for early congressional oversight of EPA's R&D efforts with respect to acid rain. See SCENR 1980a for a hearing reviewing research conducted by the Department of Energy.

23. A search in the LexisNexis database for major newspaper articles mentioning "acid rain" yielded 134 stories and abstracts published between 1972 and 1980. (There are no stories that mention acid rain before 1972.) Only two of the stories published between 1972 and 1980 criticize the acid rain science narrative. Both articles that take issue with the narrative are editorials, both published in 1980 (*Wall Street Journal* 1980; White 1980). In the preceding 8 years' of coverage of the issue, the acid rain science narrative is presented intact with no counter-narratives. In a separate search of the Historical *New York Times* database, 50 stories mentioning "acid rain" are found between 1970 and 1979 (and none before 1970). The first to include a hint of counter-narrative was published in 1979; it argued that "the damage acid rain might do is still largely a matter of conjecture" owing to a lack of quantitative data on effects (Hill 1979: E8).

24. I treat this topic in more detail in chapter 3.

25. For a detailed and lively account of the development of scientific research on global warming, see Weart 2003.

26. A brief history of the International Geophysical Year can be found at http://www.nas.edu. Miller's (2001) analysis of event leading up to the IGY demonstrates the links between post-World War II reorganization of international relations and institution building and the ideals of meteorologists aiming to create an international observational network.

27. In spite of the fact that Revelle's written statement is the most quoted, the oral comments that Revelle gave at the 1956 hearing were slightly different. What the House Committee on Appropriations heard was "Here we are perhaps making the greatest geophysical experiment in history, an experiment which could not be made in the past because we didn't have an industrial civilization and which will be impossible to make in the future because all the fossil fuels will be gone." (HCoA 1956: 473) Notably, in his oral comments Revelle does not characterize the experiment as bad, but rather as a unique opportunity for research. The same language from Revelle's written statement appears in a report submitted by Joseph Kaplan, Chair of the National Science Foundation Committee on the IGY to the Senate Committee on Appropriations (SCA 1956: 230). Later, Revelle uses the exact same language in his 1957 paper published with Hans Seuss (Revelle and Seuss 1957). Spencer Weart, in his history of climate change, specifies that Revelle added the language to the scientific paper in 1957 when he made a few last minute revisions before sending the paper off for publication (Weart 2003: 29–30). This suggests that Revelle originally composed the famous characterization with a congressional audience in mind and later included the sentence in his scientific paper.

28. According to Weart (2003: 30), "Revelle meant 'experiment' in the traditional scientific sense, a nice opportunity for the study of geophysical processes. Yet he did recognize that there might be some future risk." Revelle's mention of tropical storms on the East Coast may be an indication of that he was thinking about risks of climate change, but this point is a mere a subplot in his congressional testimony (HCoA 1956: 479).

29. For an articulation of this perspective on the relationship between the government and the scientific community, see Bush 1945. For a discussion of revisions to the "social contract for science," see Guston 2000.

30. The House Committee on Appropriations held two hearings on the progress of the IGY (HCoA 1958, 1959).

31. In 1957, Wallace Broecker proposed in his PhD thesis that shifts between glacial periods or ice ages and non-glacial or "interglacial" periods were rapid rather than gradual. The idea of rapid climate change led scientists to look for mechanisms that might drive such change (Weart 2003: 50–65). One example is the idea that melting polar ice would uncover darker surfaces. Dark surfaces absorb more solar radiation than lighter ones. Since ice is light in color, and therefore highly reflective, losing ice cover to darker surfaces would mean the Earth would absorb more energy. Thus, a warming trend that melted the Polar ice caps would then lead to more absorption of solar radiation and further warming.

32. David Hart, in an unpublished paper on climate change research (1992: 17), points out that Scandinavian scientists studying climate change since the 1950s had always viewed the issue in environmental terms. This view seemed to take hold in the US by the early 1970s, when researchers produced two reports on environmental harms in preparation for the 1972 United Nations Conference on the Human Environment (SCEP 1970; SMIC 1971). Hart discusses both of these reports (1992: 18–19).

33. Climate change was mentioned in several hearings that took place before the 1976 hearing. In a 1973 hearing on US and global food supplies, Reid Bryson raises the issue of climate change as a factor in agricultural productivity (SCANF 1973). Two years later, a NASA scientist, James Fletcher, raises the issue in the context of the negative effects of chlorofluorocarbons (CFCs) (SCASS 1975). In a separate 1975 hearing convened to discuss the only marginally related issue of chronic, low-level exposure to pollutants, scientist Helmut Landsberg grabs an opportunity to point out the long-term effects of fossil fuel consumption on the climate (HCSST 1975b). The 1976 hearing stands out because the focus of the hearing is climate.

34. For example, Reid Bryson links changes in climate to rainfall and agricultural productivity (SCANF 1973: 119–140). Stephen Schneider, who later advocates strongly for government action to mitigate climate change, argues at the 1976 hearing that climate prediction is crucial for water resource management (HCSST 1976: 37–90). Later in the same hearing, an entire panel of scientists discusses the links between climate change and food supply (ibid.: 102–131).

35. Although carbon dioxide is now one of several greenhouse gases recognized for their heat-trapping potential and for their increasing atmospheric concentrations, carbon dioxide continues to occupy center stage as the major driver of global warming. Note, for example, the emerging market in carbon credits and the emergence of the concept of an individual's "carbon footprint." For an argument against the continued focus on carbon dioxide, see Hansen et al. 2000.

36. On melting sea ice, see IPCC 2007. On the potential for climate change to increase hurricane frequency, see Goldenberg et al. 2001; Knutson, Tuleya, and Kurihara 1998.

37. For examples of the causal story for climate change across the two periods, see Revelle's discussion of the potential for global warming as a consequence of the increase in carbon dioxide in the atmosphere (HCoA: 1956: 472–3). Similar information is conveyed in a 1977 NRC report on climate change and water supply (NRC 1977a: 13): "The increasing use of fossil fuels in recent years has resulted in a global atmospheric CO_2 increase of about 0.7 percent per year. CO_2 molecules are very strong absorbers of long-wave thermal radiation at wavelengths at which the earth's atmosphere is otherwise transparent. The increased absorption tends to insulate the earth's surface from infrared heat losses to outer space, leading to higher surface temperatures (the greenhouse effect)."

38. This report also includes the causal story that links increases in greenhouse gases to global warming: "Some gaseous constituents of the atmosphere also absorb solar and infrared radiation, and carbon dioxide, water vapor, and ozone are in this category. It is well known that the CO_2 content of the global atmosphere has been rising due to the burning of fossil fuels—coal, petroleum, and natural gas—and it is expected that it will go up about another 20% by 2000 A.D." (SMIC 1971: 11)

39. Note that Broecker is paraphrasing Revelle and Seuss (1957), albeit with a negative connotation that was lacking in the original.

40. Broecker's article is published in the scientific journal *Nature*. The article appears in the "Commentary" section of the journal and is intended as an opinion piece, albeit one that marshals empirical evidence to support its central claim (1987: 124, 125).

41. Between 1980 and 2005, the only year in which Congress did not hold at least one hearing on climate change was 1983. Before 1987, there were typically only one or two hearings per year. In 1987, four hearings were held in four separate committees. In 1988, eight committees held nine hearings. In 1989, twelve committees held 21 hearings. The pattern for print media is similar. Until 1983, newspaper coverage of global warming was sporadic, with ten stories or fewer per year. In 1983 there were 23 stories; in 1984 there were 11. After 1984, the number of stories jumps dramatically each year: 22 in 1985, 59 in 1986, 75 in 1987, 462 in 1988, and more than 1,000 every subsequent year. My data for the congressional hearings and media stores are from the LexisNexis database.

42. These data are available through LexisNexis Congressional Publications database. Note, also, that in every year since 1980, excepting 1983, there is at least one substantive hearing on this issue such that the routine agenda status is not driven solely by appropriations committees reviewing federal research on climate change.

43. During hearings held in 1976 and 1977, many scientists discussed the potential for improving agricultural production through seasonal weather prediction and argued that a better understanding of climate, derived through federally supported research, might allow for such predictions (HCSST 1976, 1977). One reason that seasonal weather prediction may have fallen off both the congressional and scientific agenda is the fact that it was not very successful. Reid Bryson, a proponent of the idea of seasonal weather prediction, was forced to publicly acknowledge the limits of seasonal weather prediction after predicting a record cold winter in 1982–83, a winter that turned out to be quite warm. Bryson's prediction appeared in the *New York Times* in September 1982 (Butterfield 1982). In December, Bryson is quoted as saying "We blew it" in reference to the climatologists' prediction of an unusually harsh winter (Clifford May 1982).

44. For a list of the climate change hearings included in the qualitative analysis, see appendix D.

45. These numbers are based on searches in the Lexis-Nexis database under "General News" and "Major Papers." Search terms included "global warming" and "climate change."

46. "No matter how much pressure builds up among concerned experts," Weart argues (2003, 155), "some trigger is needed to produce and explosion of public attention. The break came in the summer of 1988." The "break" came in the form of a heat wave that provided the perfect setting for Hansen's testimony.

47. It is interesting to note that James Hansen, a NASA scientist, was associated with the 1986 NASA report and testified before Congress about that report's findings (SCEPW 1986a). Because of his role in 1986 and his evocative testimony two years later, Hansen takes on for climate change something like the role Odén played in shaping the agenda for acid rain.

48. NAPAP was funded at $500 million over a ten-year period. The USGCRP was funded at approximately $800 million in its first year of operations. The latter figure quickly grew, and the annual budget for the program between 1995 and 1998 was $1.8 billion. As has already been noted, from fiscal year 1999 to fiscal year 2004 the budget ranged between $1.65 billion and $1.82 billion per year (USGCRP 1996, 1997, 2002; USCCSP 2004).

49. The US government's commitment to scientific research on global warming slightly trailed international activity. In 1988, the World Meteorological Organization and the United Nations Environment Program jointly created the Intergovernmental Panel on Climate Change to provide periodic assessments of the most current scientific information on climate change through an international review of published scientific research. The creation of organized scientific

research efforts at both the national and international level point to scientists' persuasiveness in arguing that climate change posed a significant environmental problem that was amenable to scientific inquiry.

50. Later in the hearing, the statistician, Andrew Solow, was asked to clarify his views. He pointed out that a lack of definitive information in the present cannot rule out future warming (HCMMF 1989: 27).

51. For an overview of witness positions on climate change from 1975 to 1992, see figure 3.1. This includes data for witnesses of all education background, not just scientists.

52. The analysis of media coverage was conducted using LexisNexis database of English-language newspapers. The search for relevant stories drew from the categories "general news" and "major papers" and used the following search terms: "climate change" OR "warming" AND "carbon dioxide." The earliest story returned by this search occurs in 1975. The analysis stops after 1988 because LexisNexis will not return results that are larger than 1,000, and that number is reached in 1989 for the current search string. While it is not possible to continue the analysis beyond 1988, there is evidence to suggest that controversy about climate change begins to pick up in 1989. Several notable contrarians, including Richard Lindzen, Fred Singer, and Fred Seitz, begin to receive media coverage in 1989. Pat Michaels, also a respected voice among the contrarians, stands out among this group in that his is quoted in a story appearing in 1988. While these participants are commonly referenced in the media in the 1990s, they are notably absent before 1988.

53. These data are consistent with Baumgartner and Jones's research on periods of "Downsian mobilization," during which experts tend to dominate the way an issue is framed in the early period of media attention. They argue that issue framings that run counter to that of the experts increase with media attention (1993: 83–125).

54. Baumgartner and Jones (1993) take this term from Downs's (1972) analysis of the cyclical nature of public attention to policy problems. Downs describes the cycle as containing a period of marked public enthusiasm for tackling a policy problem that is typically followed by a more sober assessment of how difficult the problem will be to solve. For Baumgartner and Jones, however, the period of public enthusiasm is crucial in that it creates an atmosphere where new institutions can be created around a specific definition of a policy problem (1993: 86–89).

55. I explore this idealized role and its articulation in legislative and implementation policy settings in detail in the following two chapters.

56. See, e.g., Bolin et al. 1972; NRC 1981.

57. Anticipation of effects was based, in part, on the arguments in Europe concerning forest death, particularly in Germany.

58. While forest decline still may call for policy redress, the assumption that cutting sulfur dioxide emissions would reduce damage to forests is not necessarily

justified. Certainly, a number of opponents to acid rain controls in the US made this very argument, i.e., that cutting sulfur dioxide emissions will not affect lake acidification or forest decline. See, e.g., Senator Robert Byrd's comments at a hearing before the Senate Committee on Energy and Natural Resources (SCENR 1984).

59. The mixed record on crop productivity was raised during a congressional hearing by Senator Byrd, who appeared as a witness on April 30, 1984 before the Senate Committee on Energy and Natural Resources.

60. The belief that scientific research will facilitate policy making is supported by the idealized model of science in policy making where objective information, by revealing ontological truths, points decision makers toward the correct solution. Science, according to this conception, limits political debate by revealing a unique path of response with which all participants with access to the scientific truths will agree. If, however, the appropriate response cannot be read directly from scientific findings, then the mechanism for translating scientific information into policy advice must be spelled out in order to ensure that scientific research will be connected in meaningful ways to policy making needs. Such mechanisms exist in the policy-making process. For example, the "precautionary principle" instructs decision makers to err on the side of protection of human health when faced with uncertain scientific information. It is clear, however, that such mechanisms are not neutral with respect to policy outcomes (Bryner 1987). In attempting to set up a research program around acid rain that would be neutral with respect to policy outcomes, those in charge of NAPAP opened themselves up for criticisms of irrelevance.

61. This research program, called the National Acid Precipitation Assessment Program, was part of the Synthetic Fuels Act of 1980. This act, a "mammoth" piece of legislation that reputedly contained "something for everyone," passed the House with a vote of 317–93 and the Senate by a 78–12 vote (*Congressional Quarterly Almanac* 1980: 478).

62. Interview, December 2, 1998.

63. Rubin, Lave, and Morgan (1991) use NAPAP and its shortcomings as a cautionary tale in setting up research for climate change. In addition, NAPAP was criticized on more than one occasion during congressional hearings for not providing more policy-relevant information. In particular, see the hearing before the House Subcommittee on Natural Resources, Agricultural Research and Environment held on April 27, 1988, during the 100th Congress, and entitled "National Acid Precipitation Assessment Program." I address the conflict on NAPAP's attempt to remain policy neutral in their research on acid rain in chapter 3.

64. The National Research Council, in a 1977 report, predicted warming of 0.3°C for every 10% increase in CO_2 (NRC 1977a: 14). The IPCC has predicted a 1.5–4.5°C increase in global average temperature with a doubling of CO_2. Notably, the 1977 prediction falls in the center of the IPCC range. The IPCC statement of climate sensitivity has been constant across its three assessment

reports published, respectively, in 1990, 1996, and 2001 (Houghton, Jenkins, and Ephraums 1990; Houghton et al. 1996; Watson et al. 2001: 67).

65. A simple comparison of the temperature of the earth with other planets in the solar system, along with the concentrations of gases in their atmospheres, provides considerable supporting evidence for the theory (Houghton et al. 1996: 55–59).

66. These complexities arise from a number of feedbacks in the system that are not well understood. These feedbacks come from, for example, water vapor, cloud processes, and ice and snow albedo. For a summary of these, see Houghton et al. 1996: 34–35. Also uncertain are the responses of terrestrial and marine biotic systems (ibid., chapters 9 and 10).

67. Compare the IPCC reports from 1990, 1992, 1996, and 2001 (Houghton, Jenkins, and Ephraums 1990; Houghton, Callander, and Varney 1992; Houghton et al. 1996, 2001).

68. Models are also better able to handle monsoons, the El Nino Southern Oscillation (ENSO), the North Atlantic Oscillation and are even beginning to predict tracks and frequency of tropical storms (Houghton et al. 2001: 473).

69. For an evaluation of improvements in GCM capabilities and a discussion of GCM projections, see Houghton et al. 2001: 473–512. See also Stott et al. 2000. For criticisms of the reliance on GCMs as a way to approach climate policy see Brunner 1996; Shackley et al. 1998.

70. See, e.g., Conservation Foundation 1963; NRC 1976, 1977a,b. Thompson, Ellis and Wildavsky, in their work on political cultures, draw up five archetypal "myths" about nature. The "nature ephemeral" belief holds that nature is easily perturbed and must be protected to avoid significant, negative consequences. Thompson, Ellis and Wildavsky specify that each of the five beliefs about nature is partial in its understanding of nature but is held by its adherents as if it is self-evident (1990: 26–33). The assertions regarding the negative consequences of climate change that were made in the 1970s and 1980s are consistent with the "nature ephemeral" view outlined by Thompson, Ellis, and Wildavsky in that they were driven by concerns in about the scale of climate change rather than empirical evidence about how global warming would play out.

71. For example, Dr. Eric Barron expressed this view in a statement before a congressional committee: ". . . the best scientific assessments we have suggest that the changes are going to be large and that in a sense we need to look out because the future climate is going to be dramatically different than the present climate" (SCEPW 1997).

72. The criticism of NAPAP demonstrates the disconnect that can occur between scientific research programs and policy development (Roberts 1991; Rubin, Lave and Morgan 1991). For criticism focused on the ability of the USGCRP to produce policy-relevant knowledge, see Brunner 1996.

73. For example, the conference statement from the UNEP/WMO/ICSU meeting held in Villach, Austria (a meeting that collected scientists from 29 countries to

discuss climate change) includes a number of policy recommendations that call for new policies on emissions of greenhouse gases as well as support for scientific research (SCEPW: 1985b: 97–100).

74. The National Climate Program, created by legislation in 1975, is a precursor to the USGCRP. The Climate Program was created to improve scientific understanding of climate in response to several "climate anomalies" experienced in the early 1970s. Roger Pielke, in his history of the USGCRP (2000a), argues that the Climate Program was superseded by the USGCRP owing to an increasing congressional interest human-induced climate change and the insufficiency of the Climate Program for that purpose.

75. In 1985, Dean Abrahamson of the Hubert H. Humphrey Institute of Public Affairs distinguished himself by arguing that the science was sufficiently resolved to know that a policy response was required and by recommending committing resources to research on policy options rather than to more scientific research (SCEPW 1985b). Though Abrahamson was not the only proponent of action in 1985, he stands out for his view that additional scientific research would not be the most effective way to decide a course of action in response to the threat of global warming.

76. The Intergovernmental Panel on Climate Change is another organization that is predicated on the notion that scientific research will guide policy decisions about limiting emissions of greenhouse gases.

77. See Sarewitz, Pielke, and Byerly 2000.

78. The IPCC made an even stronger statement in its Third Assessment report: "An increasing body of observations gives a collective picture of a warming world and modeling studies indicate that most of the observed warming at the Earth's surface over the last 50 years is likely to have been due to human activities." (Watson and Core Writing Team 2001: 137) Several major news outlets reported on the respective IPCC statements when they were first released in draft form. See, e.g., *Wall Street Journal* 1995; Revkin 2000b.

79. Shackley and Wynne's 1997 analysis of the attempt to create a measure of global warming potentials (GWP) is instructive. They argue that scientists sought to provide policy makers with a tool that would allow them to make comparisons among greenhouse gases in deciding the most efficient way to reduce any nation's contribution to global warming. However, ambiguities in the links between radiative forcing and climate sensitivity have complicated the interpretation of the measure. In addition, scientists were criticized for not including important socio-economic variables in the tool, e.g., discount rates that would incorporate the value of making changes in the present over future changes. The debate over GWPs reveals the distance between the complexities policy makers face when making decisions about reducing greenhouse gases and the ability of scientists to model those complexities.

80. In this section, I focus on the tendency of the scientific community to assume the relevance of scientific research in solving policy dilemmas. However, this should not be read as a criticism of all scientific research conducted to inform

policy making. Rather, I wish to point to a lack of discrimination about what we can know and the often attendant assumption that all knowledge will facilitate policy making.

81. I address the stability of the science narrative during the drawn-out legislative debate over acid rain in chapter 3.

82. See, e.g.,, Wilson 1989: 179–195.

83. Interview, EPA staff member, September 14, 1998.

84. The Byrd-Hagel resolution, passed by the Senate in July 1997, stipulated that the US should not sign any resolution committing the US to greenhouse gas reductions if developing countries were not also required to reduce emissions. The Kyoto Treaty only commits developed countries to emissions reductions; if ratified, the treaty would require the US to reducing greenhouse gases to 5.2% below 1990 levels by 2012. The Kyoto Treaty came into force without US participation on February 16, 2005 after Russian ratification of the treaty in December 2004.

85. Previously, California regulators approved a measure to cut greenhouse gas emissions from automobiles by 30 percent (Hakim 2004).

86. For example, Rubin, Lave and Morgan (1991: 49) express this view in their assessment of the creation of NAPAP.

87. It is interesting to note that this dynamic of pessimistic predictions about climate change policy followed by studies of the importance of scientists in shaping policy outcomes is paralleled in the literature on acid rain policy. A number of studies seeking to explain the failure of scientists in persuading policy makers to create a regulatory program (Gould 1985; Yanerella 1985) were followed by studies that focused on the particular role of scientists in bringing about policy change (Hajer 1993; Zehr 1994a). The explanations of acid rain policy offered in the academic literature shift with the 1990 Clean Air Act Amendments. A similar trend seems to be taking place in the literature on global warming policy.

88. In comparing the two cases, mitigating acid rain requires significantly less intrusion into the economy than does climate change. Given the different in magnitude of the implied regulatory responses, one can anticipate that policy making for climate change will occur much more slowly, if at all.

Chapter 3

1. The text quoted here is taken directly from the transcript of this hearing. The two speakers are the late Senator John H. Chafee and Dr. John P. Christy, an atmospheric scientist at the University of Alabama, Huntsville. Most hearings list speakers with PhDs as "Dr.," yet this convention is not always followed. In spite of the fact that this section of hearing transcript does not make it obvious that Christy is a PhD scientist, his credentials were announced when he was introduced at the opening of the hearing.

2. Though scientists may attempt to present themselves as neutral actors (see, e.g., Hilgartner 2000), one should not assume that claims to neutrality actually indicate neutrality.

3. The visible difference in scientists' behavior in these two settings does not suggest that scientists are unaware of the idea of a boundary between science and policy making during agenda setting. *Awareness* of the boundary may not change from one setting to the next. For example, Takacs shows in his 1996 analysis that the conservation biologists he interviews are quite self-conscious about the boundary between science and politics in thinking about their efforts in advocating for protecting biodiversity. This study, on the other hand, finds that open discussion of the science/policy boundary is more likely in legislative settings than it is in agenda setting. Moreover, this research is interested in why an implicit negotiation over the boundary between science and politics becomes explicit with the shift in venue.

4. The data presented below demonstrate the over-representation of scientists in congressional hearings. This is especially true in the climate hearings.

5. Once again, inherent conflicts in scientists' role in policy making may also exist in agenda setting. To the extent that such conflicts *do* exist in agenda setting, they are less publicly visible.

6. The systemic agenda refers to the collection of issues that the public and the media consider pertinent policy issues, while the formal agenda refers to specific issues that are up for active consideration by public officials (Cobb and Elder 1983: 14). The distinction between the two was discussed in the preceding chapter.

7. The co-production view of the role of science in policy argues that scientists are not alone in creating "scientific" understandings of the world. This view is clearly supported when one studies congressional debates in which non-scientists take an active role in shaping the ways in which even technical policy issues are understood. Still, one should not assume that scientists act alone up until the point that powerful elected officials take up an issue. The formality of congressional procedure makes interactions between scientists and non-scientists more visible and more readily studied. The co-production framework, however, challenges us to find cases of co-production in settings in which the influence from scientists and non-scientists may be equally shared, albeit less visible.

8. The literature on the ability of Congress to use expertise is divided. A number of studies point to difficulties—i.e., issues of uncertainty, relevance, and timing—in incorporating analysis into congressional decision making (Jones 1976; Schick 1976; Weiss 1989). Moreover, arguments that much of congressional activity is symbolic would suggest that there is little incentive for members to worry about the effectiveness of the policies they pass and therefore not seek out relevant expertise (Edelman 1974). David Mayhew (1974: 132) explains: "The reason, of course, [for the occurrence of symbolism] is that in a large class of legislative undertakings the electoral payment is for positions rather than for effects." Adding to the picture of Congress as impervious to expertise is Ralph Huitt's

case study of the House Banking Committee, in which members did not change their positions in light of information presented in hearings. Rather, they interpreted information in ways that were consistent with their earlier beliefs (1954: 19–20). In contrast, a number of scholars point out that Congress is increasingly steeped in sources of expertise in an effort to remain independent of the Executive Branch (Polsby 1969; Jones 1976; Schick 1976; Bimber 1996). Moreover, recent research finds that interest groups have an incentive to rely on expertise to predict policy outcomes for the positions they advance given that they are instrumentally interested in the effects of proposed policies. Self-interested behavior on the part of interest groups, then, creates a "political economy of expertise" in congressional policy formation (Esterling 2004).

9. For example, a congressional staffer for the House Committee on Science whom I interviewed raised the issue of attempts by Congress to oversee agency use of science. The staffer presented these attempts as rather futile, explaining given "the use of science in legislation is sloppier than anything you'll find in the agencies" (interview, May 14, 1998).

10. See, for example the National Environmental Policy Institute's report "Enhancing Science in the Regulatory Process" which includes an appendix on ways to improve the use of scientific information in the legislative process (NEPI 1998). See also the House Committee on Science hearings entitled *Scientific Integrity and the Public Trust* (HCS 1995a–c). While these hearings focus on agency use of science, they do contain discussion of scientists' participation in hearings and, in particular, the allegation that scientists misled members of Congress about the quality of their research in order to protect the federal budgets that support their research (see especially HCS 1995b). For a response to these hearings, see Brown 1996, 1997.

11. This issue raises a distinction between *science* and *scientists* in legislative hearings. In the present chapter I am primarily interested in the role of scientists in the policy process, but I recognize that, arguably, scientists are there as representatives of an abstract body of knowledge. Transmitting this knowledge, either for practical or symbolic purposes, motivates both legislators and scientists in legislative settings. Also note, in keeping with Deborah Stone's work on agenda setting, non-scientists can also mobilize scientific framings of issues as part of their persuasive arsenal (1997).

12. For succinct reviews of the several proposed roles that hearings might play in the larger legislative process, see Huitt 1954; Diermeier and Feddersen 2002.

13. Reflecting Muskie's success in expanding the mission of the committee is the change in the name of the committee, which is now called the Senate Committee on Environment and Public Works.

14. The qualification here is that the process of transcription is subject to error. For example, when one climate change scientist testifies about albedo effects in climate change, the word appears in the record as "albito" (SCEPW 1985b: 7). In addition to noticeable errors such as this, it can be difficult to capture tone

from hearing transcripts. One aid in this endeavor is the convention of including the notation "[Laughter]" in the transcripts to note when participants laugh at some remark.

15. Reading the coverage of acid rain and climate change in major newspapers, not surprisingly, closely tracks congressional hearings. Journalists, on some occasions, react to congressional hearings by covering them as newsworthy events. Members of Congress, on occasion, react to issues that receive prominent coverage in major newspapers. Without attempting to tease out causality—does Congress follow the media or does the press follow Congress, newspaper coverage provides some triangulation for relying on the hearings as a window into the evolution of the policy debates over each issue.

16. Ralph Huitt, explaining his reliance on hearings for his study of the congressional committee, writes: "The public hearing is only a part of the activity of a committee, but it is an important and often revealing part." (1954: 341)

17. In some cases, scientific representation in the hearings is overwhelming. For example, in hearings from 1975 to 1992 that discuss climate change, scientists with PhDs in natural sciences make up 64% of witnesses appearing before Congress. When one includes all witnesses who list any postgraduate degree among their qualifications, the percentage increases to 70.4% of witnesses.

18. Richard Fenno (1973) argues that members are motivated by some combination of reelection, influence within the chamber, and good public policy. Gathering information from experts might forward any one of these three goals.

19. One of the central findings of this research is that setting or context shapes scientists' behavior. One mechanism of effect may be that each setting attracts a different subgroup of scientists. The differences one sees across the cases, therefore, might be caused by the different "types" of scientists willing to participate in a specific stage. To the extent that this mechanism is driving the observed effect, one can argue that setting changes not the individual scientist, but "the public face of scientists" who participate in the policy-making process. I discuss this in greater detail in the introduction.

20. This includes scientists who work under the auspices of the National Research Council. The NRC, the research arm of the National Academy of Sciences, was created in 1916 as a way to enlist the Academy's network of scientists in conducting studies of current knowledge on policy-relevant scientific issues. NRC reports are often produced at the request of members of Congress. Moreover, NRC scientists in charge of producing those reports often represent those reports before congressional committees. See, for example, the testimony of Thomas Dietz before the House Committee on Science, Space, and Technology to discuss the National Research Council's research on the human dimensions of global climate change (HCSST 1992).

21. Interview with congressional staffer, May 12, 1998.

22. At a 2002 meeting of the Ecological Society of America, an entire panel was devoted to the role of ecologists in policy making. A number of questions posed

to this panel focused on the risks of political engagement. More senior scientists attending the panel cautioned their more junior colleagues against political engagement until after they had been granted tenure (Alpert and Keller 2003; Keller 2002.)

23. This act created the National Acid Precipitation Assessment Program, which organized and funded scientific research on acid rain starting in 1983.

24. For a description of how data for this chapter were collected, see appendix B.

25. To avoid including in the analysis hearings in which acid rain was only discussed peripherally, a hearing is counted only if the term "acid rain" appears more than once in the Congressional Information Service summary of the hearing.

26. Though in most years after 1979 roughly 40 percent of witnesses went on record against acid rain controls, there are two outliers. In 1985 only 8% of witnesses took positions against acid rain controls, and in 1986 57% of witnesses argued against controls. These two years mark the lowest and highest percentages of witnesses taking positions against acid rain after 1979.

27. This represents a marked difference from the scientific debate over global climate change.

28. For a discussion of the resolution of several of the uncertainties of acid rain, see chapter 2.

29. For a description of the methods for data collection with respect to the hearings on climate change, see appendix B.

30. For more detail on these hearings, see note 84 to chapter 2.

31. Global cooling predictions were also based on the understanding of the greenhouse effect. Aerosol pollution released into the lower atmosphere acts to block incoming solar radiation. This *reduces* the amount of energy entering the Earth's climate system. All other things being equal, this should lead to cooling. In fact, the discrepancy between the observed warming of this century and the predicted warming from early climate models is now attributed to the fact that the models did not originally include the period of high aerosol pollution (Houghton et al. 1996: 229–284; Stott et al. 2000). This cooling effect, however, has been countered by pollution control policies of the 1970s that have improved air quality throughout industrialized countries. Confusion over the simultaneous predictions of warming and cooling caused many observers to discount scientists' claims about the ability for human action to affect the global climate. For example, Thomas Moore, an economist testifying at a subsequent congressional hearing, said "I cannot help mentioning that Steve Schneider was a great advocate of global cooling as a problem in the 1970s and since that did not sell he now sells global warming." (HCS 1995b: 237) For a similar view, see Bray 1991.

32. Sixteen committees, thus far, have held hearings on climate change, with the preponderance of hearings held by five committees. The Senate committees

holding the most hearings are Commerce, Science, and Transportation; Energy and Natural Resources; and Environment and Public Works. The House Committees holding the most hearings are Science Space, and Technology; Appropriations; and Energy and Commerce. (See table 3.2 of the present volume.)

33. The House Committee on Science, Space, and Technology held six hearings during this period, while each of the two Senate Committees held five hearings. Together, these make up 67% of the hearings held in the period 1980–1988.

34. The trend established in this figure continues into the early 1990s with both significant numbers of hearings held annually and with additional committees taking on the issue. In 1990, there were 23 hearings held by nine committees. In 1991, 24 hearings were held by nine committees. In 1992, 18 hearings were held by ten committees.

35. A number of recent studies have revised the initial methods used to calibrate satellite temperature data. Taken together, these studies show that satellite observations find warming that is consistent with observations made at the Earth's surface. For a review of this literature, see Karl et al. 2006.

36. Ultimately, the Senate passed a resolution that it would not approve the Kyoto Protocol if developing countries were not also held to strict emissions standards. Though President Clinton favored signing the protocol, he was not able to overcome congressional opposition. President Bush opposes the Kyoto Treaty, which came into force without the participation of the US in February 2005.

37. Senators Robert Byrd, Chuck Hagel, and John Ashcroft and Representatives Bill Paxon and Joe Knollenberg all introduced measures to prevent implementation of the Kyoto in advance of its adoption as a treaty by the Senate.

38. Chafee introduced his first bill on the issue, S. 2617, in 1998. This bill called for amendments to the Clean Air Act to allow for credits for voluntary reductions of greenhouse gas emissions. In 1999, Chafee introduced S. 547, a bill to provide credit for voluntary reductions without amending the Clean Air Act. Senators Joseph Lieberman and Connie Mack co-sponsored S. 2617. Co-sponsors for S. 547 were Senators Baucus, Biden, Collins, Jeffords, Lieberman, Mack, Moynihan, Reid, Voinovich, Warner, and Wyden.

39. McCain, as chair of the Senate Committee on Commerce, Science, and Transportation, chaired four hearings on climate change (SCCST 2000a–c, 2001). Lieberman introduced a bill, S. 139, with McCain cosponsoring on January 9, 2003. McCain sponsored two similar bills in 2005, with Lieberman among the 15 co-sponsors. The first, S. 342, was introduced on February 10, 2005, and the second, S. 1151, was introduced on May 26, 2005. In addition, Lieberman and McCain have offered amendments to legislation in 2003 and in 2005 that would have created an emissions trading program for greenhouse gases. Neither amendment passed.

40. In the Senate, the Commerce Committee approved a bill to increase vehicle fuel efficiency on May 8, 2007. While the bill does not explicitly address climate change, media coverage of the legislation has made the link (Simon 2007).

41. This idea clearly informed the legislation that created the National Acid Precipitation Assessment Program. Roger Pielke Jr., additionally, argues that this expectation supported the organization of the US Global Change Program to its detriment (2000a,b).

42. See, e.g., SCEPW 1983; 1986a; HCSST 1988, 1989; SCCST 2000a.

43. For a review of the literature on the shortcomings of peer review as a filter for poor research, see Jasanoff 1990: 69–76.

44. It may be that apologetic boundary crossers hope that they will be asked to give their policy positions. In such cases, being pressed by a committee member to articulate a policy position gives scientists license to change hats without appearing to be motivated to do so. Such scientists may be more "strategic" than "apologetic." I am indebted to Mark Hunter for this point.

45. Similarly, in the climate change case, Gordon MacDonald, vice president and chief scientist for the MITRE Corporation, recommends four areas for government action including controls on greenhouse gas emissions (SCEPW 1985b: 23).

46. For another example of academic scientists going on record making policy statements, see HCSST 1988, in which Likens, Goffman, and Galloway each testify that the executive summary of the 1987 NAPAP report is misleading and that there is enough scientific evidence to justify policy action.

47. Arthur Johnson of the University of Pennsylvania responded similarly to Press when he was asked, during a different hearing, to endorse the idea of regulating sulfur emissions. He made a point of saying that he was about to state his personal opinion and proceeds to tell the committee that the effects were sufficiently damaging and our knowledge was good enough to justify controls (SCEPW 1986b: 28)

48. Albritton, as an agency scientist, stands out from other agency officials who are quite willing to take policy positions during legislative testimony. See, e.g., Donna Fitzpatrick's testimony before the Senate Committee on Energy and Natural Resources, in which she calls for additional research to reduce scientific uncertainties before policy options are addressed (SCENR 1988b: 85–86). Albritton's reluctance to take a policy position in this hearing might be a function of the fact that he represents the Reagan administration and does not want to go on record with a contrary position. However, Albritton does not offer his views on policy options regarding climate change when he testifies during the Clinton administration (HCSST 1993: 4–7, 71–72, 78, 80–81; HCEC 1993: 7–10, 51–75).

49. Scientists who testify to present reports from the National Research Council—the research arm of the National Academy of Sciences—look much

like their counter parts in academia. This is not surprising; scientists involved in preparing NRC reports often come from university settings. While the NRC itself represents a link between Congress and the scientific community, the scientists involved with any specific NRC report are participating in NRC work temporarily.

50. Climate scientists involved in the US Global Change Research Program (USGCRP) have less of a presence in the climate hearings. This may be a function of the existence of the Intergovernmental Panel on Climate Change (IPCC), which has a great deal more status because of its global reach than the USGCRP. That said, research funded through the USGCRP is collected into the reports published by the IPCC and US climate researchers typically are affiliated with both organizations.

51. By contrast, academic scientists whose research is supported by NAPAP funding do not testify as NAPAP scientists but, instead, give their academic affiliations.

52. For examples in addition to the one cited above, see Christopher Bernabo's testimonies in four separate hearings (SCEPW 1983b: 24; HCSST 1983: 89; SCENR 1984; HCSST 1985) and James Mahoney's testimony about how to keep science and policy separate in future NAPAP reports (HCIIA 1984:15).

53. Both Gerald Mahlman and Daniel Albritton are listed as scientists who work for the National Oceanic and Atmospheric Administration (NOAA), which is part of the network of agencies collected under the USGCRP umbrella.

54. Hansen's statement drew considerable criticism from the science community; not for the science behind his recommendation, but for the way his statement might be perceived among decision makers who might think that CO_2 is not really a problem (Revkin 2000a).

55. One interviewee, in recounting the period at EPA under Gorsuch, reported that many the most talented researchers working on acid rain left EPA because of their disagreement with the Gorsuch-Reagan approach to environmental policy (interview, October 28, 1998).

56. Proximity to decision-making power becomes an important variable in explaining scientists' behavior during the implementation stage of decision making (see chapter 4 of the present volume) in that scientists who work in regulatory settings have to work to maintain their legitimacy by demonstrating that they have not become politicized. The effect of this is that scientists who are supposed to be producing scientific findings, spend a disproportionate amount of time defending their ability to produce good science in the political setting in which they conduct their research.

57. More recently, policy activity in the US to control greenhouse gases has emerged at the state level (Hakim 2004; DePalma 2005)

58. For a description of the database and data collection effort, see appendix B. The hearings on acid rain represent two significant cycles of policy formation including the creation of a federal research program and the eventual passage of

a regulatory program to mitigate acid rain. The coding for climate change includes one significant cycle of policy making that resulted in a federal research program to study the issue. Since then, debate about climate change in Congress has been relatively open ended in that no resolution to the debate has occurred. Given large number of hearings held on climate change and the lack of closure on the issue, only the first 17 years of climate change hearings were coded. In addition, beginning in 1990, the coding includes a random sample of 50% of the hearings held in 1990, 1991, and 1992.

59. From 1975 to 1989, 348 witnesses testified in a hearing mentioning climate change. Each of these witnesses appears in the data. From 1990 to 1992, the coding was conducted for a random sample of 50% of the hearings, in which 160 witnesses testified. This coding gives us a reliable picture of the hearings during these years, but does not represent an accurate count of the numbers of witnesses who testified.

60. In one exception in the acid rain hearings, several MDs testify about the potential for acid rain to increase the bioavailability of aluminum and, thereby, increase the risk of Alzheimer's Disease in the population. In this case, natural science PhDs would not have the appropriate expertise to speak to the issue. Notable is how rare hearings like this one are in that it is rare that a witnesses educational credentials are mentioned unless those credentials are natural science PhDs.

61. Members of Congress, quite obviously, call many witnesses to testify about each issue. This demonstrates that natural science PhDs are not the only witnesses whose perspective is sought when these issues are debated in Congress.

62. For example, in the climate change hearings coded between 1975 and 1992.

63. Witnesses who testify at these hearings but do not mention acid rain or climate change, respectively, are excluded from this analysis since these witnesses, by definition, will not take a position on the issue. A witness cannot take a position on an issue that she does not discuss.

64. Once again, government scientists are directly employed by a government agency. This group is distinguished from the larger community of scientists employed in academic or other research settings who received government grants for their research, but are not direct government employees.

65. Future research that compares scientists' careers and professional activities by their organizational affiliation would be necessary to provide a more robust answer to the question of why affiliation correlates with willingness to take a policy position. The correlation is compelling, but, by itself, cannot explain what is driving the relationship.

66. A definitive test for setting selecting type of scientist would rest on the ability to identify all the scientists involved in agenda setting. The legislative hearings do provide a record of all the scientists who participated, so determination of participation during legislation could be exhaustive. Pinning down all the

participants in agenda setting is much more difficult owing to the lack of formal procedures governing this stage of policy making.

67. For example, one agency official I interviewed explained to me that a popular scientist who had frequently been called to testify before Congress about climate change was no longer being called as a science witness given that his policy preferences with respect to global warming were so clear (interview, May 12, 1998).

68. For example, during testimony before the Senate Committee on Environment and Public Works, Richard Lindzen and Stephen Schneider agree with IPCC's claim that "the balance of evidence, from changes in global mean surface air temperature and from changes in geographical, seasonal and vertical patterns of atmospheric temperature, suggests a discernible human influence on global climate" (Houghton et al. 1996: 5). However, they take opposite stands regarding policy to reduce greenhouse gas emissions (SCEPW 1997). In an even more startling example, Sallie Baliunas testifies before a Senate Committee on Energy and Natural Resources that the bulk of the warming experienced in this century is attributable to solar activity rather than to increases in greenhouse gases (SCENR 1996: 41). When asked whether her findings are inconsistent with what is reported by the IPCC (Houghton et al. 1996), Baliunas argues that she does not disagree with the IPCC. This prompts another scientist who is testifying, V. Ramanathan, to point out that the IPCC has said there is evidence of a human influence on the climate, i.e. a warming that cannot be explained by natural variability. In this case, both scientists want to indicate that their views are supported by the science contained in the well-respected IPCC reports, yet they clearly do not agree about the report's conclusions about the cause of the observed warming in the twentieth century.

69. Tentative support for this argument comes from the testimony strategy adopted by Jerry Mahlman, director of the NOAA's Geophysical Fluid Dynamics Laboratory, who systematically refuses to take a policy position during hearings. Instead, Mahlman routinely attaches probabilities to the findings he reports as a way to indicate those in which scientists have the most confidence. See, e.g., SCENR 1994: 24.

70. For example, scientists' willingness to make policy statements may be driven by their personalities more than their view of the uncertainty of scientific claims.

71. Data on media coverage is gathered using the LexisNexis database and searching for stories in the "General News" and "Major Papers" categories. Search terms used are "Albert Gore" AND "climate" AND "carbon." For Hansen, the search terms used are "James Hansen," AND "climate" AND "carbon."

72. Figure 2.6 shows a dramatic increases in congressional attention to climate change beginning in 1987. Figure 2.7 shows a steady increase in media attention beginning in 1977.

73. The acid rain science narrative linked acid deposition to sulfur dioxide and nitrogen oxide emissions and predicted damage to surface waters, aquatic ecosystems, buildings, and potentially to forests and soils. The narrative portrayed acid rain as an important environmental policy problem. In addition, it pointed to increased scientific research as an appropriate step toward finding policy solutions. On the development of the acid rain science narrative, see chapter 2 of the present volume.

74. On the link between governmental attention to an issue and that issue's legitimacy, see Cobb and Elder 1983: 172.

75. For a detailed discussion of NAPAP's revised findings, see chapter 2 of the present volume.

76. A Harris poll conducted on May 19, 1986 asked respondents if they considered acid rain to be very serious, somewhat serious, a small problem, no problem at all, or if they weren't sure. Forty-two percent responded that acid rain was very serious, and 37 percent listed the issue as somewhat serious. In a Harris poll conducted on March 12, 1989, 68 percent of respondents said they favored federal spending for stricter control of acid rain and toxic dumping even if it meant raising taxes (Harris Poll, Institute for Social Research, University of North Carolina).

77. Cohen (1992: 42) also notes Byrd's shift: "Byrd had been the chief barrier to Senate action on acid rain legislation during the Reagan era. But in 1987, he began to understand that the political tide was turning against him and his West Virginia constituents who mined high-sulfur coal." Cohen gives a detailed discussion of the negotiations between Mitchell and Byrd that followed Byrd's change of heart (ibid.: 41–46).

78. Recall that the climate change science narrative linked greenhouse gas emissions, especially CO_2, to an increase in global average temperature and predicted a number of mostly negative consequences like drought or sea-level rise. In addition, the climate change science narrative characterized climate change and an important environmental policy problem and pointed to scientific research as an important first step in responding to the problem. On the development of the science narrative for climate change, see chapter 2 of the present volume.

79. For hearings convened in response to IPCC activity, see SCEPW 1985; SCCST 1990, 2001; SCENR 1996; HCST 2007a,b. For examples of media attention to all five of the IPCC's major assessment reports, see Whitney 1990; Stevens 1992; *New York Times* 1995; McCarthy et al. 2001; Maugh 2007.

80. The two likely contenders were the Environmental Protection Agency, which administers the acid rain emissions trading program, and the Department of Energy, which collects national data on carbon emissions (interviews, August 24 and September 14, 1998).

81. The Court handed down this decision on April 2, 2007.

82. Congressional staff report that scientists invited to testify do not always accept such invitations (interview, May 12, 1998). In addition, norms in some disciplines in the sciences steer scientists away from becoming associated with policy causes (Alpert and Keller 2003; Keller 2002).

Chapter 4

1. The data for this chapter are drawn from a set of intensive interviews with scientists and policy makers who work at the interface between science and public decision making. These interviews were conducted in 1998 and focused primarily on civil servants in the Executive Branch. In addition, a number of interviewees were affiliated with NGOs or with Congress. For a list of interviewee affiliations and interview dates, see appendix E.

2. Meyer and Rowan (1991) argue that the "institutional" level of an organization focuses primarily on interactions with the organization's environment that enhance the organization's legitimacy among its stakeholders. This institutional level, however, is buffered from the central tasks the organization performs so that external demands may be met symbolically without actually changing the organization's "technical core" (ibid.). Organizational structures designed to prevent scientists from acting politically have this symbolic quality irrespective of their effectiveness in maintaining scientists' objectivity.

3. The word "implementation," when used in the context of policy making, encompasses state activities undertaken to carry out the policies and laws enacted by the state. While states actively engage in prohibiting or limiting actions taken in the private sector, states also encourage action on the part of private actors through the selective distribution of public resources. This latter tool makes up a significant proportion of state action given that regulatory policies are difficult to pass and implement and can erode state legitimacy. This is especially in the US context where the ideal of limited government persists.

4. An outmoded view of politics suggests that the real work of policy making takes place in legislative settings and that implementation is a simple technical matter requiring no discretion on the part of agency officials. This view was discarded with Pressman and Wildavsky's 1973 analysis of the actual policy making that takes place during implementation. Certainly, Pressman and Wildavsky's point is well illustrated by highly contentious and visible battles over agency rule making. However, they did not limit their claim about the extent of policy making in the Executive Branch to regulatory agencies. For another approach that points to the distinguishing features of distributive and regulatory programs without excluding either one from the domain of policy implementation, see Wilson 1989.

5. Agenda setting, lacking even an institutional home that carries out the process, is the least formal of the stages of policy making. Legislation is, of course, a step up in formality. Yet text after text discussing the process of how a bill becomes a law must incorporate descriptions of personalities and closed-door meetings

where compromises and agreements are made. See, e.g., Birnbaum and Murray 1987; Cohen 1992; Light 1995. Perhaps as a testament to just how formalized the implementation process is, rare is the analysis of this process which focuses on personality rather than procedure in explaining outcomes. An exception that strengthens the case for reliance on the formal is Anne Gorsuch's turbulent tenure as EPA administrator. Gorsuch was forced to resign her position as EPA administrator when she became the subject of two separate investigations, one conducted by the House Committee on Energy and Commerce and one by the Justice Department. These investigations were mounted in response to her actions that contradicted the formal requirements of her role in the organization (US House Committee on Energy and Commerce 1983; Landy, Roberts, and Thomas 1990: 246–251).

6. Normative organization theory, which defined the discipline up until World War II, focused exclusively on the formal components of organizations in their pursuit of "one best way" of organizing to achieve efficiently organization goals. See for example, Gulick and Urwick's work on the principles of administration (1937) and Frederick Taylor's work on scientific management (1911, 1947).

7. See, e.g., Philip Selznick's analysis of "the nonrational dimensions of organizational behavior" (1948: 25).

8. Moe (1989) argues that regulatory agencies in the US are characterized by structures that arise out of political struggle among actors who seek to secure future regulatory outputs. The focus on structure arises out of an attempt to constrain the behavior of actors in the agency as well as those with claims on the agency's performance, e.g. members of Congress, presidents, and interest groups.

9. For a discussion of the use of procedures as a way to revise existing procedure, see Schulman's treatment of safety at the Diablo Canyon nuclear power plant (1993).

10. Review of agency rule making in the courts is quite common, especially for politically embattled agencies like the EPA. While the courts can review the substance of the agency's decision, it was common for the court, lacking the technical expertise to review the substance of the decision, to review the agency's adherence to procedure (Shapiro 1988). This practice is based on the notion that correct adherence to procedure leads to the correct decision and demonstrates clearly the link between formal procedure, the exercise of power, and legitimacy. More recently, courts have been willing to review the substance of the agencies regulatory decisions (Melnick 1983).

11. These changes grew out of the acknowledgment that administrative decision making involves the meaningful exercise of political power. The attempt to keep politics and values separate from administrative duties was championed by the Progressives and supported analytically by scholars. (See, e.g., Gulick and Urwick 1937.) Pressman and Wildavsky's 1973 work on implementation re-invigorated the study of administrative decision making as an arena of political action. More recently, Aberbach, Putnam, and Rockman (1981) show in their comparative

study of bureaucrats and politicians in Western democracies that the roles are least distinguishable in the United States when compared with Britain, France, Germany, Italy, the Netherlands and Sweden.

12. The rules of standing were expanded to allow plaintiffs who did not experience direct economic injury to sue in *Office of Communication of the United Church of Christ v. FCC*, 359 F. 2nd 944 (D.C. Cir. 1966). For a discussion of the impacts of increased standing and greater access to government information, see Wilson 1989: 129–131, 280–282.

13. American administrative decision making is unusual in its reliance on litigation as a method of resolving policy controversy (Brickman, Jasanoff, and Ilgen 1985; Kagan 2001; Miller and Barnes 2004). Though it is not clear that Americans' particularly contentious form of decision making brings about more stringent or more effective regulation (Vogel 1986), litigation itself offers yet another layer of formal procedure to the policy-making process. This additional layer of procedure creates an opportunity for extended consideration of and increased access to policy decisions.

14. Porter (1995) writes extensively on how quantification, specifically, is used in bureaucratic settings as a way to claim that political power has been exercised fairly.

15. Without asserting that scientific input is inherently part of any policy domain, I will argue in this chapter that scientific information is currently a crucial component in the legitimization of environmental policy issues. See, e.g., Jasanoff's critique of democratic bases of legitimization in environmental policy making (1990: 17).

16. Bryner, in his analysis of both scientific and economic expertise in regulatory decision making, elaborates this point: "The expectation of expertise and autonomy surrounding bureaucracy rests primarily on the idea of professional norms and political neutrality. Scientific and economic analyses are expected to legitimize the exercise of governmental power because they are 'objective' and independent of partisan considerations. As agency experts are given the primary responsibility for decision making, the decision-making process is made consonant with other political values precisely because it is, in theory, nonpolitical, interested only in the rational pursuit of scientific truth. Professional norms and peer review serve as additional checks on discretion which, in turn, reinforces the acceptability of expertise as a basis for decision-making." (1987: 55–56)

17. Jasanoff (1990) and Wagner (1995) each demonstrate the tendency for scientists attempting to portray their contributions to policy making as if they are entirely factual even when they are participating politically.

18. A number of studies undermine the notion that there is a distinct sphere for science that sets it apart from non-science. See, e.g., Gieryn 1983, 1995; Latour and Woolgar 1979. Insights regarding the inability to set any fixed boundary between science and non-science and the fundamentally social nature of scientific research have not weakened the idea of separating science from policy in the US regulatory context. Thus, one finds organizational arrangements and institu-

tional norms that continue to operate as if separate spheres are both possible and necessary.

19. The report defines risk assessment as "the characterization of the potential adverse health effects of human exposure to environmental hazard" (NRC 1983b: 18). Risk management is defined as "an agency decision-making process that entails consideration of political, social, economic, and engineering information with risk-related information to develop, analyze, and compare regulatory options and to select the appropriate regulatory response to a potential chronic health hazard" (ibid.: 19).

20. The NRC reiterates its concern about the science/policy boundary being difficult to maintain in its 1996 report on risk. In this report, the committee finds that policy considerations must be weighed through the risk-analysis process rather than as a follow up to scientific evaluations of risk (NRC 1996).

21. An interesting component of this particular demarcation is the clarity with which the assessment process is presented—four neatly delineated steps—as compared with the "fuzziness" of their discussion of risk management. Certainly, one might argue that the focus of the report is on assessment such that no articulation of the process of risk management is necessary. On the other hand, the amorphous elements of the risk-management process named in the NRC report have found their way into current agency documents as a characterization for the risk-management process (US EPA 1997: 3).

22. Reports from the Centers for Disease Control and Prevention of the Department of Health and Human Services and from the Office of Research and Development of the EPA both refer directly to the 1983 NRC report when presenting their approaches to risk analysis (NRC 1983b). The Departments of Interior, Transportation and Energy employ variants on the NRC framework that retain the distinction between risk assessment, a science-based activity, and risk management, a policy activity in their approaches to risk analysis.

23. In my interviews, I came across no other report or publication that was so widely used that it came to be referred to by a nickname that seemed to be recognized across both offices, agencies, and departments. The exception to this is the follow up report published by the NRC in 1996. Because of the report's predominantly orange cover and by extension of the nickname of the 1983 report, some had taken to calling the 1996 report "the orange book." This, however, was not a common name for the 1996 report. Rather, it was more of a joke made in reference to the original report's nickname that was shared among policy insiders dealing with risk analysis.

24. This language is used in ORACBA's pamphlet publication describing the origins and goals of the office. Similar language is also found on the office's website (http://www.usda.gov): "ORACBA's primary role is to ensure that major regulations proposed by USDA are based on sound scientific and economic analysis." In addition, an ORACBA newsletter discussing their policy, argues that risk assessment should keep science and policy separate (Carrington and Bolger 2000).

25. Gieryn (1995: 424–439) defines four types of boundary work: monopolization, expansion, expulsion, and protection. Gieryn relies of Jasanoff's 1990 study of science advisors as the exemplar of protection-type boundary work.

26. Thompson (1967) advances the idea of buffering in organizations to protect the central work of the organization or the organization's "core technology": "Under norms of rationality, organizations seek to seal off their core technologies from environmental influences." (ibid.: 19) Stockpiling, for example, is a buffering technique that enables the organization to survive a downturn in supply. The attempt to protect science from politicization may be understood in terms similar to this quite typical organizational technique. However, the growing literature on boundary work has not, to date, made use of this long-standing concept from organization theory.

27. Taking the assessment-management paradigm to a different organizational setting, the same interview contact worried about the EPA's role in allocating resources for research organizations in the government. From the interview subject's perspective, the EPA, as a regulatory body, was too deeply involved in political decision making to have the objectivity necessary to make decisions about funding for science research (interview, June 1, 1998).

28. The terms "agency science" and "academic science" denote a difference in institutional setting. The substantive differences between science conducted within regulatory settings and university settings will be addressed below.

29. Jasanoff's work on science in the environmental policy setting focuses particularly on calls for peer review of science information before it is used in policy making. Jasanoff argues that these calls rely on a technocratic model of decision making which attempts to limit political debate by shifting critical decisions about policy out of the political arena (1990: 15–16).

30. Studies demonstrating the shortcomings of the peer-review process in weeding out substandard science or even misconduct suggest that moving the determination of credibility from policy settings to academic ones substitutes one set of potential biases for another. For a succinct review of the literature on weaknesses in the peer-review process, see Jasanoff 1990: 69–76.

31. Interview, June 1, 1998 and USDHHS (1990: 1–2). See also the NIEHS website (http://ehis.niehs.nih.gov), which has information about and access to the NIEHS journal *Environmental Health Perspectives*.

32. The editorial policy of the NIEHS journal *Environmental Health Perspectives* can be accessed through the NIEHS website.

33. On one occasion, Congress tried to gain access to raw data produced by an NIEHS grantee. This access was denied according to an NIEHS policy that research results be made available only through published technical reports (interview, June 1, 1998).

34. During the G. H. W. Bush administration, EPA Administrator William Reilly created an EPA policy requiring that all major science and technological products

used to support decision making undergo peer review. This policy was re-approved by Administrator Carol Browner (interview, July 10, 1998).

35. There are a number of treatments of regulatory science (Jasanoff 1990; Irwin et al. 1997), trans-science (Weinberg 1982), and mandated science (Salter 1988). Each of these studies makes a different assumption about whether science conducted in the regulatory setting is actually less robust than academic science or is merely perceived to be less credible. Weinberg, in particular, argues that the standards of proof for trans-science *should* be relaxed given that science conducted in the regulatory setting is pushed to produce findings in areas of great uncertainty.

36. Salter, in her 1988 treatment of mandated science, argues that good science can be conducted even when values are at stake without the science itself becoming biased. Salter worries about scientists falsifying results or reaching conclusions to satisfying funders, but argues that this undesirable outcome can be avoided when science is conducted by mandate.

37. Of course, the ideal of academic science is not an accurate descriptor of how science is conducted in academic settings. For instance, academic research is heavily influenced by the availability of government funding (Greenberg 2001).

38. This perception was repeatedly raised by my interviewees. Some seemed to argue that the perception was true, but most of them characterized the charge as unwarranted.

39. Interview, July 10, 1998. In addition, Jasanoff's analysis of the peer-review process supports the claim of bias among university scientists against agency science. She argues that this bias can undermine the peer-review process that relies on university scientists to review agency-produced science. Jasanoff points out that university scientists "may . . . approach their task with an inherent bias against work produced by agency experts, who are believed by many to be less competent on average than scientists actively pursuing a research career" (1990: 79).

40. Including the comparison of policy response scenarios in NAPAP's research agenda is consistent with the EPA's view that much of what is conducted under the aegis of risk management is heavily scientific or technical and can be improved by involving scientific evaluation (US EPA 1997: 2–5).

41. I discuss these instances in chapter 3.

42. I am indebted to an anonymous reviewer for this point.

43. See, e.g., Brunner 1996.

44. Price (1965) argues that those who leave the academic setting and enter policy making change roles and act as professionals who accept the constraints imposed by the norms of the profession or as administrators who accept constraint in the form of political oversight. These constraints are imposed to ensure that these actors act responsibly in the policy-making process. My argument is distinct from Price's in that I find scientists accepting constraints on their

participation as a way to ensure the preservation of their role as *scientists* rather than as professionals or administrators.

45. Two of my interview subjects independently made unprompted comparisons between science at the NIEHS and the EPA (June 1, 1998 and July 10, 1998). A third interview subject when asked directly about the comparability of NIEHS and ORD, the research arm of the EPA, responded favorably to the comparison both in terms of their organization within a larger policy organization—HHS and the EPA, respectively—and the subject matter of the research conducted–environmental health (July 16, 1998).

46. ORD has a larger research agenda in that environmental issues that do not have a human health component are part of the EPA's statutory mandate. However, the bulk of EPA regulations are written with the goal of improving public health.

47. Note that NIEHS, though organizationally part of the National Institutes of Health, is located not in Bethesda, Maryland, but in Research Triangle Park, North Carolina. For the most part, the National Institutes of Health engage in "distributive politics," i.e., dolling out federal grants. Distributive politics are far less contentious than regulatory politics (Lowi 1964, 1972)—something that may account for NIEHS's alternate location.

48. The Centers for Disease Control and Prevention (CDC), which are located in Atlanta, once faced the possibility of being relocated to Washington. Leadership at the CDC at the time argued vociferously and successfully against the move. Their reasoning was that their scientific and technical credibility would be higher if they were not located in the nation's capital (Etheridge 1992). The CDC example suggests that NIEHS is not the only agency within the Executive Branch that views proximity to centers of policy making as threatening.

49. The report referred to here is actually published by the NRC (1983b). The NRC is the operating arm of both the National Academy of Sciences, and the National Academy of Engineering and was created by Congress to provide scientific information of interest to decision makers. However, "the National Academy of Sciences" or "the Academy" is often used to refer to the entire organization, probably because the NAS predates the other affiliated organizations including the Institutes of Medicine.

50. Notably, Guston (2000) develops his concept of boundary organizations specifically in the arena of distributive politics where governments and the scientific community are involved in interactions around the distribution of research dollars.

51. Mahoney made these statements as the new director of NAPAP. The previous director, Lawrence Kulp, had resigned in the furor over the executive summary of the 1987 report.

52. Representative Dana Rohrabacher, who chaired these hearings, referred to theories about global warming as "liberal claptrap" (*New York Times* 1995).

53. For example, in the year in which the IPCC produced its first of three assessment reports, there were 86 stories about the organization in major newspapers. The USGCRP's first report, published in 2000, generated 10 stories. These numbers might suggest that climate change was a more salient issue in 1992 than in 2000. Yet in 2000, a year in which the IPCC did not release one of its three major assessments, it generated 82 stories. These data are drawn from the Lexis-Nexis newspaper database for "General News" in "Major Papers." Full-text searchers for "USGCRP" and "IPCC," respectively, were used to search the database.

54. See, e.g., NAPAP 1991, 1998. The priority given ecological effects over health effects is replicated at NAPAP's website (http://www.oar.noaa.gov). Also, in one of NAPAP's annual reports to Congress, though health effects are treated in the report, a list of NAPAP task groups at the time shows that no task group was convened on health effects (NAPAP 1990: unnumbered page preceding table of contents).

55. A number of studies make the case that nitrous oxide emissions reductions set out in the Clean Air Act Amendments of 1990 are not strict enough to protect lakes, forests and soils (interviews, September 14 and December 2, 1998; USGAO 2000).

56. Recall that the executive summary of the 1987 report was quite controversial.

57. This requirement is included in Title IV of the 1990 Clean Air Act Amendments that initiated the Acid Rain Program.

58. See, e.g., HSCA 1983.

59. Interviews, September 14, October 28, and December 2, 1998.

60. In a congressional review of the Acid Rain Program, human health effects were argued as one of the main benefits derived from the program (JEC 1997). In general, the acid rain program construes human health as the primary benefit from the program (interviews, October 28 and December 2, 1998).

61. An additional example of scientists ceding the role of persuasion comes from Karen Litfin's treatment of the policy debates around ozone depletion. Litfin notes that "knowledge brokers," in this case officials from the EPA, offered persuasive frames about how to understand the patchy scientific evidence about ozone loss. Scientists, according to Litfin, who might have offered such frames, stuck closely to scientifically defensible statements about ozone loss and were reluctant to draw policy implications (1994: 115). Notably, the examples she gives of scientists talking about ozone loss come from formal policy settings, such as congressional hearings. Because Litfin excludes the early statements scientists made about ozone depletion from her analysis, she does not address the distinctions between the early and the later, more formal statements from scientists. The statements from scientists that she includes in her analysis are quite different from their earliest warnings about ozone loss, which contained explicit policy recommendations—most notably that the use of CFCs should be banned.

(For Molina's description of his and Rowland's policy position on CFCs, see note 34 to this chapter). In both cases, we see scientists initiate debate with policy-relevant, persuasive arguments and then relinquish this role to others in order to project a more objective stance in the process

62. There are a number of examples of scientists taking strong policy positions on global warming. Steve Schneider has been a notable voice from the science community in advocating for policy action. The IPCC's 1995 update includes controversial language in its executive summary linking the observed warming to human action (Houghton et al. 1996). Prior to the IPCC 1995 update, Jim Hansen testified before the US Senate that the heat of the summer of 1988 was linked to global warming. At the time Hansen's claim was widely criticized by his professional colleagues as premature. More recently, Hansen has published a report through the National Academy of Sciences that argues for a focus on non-carbon based climate forcing gases (Hansen et al. 2000). Again, Hansen has drawn criticism from fellow scientists, this time for allowing space for contrarians to argue that global warming fears are exaggerated (Revkin 2000a). What is especially interesting about Hansen's statement is that he works in NASA's Goddard Institute for Space Studies, one of the organizations operating under the umbrella of the USGCRP. The fact that his statements were made by the non-governmental National Academy of Sciences removes him from the USGCRP prohibition from recommending policies on global change issues.

63. Scientists' participation in debates over pursuing the hydrogen bomb or supersonic transport are examples.

64. Kelly Moore's 1996 analysis looks specifically and mediating organizations—public-interest organizations—that attempt to link scientific and political considerations in a way that preserves two crucial but potentially contradictory images of the scientist as objective and useful. From policy circles comes the NRC report on risk analysis which addresses the specific question of whether risk analysis is better conducted by an organization that is independent of agencies and departments with regulatory power. The NRC rejects this solution and argues instead for a procedural rather than an organizational separation of science and policy making (1983b).

Conclusion

1. Thompson, Ellis, and Wildavsky (1990) argue that political cultures are based on value structures that are derived from deep-seated views of nature. According to one story about nature, nature is robust and can withstand small perturbations—clearly the perspective from which many industry groups operate. The conflicting story, that nature is fragile, shapes environmentalists' response to information about environmental damage.

2. Schattschneider (1961: 68) makes a strong case for the important of agenda setting: "He who determines what politics is about runs the country, and the choice of conflicts allocates power."

3. Baumgartner and Jones (1994) argue that policy change often requires the emergence of novel venues that create a space for novel ideas to be debated. Absent such venues, policy change tends to be incremental and dominated by deeply institutionalized approaches. Litfin (1994) demonstrates this in the case of ozone depletion. Since the issue was originally framed in terms of its potential to increase skin cancers and damage aquatic food chains, the discovery that CFCs were not only ozone destroyers but also greenhouse gases hardly made a dent in the deliberations over whether or not to limit CFC production.

4. Herbert Simon emphasizes this in his seminal work on organizations (1976). Members of an organization suffer from "bounded rationality" in that the organization predisposes them to approach problem solving in particular ways that place in relief some types of information while obscuring others. Simon was surely correct in pointing out that selective attention makes decision making possible. We could not act if we made no assumptions about the world and treated everything as open to question.

5. In the case of acid rain, for example, the policy innovation that turned the tide in legislative debate—emissions trading—came from economists via an attentive lawyer at the National Resources Defense Council, not from atmospheric physicists and chemists instrumental in putting acid rain on the policy map.

6. See chapter 3 of the present volume.

7. Jasanoff makes a similar point about the regulatory political environment as an arena in which the deconstruction of scientific arguments is commonplace (1990: 13).

8. For example, NAPAP's attempt to remain objective isolated the organization from decision makers who were grappling with a number of value conflicts in making decisions about acid rain policy. I discuss this in chapters 3 and 4.

9. Recall the discussion in chapter 3.

10. I did not interview either of these people. Their respective association with the two issues is appears in the public record.

11. An additional question that is raised by considering the domain of distributive policy is the difference between producing science in policy-making settings versus producing technology in policy-making settings. This is a much larger question that is beyond the scope of the present volume.

12. I discuss reliance on scientific information in public records of decision making in chapter 2.

13. Robert Kagan (2001) also expresses concern about the time and cost involved in the adversarial approach to policy formation in the US.

14. I discuss the incentives for members of Congress to engage in symbolic acts in chapter 3. The role of science, while it can fulfill its stated aims, can also be used in this more symbolic manner, in which the statement of goals is more important than their actual achievement.

Appendix A

1. The critics of the original experiment agreed that one of the six negative experiments was a good refutation of the original results. However, the original experimenter and one other scientist who sympathetic to the original experiment were critical of the attempted replication that the critics supported (Collins 1981: 42).

2. Robert Merton (1942) set out four norms that, he argued, govern science and provide for its unique capacity to explain the natural world: universalism, communism, disinterestedness, and organized skepticism.

3. Kuhn's book *The Structure of Scientific Revolutions* was originally published in 1962.

4. Latour elaborates the importance of networks in subsequent work (1983, 1987, 1988, 1999b).

5. Collins (1981) stands out among these scholars mentioned here in that he does argue from a relativist position.

Appendix B

1. For access to the data on acid rain hearings, contact the author (annk@ berkeley.edu).

2. Appropriations hearings were excluded in the original search after finding in the acid rain hearings that scientists rarely appear in appropriations hearings and that issues of science were almost never debated in this context.

3. There have, of course, been oversight hearings on acid rain since the passage of the Clean Air Act Amendments of 1990. However, these are not hearings that involve scientists in debates about scientific knowledge and potential policy action. Given that, these hearings are not included in the sample. Since the passage of the Clean Air Act Amendments of 1990, there has been no congressional debate on revisions to the existing regulatory program for acid rain. In fact, most of the oversight hearings on acid rain hail the program as a success.

4. For access to the data on climate change hearings, contact the author (annk@ berkeley.edu).

Bibliography

Aberbach, Joel D., Robert D. Putnam, and Bert A. Rockman. 1981. *Bureaucrats and Politicians in Western Democracies*. Harvard University Press.

Peter Alpert, and Ann Keller. 2003. The ecology-policy interface: How close is too close? *Frontiers in Ecology and the Environment* 1, no. 1: 45–46.

Arrhenius, Svante. 1896. On the influence of carbonic acid in the air upon the temperature of the ground. *Philosophical Magazine and Journal of Science* 41: 237–276.

Bachrach, Peter, and Morton Baratz. 1962. Two faces of power. *American Political Science Review* 56: 948.

Balfour, Daniel L., and William Mesaros. 1994. Connecting the local narratives: Public administration as hermeneutic science. *Public Administration Review* 54, no. 6: 559–564.

Barnes, Robert, and Juliet Eilperin. 2007. High Court faults EPA inaction on emissions. *Washington Post*, April 3.

Barringer, Felicity. 2006. Officials reach California deal to cut emissions. *New York Times*, August 31.

Baumgartner, Frank R., and Bryan D. Jones. 1993. *Agendas and Instability in American Politics*. University of Chicago Press.

Baumgartner, Frank R., Bryan D. Jones, and Michael C. MacLeod. 2000. The evolution of legislative jurisdictions. *Journal of Politics* 62 (May): 321–349.

Beamish, Richard J., and Harold H. Harvey. 1972. Acidification of the La Cloche Mountain Lakes, Ontario, and resulting fish mortalities. *Journal of Fisheries Research Board of Canada* 29: 1131–1143.

Berger, Peter L., and Thomas Luckmann. 1966. *The Social Construction of Reality: A Treatise in the Sociology of Knowledge*. Doubleday.

Berry, Jeffrey. 1999. *The New Liberalism: The Rising Power of Citizen's Groups*. Brookings Institution Press.

Bimber, Bruce. 1996. *The Politics of Expertise in Congress: The Rise and Fall of the Office of Technology Assessment*. State University of New York Press.

Birnbaum, Jeffrey H., and Alan S. Murray. 1987. *Showdown at Gucci Gulch: Lawmakers, Lobbyists, and the Unlikely Triumph of Tax Reform.* Vintage Books.

Boehmer-Christiansen, Sonja. 1988. Black mist and the acid rain: Science as figleaf of policy. *Political Quarterly* 59, no. 2: 145–160.

Boehmer-Christiansen, Sonja. 1996. The international research enterprise and global environmental change: Climate-change as a policy research process. In *The Environment and International Relations*, ed. J. Vogler and M. Imber. Routledge.

Boffey, Philip M. 1975. *The Brain Bank of America: An Inquiry into the Politics of Science.* McGraw-Hill.

Bolin, Bert, and R. B. Cook, eds. 1983. *The Major Biochemical Cycles and Their Interactions.* Wiley.

Bolin, Bert, et al. 1972. *Air Pollution across National Boundaries: The Impact on the Environment of Sulfur in Air and Precipitation.* Royal Ministry for Foreign Affairs and Royal Ministry for Agriculture, Stockholm.

Bowker, Geoffrey C., and Susan Leigh Star. 1999. *Sorting Things Out: Classification and Its Consequences.* MIT Press.

Bray, Anna J. 1991. The ice age cometh: Global cooling scare once dominated media and policymakers' minds. *Policy Review* 58, fall: 82–84.

Brickman, Ronald, Sheila Jasanoff, and Thomas Ilgen. 1985. *Controlling Chemicals: The Politics of Regulation in Europe and the United States.* Cornell University Press.

Brody, Richard A. 1991. *Assessing the President: The Media, Elite Opinion, and Public Support.* Stanford University Press.

Broecker, William. 1987. Unpleasant surprises in greenhouse? *Nature* 328, July 9: 123–126.

Brooks, Harvey. 1964. The scientific advisor. In *Scientists and National Policy-Making*, ed. R. Gilpin and C. Wright. Columbia University Press.

Brown, George E., Jr. 1996. *Environmental Science Under Siege: Fringe Science and the 104th Congress.* Report by Rep. George E. Brown Jr., US House of Representatives, October 23.

Brown, George E., Jr. 1997. Environmental science under siege in the U.S. Congress. *Environment* 39, no. 2: 12–30.

Brown, Phil. 1992. Popular epidemiology and toxic waste contamination: Lay and professional ways of knowing. *Journal of Health and Social Behavior* 33, September: 267–281.

Brunner, Ronald D. 1996. Policy and global change research: A modest proposal. *Climatic Change* 32: 121–147.

Bryner, Gary C. 1987. Scientific and economic analysis in administrative rule making. In *Bureaucratic Discretion: Law and Policy in Federal Regulatory Agencies.* Pergamon.

Bryner, Gary C. 1993. *Blue Skies, Green Politics: The Clean Air Act of 1990.* CQ Press.

Bush, Vannevar. 1945. *Science, the Endless Frontier.* U.S. Government Printing Office.

Butterfield, Fox. 1982. Unusually cold winter is forecast by analysts. *New York Times*, September 20.

Callon, Michel. 1985. Some elements of a sociology of translation: Domestication of the scallops and the fishermen of St. Brieuc. In *Power, Action and Belief*, ed. J. Law. Routledge and Kegan Paul.

Callon, Michel, and John Law. 1982. On interests and their transformation: Enrollment and counter-enrollment. *Social Studies of Science* 12: 615–625.

Carpenter, Daniel P., Kevin M. Esterling, and David Lazer. 1998. The strength of weak ties in lobbying networks: Evidence of health care politics. *Journal of Theoretical Politics* 10: 417–444.

Carrington, Clark, and Michael Bolger. 2000. Safety assessment and risk assessment: Sometimes more is less. *ORACBA News* 5, no. 2: 1–3. Carson, Nancy, and Don Munton. 2000. Flaws in the conventional wisdom on acid deposition: NAPAP biennial report to Congress: An integrated assessment. *Environment* 42, March: 33–35.

Carson, Rachel. 1962. *Silent Spring.* Fawcett Crest.

Chapin, Steven. 1995. Cordelia's love: Credibility and the social studies of science. *Perspectives on Science* 3, fall: 255–275.

Charney, Jule G., et al. 1979. *Carbon Dioxide and Climate: A Scientific Assessment: Report of an Ad Hoc Study Group on Carbon Dioxide and Climate.* National Academy of Sciences.

CIA (Central Intelligence Agency). 1974. *Potential Implications of Trends in Food, Population, and Climate.* Government Printing Office.

Cigler, Allan J., and Burdett A. Loomis, eds. 2002. *Interest Group Politics*, sixth edition. CQ Press.

Clarke, Adele. 1990. A social worlds research adventure: The case of reproductive science. In *Theories of Science in Society*, ed. S. Cozzens and T. Gieryn. Indiana University Press.

Cobb, Roger W., and Charles D. Elder. 1983. *Participation in American Politics: The Dynamics of Agenda Building*, second edition. Johns Hopkins University Press.

Cobb, Roger W., and Marc Howard Ross. 1997. Agenda setting and the denial of agenda access: Key concepts. In *Cultural Strategies of Agenda Denial*, ed. R. Cobb and M. Ross. University Press of Kansas.

Cogbill, Charles V., and Gene E. Likens. 1974. Acid precipitation in the northeastern United States. *Water Resources Research* 10, December: 1133–1137.

Cohen, Michael D., James G. March, and Johan P. Olsen. 1972. A garbage can model of organizational choice. *Administrative Science Quarterly* 17: 1–25.

Cohen, Richard E. 1995. *Washington at Work: Back Rooms and Clean Air*, second edition. Macmillan.

Cole, Stephen, Jonathan Cole, and Gary A. Simon. 1981. Chance and consensus in peer review. *Science* 214: 881–886.

Collingridge, David, and Colin Reeve. 1986. *Science Speaks to Power: The Role of Experts in Policy Making*. St. Martin's Press.

Collins, H. M. 1981. Son of seven sexes: The social destruction of a physical phenomenon. *Social Studies of Science* 11: 33–62.

Collins, Harry. 1985. *Changing Order: Replication and Induction in Scientific Practice*. Sage.

Congressional Quarterly Almanac. 1980. *96th Congress, Second Session, 1980*, volume 36. Congressional Quarterly Inc.

Conservation, Foundation. 1963. *Implications of Rising Carbon Dioxide Content of the Atmosphere*.

Cowling, Ellis B. 1982. Acid precipitation in historical perspective. *Environmental Science & Technology* 16, February: 110A–123A.

Crandall, Robert W., and Lester B. Lave, eds. 1981. *The Scientific Basis of Health and Safety Regulation*. Brookings Institution.

Daemmrich, Arthur. 2004. *Pharmacopolitics: Drug Regulation in the United States and Germany*. University of North Carolina Press.

Dahl, Robert A. 1956. *A Preface to Democratic Theory*. University of Chicago Press.

DeGregorio, Christine. 1992. Leadership approaches in congressional committee hearings. *Western Political Quarterly* 45, December: 971–983.

deLeon, Peter. 1999. The stages approach to the policy process. In *Theories of the Policy Process*, ed. P. Sabatier. Westview.

Demerrit, David. 1999. Global climate change and the cultural politics of science. Paper presented at Berkeley Workshop on Environmental Politics.

DePalma, Anthony. 2005. Nine states in plan to cut emissions by power plants. *New York Times*, August 24.

Diermeier, Daniel, and Timothy J. Feddersen. 2000. Information and congressional hearings. *American Journal of Political Science* 44, January: 51–65.

D'Itri, Frank M., ed. 1982. *Acid Precipitation Effects on Ecological Systems*. Ann Arbor Science Publishers.

Downs, Anthony. 1972. Up and down with ecology: The issue attention cycle. *The Public Interest* 28: 38–50.

Eckstein, Harry. 1975. Case study and theory in political science. In *Handbook of Political Science*, volume 7, ed. F. Greenstein and N. Polsby. Addison-Wesley.

Epstein, Steven. 1996. *Impure Science: AIDS, Activism, and the Politics of Knowledge*. University of California Press.

Epstein, Steven. 2000. Democracy, expertise, and AIDS treatment activism. In *Science, Technology, and Democracy*, ed. D. Kleinman. State University of New York Press.

Esterling, Kevin M. 2004. *The Political Economy of Expertise: Information and Efficiency in American National Politics*. University of Michigan Press.

Etheridge, Elizabeth W. 1992. *Sentinel for Health: A History of the Centers for Disease Control*. University of California Press.

Evelyn, J. 1661. *Fumifugium*. Bedel and Collins.

Ezrahi, Yaron. 1980. Utopian and pragmatic rationalism: The political context of scientific advice. *Minerva* 18, spring: 111–131.

Ezrahi, Yaron. 1990. *The Descent of Icarus: Science and the Transformation of Contemporary Democracy*. Harvard University Press.

Farnsworth, Clyde H. 1970. Norse seek curb on acid rainfall. *New York Times*, November 27.

Fenno, Richard F., Jr. 1966. *The Power of the Purse: Appropriations Politics in Congress*. Little, Brown.

Fenno, Richard F., Jr. 1973. *Congressmen in Committees*. Little, Brown.

Fenno, Richard F., Jr. 1978. *Home Style: House Members in Their Districts*. Little, Brown.

Fiorina, Morris P. 1989. *Congress: Keystone of the Washington Establishment*. Yale University Press.

Fischer, Frank, and John Forester. 1993. *The Argumentative Turn in Policy Analysis and Planning*. Duke University Press.

Fleagle, Robert G. 1994. *The Global Environmental Change: Interactions of Science, Policy, and Politics in the United States*. Praeger.

Fritschler, A. Lee, and James M. Hoefler. 1996. *Smoking and Politics: Policy Making and the Federal Bureaucracy*, fifth edition. Prentice-Hall.

Fujimura, Joan. 1988. The molecular biological bandwagon in cancer research: Where social worlds meet. *Social Problems* 35: 261–283.

Fujimura, Joan. 1992. Crafting science: Standardized packages, boundary objects and "translation." In *Science as Practice and Culture*, ed. A. Pickering. University of Chicago Press.

Fujimura, Joan, and Danny Chou. 1994. Dissent in science: styles of scientific practice and the controversy over the cause of AIDS. *Social Science & Medicine* 38, April 15: 1017–1036.

Galloway, James, et al. 1978. A National Program for Assessing the Problem of Atmospheric Deposition (Acid Rain). National Atmospheric Deposition Program. National Resource Ecology Laboratory, Fort Collins, Colorado.

Gieryn, Thomas F. 1983. Boundary work and the demarcation of science from non-science: Strains and interests in professional ideologies of scientists. *American Sociological Review* 48, December: 781–795.

Gieryn, Thomas F. 1995. Boundaries of science. In *Handbook of Science and Technology Studies*, ed S. Jasanoff et al. Sage.

Gieryn, Thomas F. 1999. *Cultural Boundaries of Science*. University of Chicago Press.

Gilpin, Robert. 1962. *American Scientists and Nuclear Weapons Policy*. Princeton University Press.

Gilpin, Robert, and Christopher Wright, eds. 1964. *Scientists and National Policy-Making*. Columbia University Press.

Goldenberg, Stanley B., et al. 2001. The recent increase in Atlantic hurricane activity: Causes and implications. *Science* 293, July: 474–479.

Gordon, A. J., and Eville Gorham. 1963. Ecological aspects of air pollution from an iron-sintering plant at Wawa, Ontario. *Canadian Journal of Botany* 41: 1063–1078.

Gorham, Eville. 1981. Scientific understanding of atmosphere-biosphere interactions: A historical overview. In *Atmosphere-Biosphere Interactions: Toward a Better Understanding of the Ecological Consequences of Fossil Fuel Combustion*. National Academy Press.

Gould, Roy R. 1983. Midwestern contributions to acid rain. *New York Times*, August 9.

Gould, Roy. 1985. *Going Sour: Science and the Politics of Acid Rain*. Birkhauser.

Greenberg, Daniel. 1967. *The Politics of Pure Science*. New American Library.

Greenwood, Ted. 1984. *Knowledge and Discretion in Government Regulation*. Praeger.

Grobstein, Clifford. 1981. Saccharin: A scientist's view. In *The Scientific Basis of Health and Safety Regulation*, ed. R. Crandall and L. Lave. Brookings Institution.

Grundmann, Reiner. 2006. Ozone and climate: Scientific consensus and leadership. *Science, Technology, and Human Values* 31, January: 73–101.

Gulick, Luther, and L. Urwick, eds. 1937. *Papers on the Science of Administration*. Institute of Public Administration.

Guston, David. 1999. Stabilizing the boundary between U.S. politics and science: The role of the Office of Technology Transfer as a boundary organization. *Social Studies of Science* 29, no. 1: 87–111.

Guston, David. 2000. *Between Politics and Science: Assuring the Integrity and Productivity of Research*. Cambridge University Press.

Haas, Peter. 1990. *Saving the Mediterranean: The Politics of International Environmental Cooperation*. Columbia University Press.

Haas, Peter. 1992. Banning chlorofluorocarbons: Epistemic community efforts to protect stratospheric ozone. *International Organization* 46, winter: 187–224.

Hajer, Maarten A. 1993. Discourse coalitions and the institutionalization of practice: The case of acid rain in Great Britain. In *The Argumentative Turn in Policy Analysis and Planning*, ed. F. Fischer and J. Forester. Duke University Press.

Hajer, Maarten A. 1995. *The Politics of Environmental Discourse: Ecological Modernization and the Policy Process*. Clarendon.

Hakim, Danny. 2004. California backs plan for big cut in car emissions. *New York Times*, September 24.

Hall, Richard L., and Bernard Grofman. 1990. The committee assignment process and the conditional nature of committee bias. *American Political Science Review* 84: 1149–1166.

Hamburg, Stephen P., et al. 1999. *Common Questions About Climate Change*. United Nations Environment Programme and World Meteorological Organization.

Hansen, James, et al. 2000. Global warming in the twenty first century: An alternative scenario. *Proceedings of the National Academy of Sciences 97*, no. 18: 9875–9880.

Hart, David. 1992. Strategies of Research Policy Advocacy: Anthropogenic Climatic Change Research, 1957–1974. Working Paper 92-08, Center for Science and International Affairs, John F. Kennedy School of Government, Harvard University.

HCA (House Committee on Agriculture). 1986. *Effects of Acid Deposition and Air Pollutants on Forest Productivity: Hearing before the Subcommittee on Forests, Family Farms, and Energy of the House Committee on Agriculture*. 99th Congress, 2nd Session. Government Printing Office.

HCA. 1987. *Forest Ecosystems and Atmospheric Pollution Research Act of 1987: Hearing before the Subcommittee on Forests, Family Farms, and Energy of the House Committee on Agriculture*. 100th Congress, 1st Session. Government Printing Office.

HCoA (House Committee on Appropriations). 1956. *Second Supplemental Appropriation Bill, 1956. Hearings before the House Committee on Appropriations*. 84th Congress, Second Session. Government Printing Office.

HCoA. 1957. *National Science Foundation. Report on International Geophysical Year. Hearings before the House Committee on Appropriations*. 85th Congress, First Session. Government Printing Office.

HCoA. 1958. *National Science Foundation. Review of the First Eleven Months of the International Geophysical Year. Hearings before the House Committee on Appropriations*. 85th Congress, Second Session. Government Printing Office.

HCoA. 1959. *National Science Foundation; National Academy of Sciences. Report on the International Geophysical Year (February 1959). Hearings before the House Committee on Appropriations*. 86th Congress, First Session. Government Printing Office.

HCBFUA (House Committee on Banking, Finance, and Urban Affairs). 1990. *Impact of Proposed Clean Air Act Legislation on Energy Security and Economic Stability. Hearings before the House Committee on Banking, Finance, and Urban Affairs.* 101st Congress, 2nd Session. Government Printing Office.

HCEC (House Committee on Energy and Commerce). 1981a. *Acid Precipitation (Part 1): Hearings before the Subcommittee on Heath and the Environment of the House Committee on Energy and Commerce.* 97th Congress, 1st Session. Government Printing Office.

HCEC. 1981b. *Acid Precipitation (Part 2): Hearings before the Subcommittee on Heath and the Environment of the House Committee on Energy and Commerce.* 97th Congress, 1st Session. Government Printing Office.

HCEC. 1983. *Future of Coal: Hearings before the Subcommittee on Fossil and Synthetic Fuels of the House Committee on Energy and Commerce.* 98th Congress, 1st Session. Government Printing Office.

HCEC. 1984. *Clean Air Act Reauthorization (Part 1): Hearings before the House Committee on Energy and Commerce.* 98th Congress, 2nd Session. Government Printing Office.

HCEC. 1986. *Acid Deposition Control Act of 1986 (Part 2): Hearings before the House Committee on Energy and Commerce.* 99th Congress, 2nd Session. Government Printing Office.

HCEC. 1987. *Acid Deposition Control Act of 1987: Hearings before the House Committee on Energy and Commerce.* 100th Congress, 1st Session. Government Printing Office.

HCEC. 1988a. Acid Rain Oversight: *Hearings before the Subcommittee on Heath and the Environment of the House Committee on Energy and Commerce.* 100th Congress, 2nd Session. Government Printing Office.

HCEC. 1988b. *Energy Policy Implications of Global Warming: Hearings before the Subcommittee on Heath and the Environment of the House Committee on Energy and Commerce.* 100th Congress, 2nd Session. Government Printing Office.

HCEC. 1993. Global Warming (Part 1). Hearings before the Subcommittee on Energy and Power. 103rd Congress, 1st Session. Government Printing Office.

HCFA (House Committee on Foreign Affairs). 1981. *United States-Canadian Relations and Acid Rain: Hearing before the Subcommittee on Human Rights and International Organizations and on Inter-American Affairs of the House Committee on Foreign Affairs.* 97th Congress, 1st Session. Government Printing Office.

HCGR (House Committee on Government Reform). 1998a. *Kyoto Protocol: Is the Clinton-Gore Administration Selling Out Americans? Parts I-VI: Hearings before the Subcommittee on National Economic Growth, Natural Resources, and Regulatory Affairs.* 105th Congress, 2nd Session. Government Printing Office.

HCGR. 1998b. *Will the Administration Implement the Kyoto Protocol through the Back Door? Hearing before the Subcommittee on National Economic Growth, Natural Resources, and Regulatory Affairs of the House Committee on Government Reform and Oversight.* 105th Congress, 2nd Session. Government Printing Office.

HCGR. 1999. *Is CO_2 a Pollutant and Does EPA Have the Power To Regulate It. Joint Hearings before the Subcommittee on National Economic Growth, Natural Resources, and Regulatory Affairs of the House Committee on Government Reform and the Subcommittee on Energy and Environment of the House Committee on Science.* 106th Congress, 1st Session. Government Printing Office.

HCIFC (House Committee on Interstate and Foreign Commerce). 1958. *International Geophysical Year. Hearing before the House Committee on Interstate and Foreign Commerce.* 85th Congress, 2nd Session. Government Printing Office.

HCIFC. 1980. *Acid Rain: Hearing before the Subcommittee on Oversight and Investigations of the House Committee on Interstate and Foreign Commerce.* 96th Congress, 2nd Session. Government Printing Office.

HCIIA (House Committee on Interior and Insular Affairs). 1984. *Effects of Air Pollution and Acid Rain on Forest Decline: Hearing Before the Subcommittee on Mining, Forest Management, and Bonneville Power Administration of the House Committee on Interior and Insular Affairs.* 98th Congress, 2nd Session. Government Printing Office.

HCMMF (House Committee on Merchant Marine and Fisheries). 1989. *Global Climate Change: Hearing before the Subcommittee on Oceanography and the Great Lakes of the House Committee on Merchant Marine and Fisheries.* 101st Congress, 1st Session. Government Printing Office.

HCR (House Committee on Resources). 2003. *Kyoto Global Warming Treaty's Impact on Ohio's Coal-Dependent Communities.* 108th Congress, 1st Session. Government Printing Office.

HCS (House Committee on Science). 1995a. *Scientific Integrity and the Public Trust: The Science Behind Federal Policies and Mandates: Case Study 1—Stratospheric Ozone: Myths and Realities: Hearings before the Subcommittee on Energy and Environment of the House Committee on Science.* 104th Congress, 1st Session. Government Printing Office.

HCS. 1995b. *Scientific Integrity and the Public Trust: The Science behind Federal Policies and Mandates: Case Study 2—Climate Models and Projections of Potential Impacts of Global Climate Change: Hearings before the Subcommittee on Energy and Environment of the House Committee on Science.* 104th Congress, 1st Session. Government Printing Office.

HCS. 1995c. *Scientific Integrity and the Public Trust: The Science Behind Federal Policies and Mandates: Case Study 3—EPA's Dioxin Risk Assessment: Hearings before the Subcommittee on Energy and Environment of the House*

Committee on Science. 104th Congress, 1st Session. Government Printing Office.

HCS. 1996. *U.S. Global Change Research Programs: Data Collection and Scientific Priorities. Hearings before the House Committee on Science.* 104th Congress, 2nd Session. Government Printing Office.

HCS. 1997. *Countdown to Kyoto, Parts I-III, Vol. I. Hearings before the Subcommittee on Energy and Environment of the House Committee on Science. 105th Congress, 1st Session.* Government Printing Office.

HCSB (House Committee on Small Business). 1989. *Effects of Proposed Acid Rain Legislation on Workers and Small Business in the High-Sulfur Coal Industry. Hearings before the House Committee on Small Business.* 101st Congress, 1st Session. Government Printing Office.

HCSB. 1998a. *Oversight Hearing on the Kyoto Protocol: The Undermining of American Prosperity: Hearings before the House Committee on Small Business.* 105th Congress, 2nd Session. Government Printing Office.

HCSB. 1998b. *Kyoto Protocol: The Undermining of American Prosperity—The Science: Hearings before the House Committee on Small Business.* 105th Congress, Second Session. Government Printing Office.

HCSB. 1999. *Effect of the Kyoto Protocol on American Small Business: Hearings before the House Committee on Small Business.* 106th Congress, First Session. Government Printing Office.

HCSST (House Committee on Science, Space and Technology). 1975a. *Research and Development Related to Sulphates in the Atmosphere: Hearings before the Subcommittee on the Environment and the Atmosphere of the House Committee on Science, Space, and Technology.* 94th Congress, 1st Session. Government Printing Office.

HCSST. 1975b. *Costs and Effects of Chronic Exposure to Low-Level Pollutants in the Environment: Hearings before the Subcommittee on Environment and the Atmosphere of the House Committee on Science, Space, and Technology.* 94th Congress, 1st Session. Government Printing Office.

HCSST. 1976. *The National Climate Program Act: Hearings before the Subcommittee on the Environment and the Atmosphere of the House Committee on Science, Space, and Technology.* 94th Congress, 2nd Session. Government Printing Office.

HCSST. 1977. *National Climate Program: Hearings before the Subcommittee on the Environment and the Atmosphere of the House Committee on Science, Space, and Technology.* 95th Congress, 1st Session. Government Printing Office.

HCSST. 1979. *Implementation of the Climate Act: Hearings before the Subcommittee on Natural Resources and Environment of the House Committee on Science, Space, and Technology.* 96th Congress, 1st Session. Government Printing Office.

HCSST. 1980. *Authorization for the Office of Research and Development, Environmental Protection Agency. Hearings before the House Committee on Science, Space, and Technology.* 96th Congress, 2nd Session. Government Printing Office.

HCSST. 1981. *Acid Rain: Hearings before the Subcommittee on Natural Resources, Agriculture Research and Environment of the House Committee on Space, Science, and Technology.* 97th Congress, 1st Session. Government Printing Office.

HCSST. 1983. *Acid Rain: Implications for Fossil Fuel R&D: Hearings before the Subcommittee on Energy Development and Applications and the Subcommittee on Natural Resources, Agriculture Research, and Environment of the House Committee on Science, Space, and Technology.* 98th Congress, 1st Session. U.S. Government Printing Office.

HCSST. 1985. *Acid Rain Research: Hearing before the Subcommittee on Natural Resources, Agricultural Research and Environment of the House Committee on Science, Space, and Technology.*

HCSST. 1988. *National Acid Precipitation Assessment Program: Hearing before the Subcommittee on Natural Resources, Agriculture Research and Environment of the House Committee on Science, Space and Technology.* 100th Congress, 2nd Session. Government Printing Office.

HCSST. 1989. *Air Pollution Research and Development Needs: Hearing before the Subcommittee on Natural Resources, Agriculture Research and Environment of the House Committee on Science, Space and Technology.* 101st Congress, 1st Session. Government Printing Office.

HCSST. 1992. *U.S. Global Change Research Program. Hearing before the Subcommittee on Environment of the House Committee on Science, Space and Technology.* 102nd Congress, 2nd Session. Government Printing Office.

HCSST. 1993. *Global Change Research Program: Key Scientific Uncertainties. Hearing before the Subcommittee on Space.* 103rd Congress, 1st Session. Government Printing Office.

HCST (House Committee on Science and Technology). 2007a. *State of Climate Change Science 2007: The Findings of the Fourth Assessment Report by the Intergovernmental Panel on Climate Change (IPCC), Working Group I Report. Hearings before the House Committee on Science and Technology.* 110th Congress, 1st Session. Government Printing Office.

HCST. 2007b. *State of Climate Change Science 2007: The Findings of the Fourth Assessment Report by the Intergovernmental Panel on Climate Change (IPCC), Working Group III: Mitigation of Climate Change. Hearings before the House Committee on Science and Technology.* 110th Congress, 1st Session. Government Printing Office.

Heclo, Hugh. 1978. Issue networks and the executive establishment. In *The New American Political System*, ed. A. King. American Enterprise Institute.

Herrick, Charles, ed. 1987. *NAPAP Interim Assessment: The Causes and Effects of Acidic Deposition*, volume II: *Emissions and Controls*. National Acid Precipitation Assessment Program, Office of the Director of Research.

Herrick, Charles. 2000. Predictive modeling of acid rain: Obstacles to generating useful information. In *Prediction: Science, Decision Making and the Future of Nature*, ed. D. Sarewitz et al. Island.

Hess, David J. 1997. *Science Studies: An Advanced Introduction*. New York University Press.

Hilgartner, Stephen. 2000. *Science on Stage: Expert Advice as Public Drama*. Stanford University Press.

Hill, Gladwin. 1979. Acid rain—no one really knows yet how bad it really is. *New York Times*, August 12.

Hird, John A. 2005. *Power, Knowledge, and Politics: Policy Analysis in the States*. Georgetown University Press.

Houghton, J. T., B. A. Callander, and S. K. Varney, eds. 1992. *Climate Change 1992: The Supplementary Report to the IPCC Scientific Assessment*. Cambridge University Press.

Houghton, J. T., G. J. Jenkins, and J. J. Ephraums, eds. 1990. *Climate Change: The IPCC Scientific Assessment*. Cambridge University Press.

Houghton, J. T., et al., eds. 1996. *Climate Change 1995: The Science of Climate Change*. Cambridge University Press.

Houghton, J. T., et al., eds. 2001. *Climate Change 2001: The Scientific Basis*. Cambridge University Press.

HSCA (House Select Committee on Aging). 1983. *Alzheimer's Disease: Is There an Acid Rain Connection? Hearing before the Subcommittee on Human Services of the House Select Committee on Aging*. 98th Congress, 1st Session. Government Printing Office.

Huitt, Ralph K. 1954. The congressional committee: A case study. *American Political Science Review* 48: 340–365.

ICSU, UNEP, and WMO (International Council for Science, United Nations Environment Program, and World Meteorological Organization). 1986. *Report of the International Conference on the Assessment of the Role of Carbon Dioxide and Other Greenhouse Gases in Climate Variations and Assorted Impacts*. WMO Document No. 661.

IPCC (Intergovernmental Panel on Climate Change). 2007. *Climate Change 2007. The Physical Science Basi*s, ed. S. Solomon et al. Cambridge University Press.

Irwin, Alan, Henry Rothstein, Steven Yearly, and Elaine McCarthy. 1997. Regulatory science—Towards a sociological framework. *Futures* 29, no. 1: 17–31.

Jasanoff, Sheila. 1990. *The Fifth Branch: Science Advisors as Policy Makers*. Harvard University Press.

Jasanoff, Sheila. 1993. Skinning scientific cats. *New Statesman & Society* 26, February: 29–30.

Jasanoff, Sheila. 2004a. Ordering knowledge, ordering society. In Jasanoff, *States of Knowledge: The Co-Production of Science and Social Order.* Routledge.

Jasanoff, Sheila. 2004b. Heaven and Earth. In *Earthly Politics: Local and Global in Environmental Governance,* ed. S. Jasanoff and M. Long Martello. MIT Press.

Jasanoff, Sheila. 2005a. *Designs on Nature: Science and Democracy in Europe and the United States.* Princeton University Press.

Jasanoff, Sheila. 2005b. Judgment under siege: The three-body problem of expert legitimacy. In *Democratization of Expertise? Exploring Novel Forms of Scientific Advice in Political Decision-Making,* ed. S. Maasen and P. Weingart. Springer.

Jasanoff, Sheila, and Brian Wynne. 1998. Science and decisionmaking. In *Human Choice and Climate Change,* volume I: *The Societal Framework,* ed. S. Rayner and E. Malone. Battelle Press.

JEC (Joint Economic Committee of U.S. Congress). 1997. *Tradable Emissions. Hearings before the Joint Economic Committee.* S. Hrg. 105–167.

Jenkins-Smith, Hank. 1990. *Democratic Politics and Policy Analysis.* Brooks/Cole.

Jones, Charles O. 1976. Why Can't Congress Do Policy Analysis (or words to that effect). *Policy Analysis* 2, spring: 251–264.

Kagan, Robert. 2001. *Adversarial Legalism: The American Way of Law.* Harvard University Press.

Keeling, Charles D. 1960. The concentration of isotopic abundances of carbon dioxide in the atmosphere. *Tellus* 12: 200–203.

Keller, Ann. 2002. Risky business: Government-sponsored research and the search for policy-relevant science. Presented at annual meeting of Ecological Society of America, Tucson.

Kingdon, John W. 1984. *Agendas, Alternatives, and Public Policies* (second edition: Little, Brown, 1996).

Klein, Gary A., et al., eds. 1995. *Decision Making in Action.* Ablex.

Kleinman, Daniel, ed. 2000. *Science, Technology, and Democracy.* State University of New York Press.

Knott, John W., and Gary J. Miller. 1987. *Reforming Bureaucracy: The Politics of Institutional Choice.* Prentice-Hall.

Knutson, Thomas R., Robert E. Tuleya, and Yoshio Kurihara. 1998. Simulated increase of hurricane intensities in a CO_2-warmed climate. *Science* 279, February: 1018–1021.

Krehbiel, Keith. 1991. *Information and Legislative Organization.* University of Michigan Press.

Krimsky, Sheldon. 2000. *Hormonal Chaos: Scientific and Social Origins of the Environmental Endocrine Hypothesis.* Johns Hopkins University Press.

Kuhn, Thomas S. 1970. *The Structure of Scientific Revolutions,* second edition, enlarged. University of Chicago Press.

Lambright, W. Henry. 1997. The rise and fall of interagency cooperation: The U.S. Global Change Research Program. *Public Administration Review* 57, January-February: 36–44.

Landy, Marc K., Marc J. Roberts, and Stephen R. Thomas. 1994. *The Environmental Protection Agency: Asking the Wrong Questions from Nixon to Clinton.* Oxford University Press.

LaPorte, Todd, and Ann Keller. 1996. Assuring institutional constancy: Requisite for managing long-lived hazards. *Public Administration Review* 56, November-December: 535–544.

Lasswell, Harold D. 1956. *The Decision Process: Seven Categories of Functional Analysis.* University of Maryland Press.

Latour, Bruno. 1983. Give me a laboratory and I will raise the world. In *Science Observed: Perspectives on the Social Study of Science,* ed. K. Knorr Cetina and M. Mulkay. Sage.

Latour, Bruno. 1987. *Science in Action: How to Follow Scientists and Engineers through Society.* Harvard University Press.

Latour, Bruno. 1988. *The Pasteurization of France.* Harvard University Press.

Latour, Bruno. 1990. Drawing things together. In *Representation in Scientific Practice,* ed. M. Lynch and S. Woolgar. MIT Press.

Latour, Bruno. 1999a. *Politiques de la Nature: Comment Faire Entrer les Sciences en Démocratie.* Editions la Découverte.

Latour, Bruno. 1999b. *Pandora's Hope: Essays on the Reality of Science Studies.* Harvard University Press.

Latour, Bruno. 2000. The End of Nature as a Way to Organize our Polity. Avenali Lecture, Townsend Center for the Humanities, University of California, Berkeley.

Latour, Bruno, and Steve Woolgar. 1979. *Laboratory Life: The Social Construction of Scientific Facts.* Sage.

Law, John. 1987. Technology, closure and heterogeneous engineering: The case of the Portuguese expansion. In *The Social Construction of Technological Systems,* ed. W. Bijker et al. MIT Press.

Leonhardt, David. 1996. Thalidomide: It's back. *Business Week* no. 3472, April 22: 46.

Leyden, Kevin M. 1995. Interest group resources and testimony and congressional hearings. *Legislative Studies Quarterly* 20: 431–440.

Light, Paul. 1995. *Still Artful Work: The Continuing Politics of Social Security Reform, Second Edition*. McGraw-Hill.

Likens, Gene E., F. H. Bormann, and N. M. Johnson. 1972. Acid rain. *Environment* 14, no. 2: 33–40.

Lindblom, Charles E. 1959. The "science" of muddling through. *Public Administration Review* 19, spring: 79–88.

Lindblom, Charles E. 1979. Still muddling, not yet through. *Public Administration Review* 39, November-December: 517–526.

Litfin, Karen T. 1994. *Ozone Discourses: Science and Politics in Global Environmental Cooperation*. Columbia University Press.

Lock, Stephen. 1985. *A Difficult Balance: Editorial Peer Review in Medicine*. Nuffield Provisional Hospitals Trust.

Londregan, John, and James M. Snyder Jr. 1994. Comparing committee and floor preferences. *Legislative Studies Quarterly* 19: 233–267.

Lowi, Theodore J. 1964. American business, public policy, case studies, and political theory. *World Politics* 16, July: 677–715.

Lowi, Theodore J. 1972. Four systems of policy, politics, and choice. *Public Administration Review* 32, July-August: 298–310.

Mahoney, Michael J. 1977. Publication prejudices: An experimental study of confirmatory bias in the peer review system. *Cognitive Therapy and Research* 1: 161–175.

Majone, Giandomenico. 1989. *Evidence, Argument, and Persuasion in the Policy Process*. Yale University Press.

March, James G., and Herbert A. Simon. 1958. *Organizations*. Wiley.

Marshall, Jeanmarie. 1994. *Breast Cancer Action Newsletter* no. 24, June.

Martin, Mark. 2006. State's war on warming: Governor signs measure to cap greenhouse gas emissions. *San Francisco Chronicle*, September 28.

May, Clifford D. 1982. As snow clogs Denver, daffodils stir on L.I. *New York Times*, December 27.

Mayhew, David R. 1974. *Congress: The Electoral Connection*. Yale University Press.

Mazur, Allan. 1973. Disputes between experts. *Minerva* 11: 243–262.

Mazur, Allan. 1981. *The Dynamics of Technical Controversy*. Communications Press.

McFadyen, Richard E. 1976. Thalidomide in America: A brush with tragedy. *Clio Medica* 11: 79–93.

Melnick, R. Shep. 1983. *Regulation and the Courts: The Case of the Clean Air Act*. Brookings Institution.

Merton, Robert K. 1942. The normative structure of science. In *The Sociology of Science*, ed. N. Storer. University of Chicago Press.

Merton, Robert K. 1968. The Matthew Effect in science. *Science* 159: 56–63.

Merton, Robert K. 1973. *The Sociology of Science: Theoretical and Empirical Investigations.* University of Chicago Press.

Meyer, John W., and Brian Rowan. 1991. Institutionalized organizations: Formal structure as myth and ceremony. In *The New Institutionalism in Organizational Analysis*, ed. W. Powell and P. Dimaggio. University of Chicago Press.

Miller, Clark. 2000. The dynamics of framing environmental values and policy: Four models of societal processes. *Environmental Values* 9, May: 211–233.

Miller, Clark. 2001. Scientific internationalism in American foreign policy: The case of meteorology. In *Changing the Atmosphere: Expert Knowledge and Environmental Governance*, ed. C. Miller and P. Edwards. MIT Press.

Miller, Clark. 2004a. Climate science and global political order. In *States of Knowledge: The Co-Production of Science and Social Order*, ed. S. Jasanoff. Routledge.

Miller, Clark. 2004b. Resisting empire: Globalism, relocalization, and the politics of knowledge. In *Earthly Politics: Local and Global in Environmental Governance*, ed. S. Jasanoff and M. Long Martello. MIT Press.

Miller, Clark, and Paul N. Edwards. 2001. Introduction: The globalization of climate science and climate politics. In *Changing the Atmosphere: Expert Knowledge and Environmental Governance*, ed. Miller and Edwards. MIT Press.

Moe, Terry M. 1989. The politics of bureaucratic structure. In *Can the Government Govern?* ed. J. Chubb and P. Peterson. Brookings Institution.

Mohnen, Volker A. 1983. Defects in legislation on acid rain. *New York Times*, July 29.

Molina, M. J., and F. S. Rowland. 1974. Stratospheric sink for chlorofluoromethanes-chlorine atom catalyzed destruction of ozone. *Nature* 249: 810–812.

Monton, Don. 1998. Dispelling the myths of the acid rain story, part 2. *Environment* 40, July: 4–15.

Moore, Kelly. 1996. Organizing integrity: American science and the creation of public interest organizations, 1955–1975. *American Journal of Sociology* 101, May: 1592–1627.

Moore, Mike. 1995. Midnight never came: How the clock on the cover of the *Bulletin of the Atomic Scientists* represented nuclear tensions. *Bulletin of the Atomic Scientists* 51, no. 6: 16–35.

Morrissey, Wayne A. 1998. Global Climate Change: A Concise History of Negotiations and Chronology of Major Activities Preceding the 1992 U.N. Framework Convention. CRS Report 98-431.

Morrissey, Wayne A. 1999. Global climate change: Congressional concern about "back door" implementation of the 1997 U.N. Kyoto Protocol. Congressional Research Service Report for Congress 98-664. Government Printing Office.

Murphy, Kim. 2004. Russia takes first steps toward joining Kyoto Treaty. *Los Angeles Times*, September 24.

Mydans, Seth, and Andrew C. Revkin. 2004. With Russia's nod, treaty on emissions clears last hurdle. *New York Times*, September 30.

Nakamura. Robert T. 1975. *Information and the Policy Process: Experts and Decision-makers in California School Tax Legislation*. University of California, Berkeley.

NAPAP (National Acid Precipitation Assessment Program). 1987. *NAPAP Interim Assessment: The Causes and Effects of Acidic Deposition, Volume I, Executive Summary*. Government Printing Office.

NAPAP. 1990. *Annual Report, 1989 and Findings Update*.

NAPAP. 1991. The U.S. National Acid Precipitation Assessment Program: 1990 Integrated Assessment Report.

NAPAP. 1998. *NAPAP Biennial Report to Congress: An Integrated Assessment*.

NAST (National Assessment Synthesis Team). 2000. *Climate Change Impacts on the United States: The Potential Consequences of Climate Variability and Change*. U.S. Global Change Research Program.

National Academy of Science. 1992. *Policy Implications of Greenhouse Warming: Mitigation, Adaptation, and the Science Base*. National Academy Press.

National Academy of Science. 2005. *International Geophysical Year*. Available at http://www.nas.edu.

National Environmental Policy Institute. 1998. *Enhancing Science in the Regulatory Process: A Guide for Congress, Federal Agencies, and Others Interested in Improving the Use of Scientific Knowledge in Public Policy Decisions*.

NRC (National Research Council). 1966. *Weather and Climate Modification Problems And Prospects: Final Report of the Panel on Weather and Climate Modification*. National Academy Press.

NRC. 1976. *Climate and Food: Climatic Fluctuation and U.S. Agricultural Production*. National Academy Press.

NRC. 1977a. *Climate, Climatic Change, and Water Supply*. National Academy Press.

NRC. 1977b. *Energy and Climate*. National Academic of Sciences.

NRC. 1981. *Atmosphere-Biosphere Interactions: Toward a Better Understanding of the Ecological Consequences of Fossil Fuel Combustion*. National Academy Press.

NRC. 1983a. *Acid Deposition: Atmospheric Processes in Eastern North America: A Review of Current Scientific Understanding*. National Academy Press.

NRC. 1983b. *Risk Assessment in the Federal Government: Managing the Process*. National Academy Press.

NRC. 1994. *Science and Judgment in Risk Assessment*. National Academy Press.

NRC. 1996. *Understanding Risk*. National Academy Press.

Nelkin, Dorothy, ed. 1979. *Controversy: Politics of Technical Decisions*. Sage.

New York Times. 1951. Is the climate changing? July 22.

New York Times. 1985. Action is urged to avert global climate shift. December 11.

New York Times. 1995. Global warming heats up. September 18.

North, Douglass C. 1990. *Institutions, Institutional Change and Economic Performance*. Cambridge University Press.

North Carolina State University Acid Deposition Program for National Acid Precipitation Assessment Program. 1983. *International Directory of Acid Deposition Researchers, 1983 Edition*. Acid Rain Foundation.

North Carolina State University Acid Deposition Program for National Acid Precipitation Assessment Program. 1986. *International Directory of Acid Deposition Researchers, 1985–86 Edition*. Acid Rain Foundation.

O'Connor, Karen, and Lee Epstein. 1983. Beyond legislative lobbying: Women's rights groups and the Supreme Court. *Judicature*, September: 134–145.

Odén, Svante. 1964. Aspects of the Atmosphere Corrosion Climate. In *Current Corrosion Research in Scandinavia: Lectures Held at the Fourth Scandinavian Corrosion Congress*, ed. J. Larinkari.

Odén, Svante. 1967. *Dagens Nyheter*, Stockholm, October 24.

Odén, Svante, 1968. The Acidification of Air and Precipitation and Its Consequences in the Natural Environment. Ecology Community Bulletin no. 1, National Science Research Council, Stockholm.

Odén, Svante. 1976. The acidity problem: An outline of concepts. In *Proceedings of the First International Symposium on Acid Precipitation and the Forest Ecosystem*, General Technical Report NE-23, USDA Forest Service.

Odén, Svante. 1980. On experiences with acid rain in Europe. Testimony before the House Subcommittee on Oversight and Investigation, February 26, 96th Congress, second session.

Oleszek, Walter J. 1989. *Congressional Procedures and the Policy Process*. CQ Press.

Oppenheimer, Michael. 1995. Global warming, unfortunately, is all too real. *New York Times*, September 26.

Osborne, James. 2003. Italy offers Russia Kyoto carrots. Moscowtimes.com, December 8.

Osterlund, Peter. 1985. Taking a new look at how Earth works. *Christian Science Monitor*, January 8.

Parson, Edward A. 2003. *Protecting the Ozone Layer: Science and Strategy.* Oxford University Press.

Parthasarathy, Shobita. 2004. Regulating risk: Defining genetic privacy in the United States and Britain. *Science, Technology, & Human Values* 29, summer: 332–352.

Passell, Peter. 1989. Sale of air pollution permits is part of Bush acid-rain plan. *New York Times*, May 17.

Paterson, Matthew. 1996. Neorealism, neoinstitutionalism and the Climate Change Convention. In *The Environment and International Relations*, ed. J. Vogler and M. Imber. Routledge.

Paulson, William. 1994. Chance, complexity and narrative explanation. *SubStance* 74: 5–21.

Penick, et al., eds. 1965. *The Politics of American Science: 1939 to the Present.* Rand McNally.

Peters, Douglas P., and Stephen J. Ceci. 1982. Peer review practices of psychological journals: The fate of published articles submitted again. *Behavioral and Brain Sciences* 5: 187–195.

Pianin, Eric. 2003. Senate rejects mandatory cap on greenhouse gas emissions. *Washington Post*, October 31.

Pielke, Roger A. 2000a. Policy history of the US Global Change Research Program: Part I. Administrative development. *Global Environmental Change* 10: 9–25.

Pielke, Roger A. 2000b. Policy history of the US Global Change Research Program: Part II. Legislative process. *Global Environmental Change* 10: 133–144.

Pilkey, Orrin. 1987. Coastal geology: Don't stop the ocean, move the light. *Washington Post*, January 4.

Plass, Gilbert N. 1956. Carbon dioxide and the climate. *American Scientist* 44: 302–316.

Polsby, Nelson W. 1969. *Policy Analysis and Congress.* Institute of Governmental Studies, University of California, Berkeley.

Polsby, Nelson W. 1984. *Political Innovation in America: The Politics of Policy Initiation.* Yale University Press.

Popper, Karl. 1963. *Conjectures and Refutations.* Routledge and Kegan Paul.

Porter, Theodore M. 1995. *Trust in Numbers: The Pursuit of Objectivity in Science and Public Life.* Princeton University Press.

Powell, Mark R. 1999. *Science at EPA: Information in the Regulatory Process.* Resources for the Future.

Pressman, Jeffrey L., and Aaron B. Wildavsky. 1973. *Implementation: How Great Expectations in Washington Are Dashed in Oakland.* University of California Press.

Price, Don K. 1965. *The Scientific Estate*. Belknap.

Primack, Joel, and Frank von Hippel. 1974. *Advice and Dissent: Scientists in the Political Arena*. Basic Books.

Regens, James L. 1993. Acid deposition. In *Keeping Pace with Science and Engineering*, ed. M. Uman. National Academy Press.

Regens, James L., and Robert W. Rycroft. 1988. *The Acid Rain Controversy*. University of Pittsburgh Press.

Reichhardt, Tony. 1995. Earth observation programme "needs tighter coordination." *Nature* 377, no. 6546: 191.

Revelle, Roger, and Hans Suess. 1957. Carbon dioxide exchange between the atmosphere and ocean and the question of an increase of atmospheric CO_2 during the past decade. *Tellus* 9: 18.

Revkin, Andrew C. 2000a. Debate rises over quick(er) climate fix. *New York Times*, October 2.

Revkin, Andrew C. 2000b. A shift in stance on global warming theory. *New York Times*, October 26.

Ricci, David M. 1993. *The Transformation of American Politics: The New Washington and the Rise of Think Tanks*. Yale University Press.

Roberts, Leslie. 1991. Learning from an acid rain program. *Science* 251, March 15: 1302–1305.

Rosaldo, Renato. 1989. *Culture and Truth*. Beacon.

Rubin, Edward S., Lester B. Lave, and Granger Morgan. 1991. Keeping climate research relevant. *Issues in Science and Technology* 8, winter: 47–55.

Salter, Liora. 1988. *Mandated Science: Science and Scientists in the Making of Standards*. Kluwer.

Sarewitz, Daniel. 1996. *Frontiers of Illusion: Science, Technology, and the Politics of Progress*. Temple University Press.

Sarewitz, Daniel, Roger A. Pielke Jr., and Radford Byerly Jr., eds. 2000. Introduction: Death, taxes, and environmental policy. In *Prediction: Science, Decision Making and the Future of Nature*, ed. Sarewitz et al. Island.

Saunders, Craig. 1999. Money to burn: Petroleum companies embrace carbon emissions trading system. *This Magazine*, May–June: 32–37.

SCA (Senate Committee on Appropriations). 1956. *Second Supplemental Appropriation Bill, 1956. Hearings before the Senate Committee on Appropriations*. 84th Congress, Second Session. Government Printing Office.

SCANF (Senate Committee on Agriculture, Nutrition and Forestry). 1973. *U.S. and World Food Situation: Hearing before the Senate Committee on Agriculture, Nutrition and Forestry*. 93rd Congress, 1st Session. Government Printing Office.

SCANF. 1989. *Global Climate Change Prevention Act of 1989—S. 1610: Hearing before the Senate Committee on Agriculture, Nutrition and Forestry*. 101st Congress, 1st Session. Government Printing Office.

SCASS (Senate Committee on Aeronautical and Space Sciences). 1975. *Strato-spheric Ozone Depletion, Part 1: Hearings before the Subcommittee on the Upper Atmosphere of the Senate Committee on Aeronautical and Space Sciences.* 94th Congress, 1st Session. Government Printing Office.

SCCST (Senate Committee on Commerce, Science and Transportation). 1977. *National Climate Program Act: Hearings before the Subcommittee on Science, Technology, and Space of the Senate Committee on Commerce, Science, and Transportation.* 95th Congress, 1st Session. Government Printing Office.

SCCST. 1987. *Global Environmental Change Research: Hearing before the Subcommittee on Science, Technology and Space and the National Ocean Policy Study of the Senate Committee on Commerce, Science and Transportation.* 100th Congress, 1st Session. Government Printing Office.

SCCST. 1990. *Global Climate Change: Seeking a Global Consensus: Hearing before the Senate Committee on Commerce, Science and Transportation.* 101st Congress, 2nd Session. Government Printing Office.

SCCST. 1991a. *Policy Implications of Greenhouse Warming. Hearings before the Senate Committee on Commerce, Science and Transportation.* 102nd Congress, 1st Session. Government Printing Office.

SCCST. 1991b. Global Change Research: The Role of Clouds in Climate Change. *Hearings before the Senate Committee on Commerce, Science and Transportation.* 102nd Congress, 1st Session. Government Printing Office.

SCCST. 1992. *Global Change Research: Global Warming and the Biosphere: Hearing before the Senate Committee on Commerce, Science and Transportation.* 102nd Congress, 2nd Session. Government Printing Office.

SCCST. 2000a. *Science Behind Global Warming. Hearings before the Senate Committee on Commerce, Science and Transportation.* 106th Congress, 2nd Session. Government Printing Office.

SCCST. 2000b. *Climate Change Impacts to the U.S. Hearings before the Senate Committee on Commerce, Science and Transportation.* 106th Congress, 2nd Session. Government Printing Office.

SCCST. 2000c. *Solutions to Climate Change. Hearings before the Senate Committee on Commerce, Science and Transportation.* 106th Congress, 2nd Session. Government Printing Office.

SCCST. 2001. *Intergovernmental Panel on Climate Change (IPCC) Third Assessment Report. Hearings before the Senate Committee on Commerce, Science and Transportation.* 107th Congress, 1st Session. Government Printing Office.

SCENR (Senate Committee on Energy and Natural Resources). 1980a. *Department of Energy FY81–FY82 Authorization (Civilian Applications): Hearings before the Senate Committee on Energy and Natural Resources.* 96th Congress, 2nd Session. Government Printing Office.

SCENR. 1980b. *Effects of Carbon Dioxide Buildup in the Atmosphere: Hearings before the Senate Committee on Energy and Natural Resources.* 96th Congress, 2nd Session. Government Printing Office.

SCENR. 1980c. *Powerplant Fuels Conservation Act of 1980: Hearings before the Senate Committee on Energy and Natural Resources.* 96th Congress, 2nd Session. Government Printing Office.

SCENR. 1980d. *Effects of Acid Rain, Part 2: Hearings before the Subcommittee on Energy Conservation and Supply of the Senate Committee on Energy and Natural Resources.* 96th Congress, 2nd Session. Government Printing Office.

SCENR. 1982. *Acid Precipitation and the Use of Fossil Fuels: Hearings before the Senate Committee on Energy and Natural Resources.* 97th Congress, 2nd Session. Government Printing Office.

SCENR. 1983. *Enhanced Coal Technology. Hearings before the Senate Committee on Energy and Natural Resources.* 98th Congress, 1st Session. Government Printing Office.

SCENR. 1984. *Implementation of the Acid Precipitation Act of 1980: Hearing before the Senate Committee on Energy and Natural Resources.* 98th Congress, 2nd Session. Government Printing Office.

SCENR. 1988a. *Greenhouse Effect and Global Climate Change, Part 2: Hearings before the Senate Committee on Energy and Natural Resources.* 100th Congress, 2nd Session. Government Printing Office.

SCENR. 1988b. *National Energy Policy Act of 1988 and Global Warming.* 100th Congress, 2nd Session. Government Printing Office.

SCENR. 1992. *Global Climate Change. Hearings before the Senate Committee on Energy and Natural Resources.* 102nd Congress, 2nd Session. Government Printing Office.

SCENR. 1994. *Science Concerning Global Climate Change: Hearing before the Senate Committee on Energy and Natural Resources.* 103rd Congress, 2nd Session. Government Printing Office.

SCENR. 1996. *Global Climate Change: Hearing before the Senate Committee on Energy and Natural Resources.* 104th Congress, 2nd Session. Government Printing Office.

SCENR. 1999. *Global Climate Change: Hearing before the Senate Committee on Energy and Natural Resources.* 106th Congress, 1st Session. Government Printing Office.

SCEP (Study of Critical Environmental Problems). 1970. *Man's Impact on the Global Environment.* MIT Press.

SCEPW (Senate Committee on Environment and Public Works). 1979. *FY 80 Budget Review.* 96th Congress, 1st Session. Government Printing Office.

SCEPW. 1981a. Clean Air Act Oversight (Field Hearings) Part 6. *Hearing before the Senate Committee on Environment and Public Works.* 97th Congress, 1st Session. Government Printing Office.

SCEPW. 1981b. *Acid Rain: Hearing before the Senate Committee on Environment and Public Works.* 97th Congress, 1st Session. Government Printing Office.

SCEPW. 1982. *Acid Rain: A Technical Inquiry: Hearing before the Senate Committee on Environment and Public Works.* 97th Congress, 2nd Session. U.S. Government Printing Office.

SCEPW. 1983a. *Acid Rain, 1983: Hearings before the Senate Committee on Environment and Public Works.* 98th Congress, 1st Session. Government Printing Office.

SCEPW. 1983b. *Environmental Research and Development, Part 2. Hearing before the Senate Committee on Environment and Public Works,* 98th Congress, 1st Session. Government Printing Office.

SCEPW. 1985a. Acid Rain in the West: *Hearing before the Senate Committee on Environment and Public Works.* 99th Congress, 1st Session. Government Printing Office.

SCEPW. 1985b. *Global Warming: Hearing before the Subcommittee on Toxic Substances and Environmental Oversight of the Senate Committee on Environment and Public Works.* 99th Congress, 1st Session. Government Printing Office.

SCEPW. 1986a. *Ozone Depletion, the Greenhouse Effect, and Climate Change: Hearing before the Committee on Environment and Public Works, United States Senate.* 99th Congress, 2nd Session. Government Printing Office.

SCEPW. 1986b. *Acid Deposition and Related Air Pollution Issues: Hearing before the Committee on Environment and Public Works, United States Senate.* 99th Congress, 2nd Session. Government Printing Office.

SCEPW. 1986c. New Clean Air Act: *Hearing before the Committee on Environment and Public Works, United States Senate.* 99th Congress, 2nd Session. Washington: Government Printing Office.

SCEPW. 1986d. *Review of the Federal Government's Research Program on the Causes and Effects of Acid Rain: Hearing before the Committee on Environment and Public Works, United States Senate.* 99th Congress, 2nd Session. Washington: Government Printing Office.

SCEPW. 1987a. *Health Effects of Acid Rain Precursors: Hearing before the Subcommittee on Environmental Protection of the Senate Committee on Environment and Public Works.* 100th Congress, 1st Session. Government Printing Office.

SCEPW. 1987b. *Acid Rain Control Technologies: Existing and Emerging Acid Rain Control Technologies: Hearing before the Subcommittee on Environmental Protection of the Senate Committee on Environment and Public Works.* 100th Congress, 1st Session. Government Printing Office.

SCEPW. 1987c. *Acid Rain Control Technologies: Clean Coal and the US and Canada's Acid Rain Envoys' Report: Hearing before the Subcommittee on Environmental Protection of the Senate Committee on Environment and Public Works.* 100th Congress, 1st Session. Government Printing Office.

SCEPW. 1987d. *Acid Rain and Nonattainment Issues: Hearing before the Subcommittee on Environmental Protection of the Senate Committee on Environment and Public Works.* 100th Congress, 1st Session. Government Printing Office.

SCEPW. 1987e. *Clean Air Act Amendments of 1987, Part 1: Hearings before the Subcommittee on Environmental Protection of the Senate Committee on Environment and Public Works.* 100th Congress, 1st Session. Government Printing Office.

SCEPW. 1988. *Greenhouse Effect and Global Climate Change, Part 2: Hearings before the Senate Committee on Environment and Public Works.* 100th Congress, 2nd Session. Government Printing Office.

SCEPW. 1989. *Responding to the Problem of Global Warming: Hearing before the Subcommittee on Environmental Protection of the Senate Committee on Environment and Public Works.* 101st Congress, 1st Session. Government Printing Office.

SCEPW. 1991. *Global Warming and Other Consequences of Energy Strategies: Hearing before the Subcommittee on Environmental Protection of the Senate Committee on Environment and Public Works.* 102nd Congress, 1st Session. Government Printing Office.

SCEPW. 1997. *Global Climate Change: Hearing before the Senate Committee on Environment and Public Works.* 105th Congress, 1st Session. Government Printing Office.

SCEPW. 2002. *Clean Air Act: Risks from Greenhouse Gas Emissions. Hearing before the Senate Committee on Environment and Public Works.* 107th Congress, 2nd Session. Government Printing Office.

SCFR (Senate Committee on Foreign Relations). 1982. *Acid Rain: Hearing before the Subcommittee on Arms Control, Oceans, International Operations and Environment of the Senate Committee on Foreign Relations.* 97th Congress, 2nd Session. Government Printing Office.

Schattschneider, E. E., 1961. *The Semi-Sovereign People.* Holt, Rinehart and Winston.

Scheberle, Denise. 1994. Radon and asbestos: A study of agenda setting and causal stories. *Policy Studies Journal* 22, no. 1: 74–86.

Schick, Allen. 1976. The supply and demand for analysis on Capitol Hill. *Policy Analysis* 2, spring: 215–234.

Schulman, Paul R. 1989. The "logic" of organizational irrationality. *Administration and Society* 21, May: 31–53.

Schulman, Paul R. 1993. The negotiated order of organizational reliability. *Administration and Society* 25, November: 353–372.

Science Daily. 2008. 2007 was tied as Earth's second warmest year (January 17).

Selznick, Philip. 1948. Foundations of the theory of organization. *American Sociological Review* 13: 25–35.

Seppa, N. 1999. Thalidomide combats myeloma blood cancer. *Science News* 156, no. 21: 326.

Shabecoff, Philip. 1982a. Acid rain debate tells as much about Washington as science. *New York Times*, February 9.

Shabecoff, Philip. 1982b. A debate: Are enough data in hand to act against acid rain? *New York Times*, November 14.

Shabecoff, Philip. 1985. Scientists warn of earlier rise in sea levels. *New York Times*, November 3.

Shabecoff, Philip. 1986. Scientists warn of effects of human activity on atmosphere. *New York Times*, January 12.

Shabecoff, Philip. 1987. Government acid rain report comes under sharp attack. *New York Times*, September 22.

Shabecoff, Philip. 1990. Acid rain report unleashes a torrent of criticism. *New York Times*, March 20.

Shackley, Simon, and Brian Wynne. 1995. Global climate change: The mutual construction of an emergent science-policy domain. *Science and Public Policy* 22, August: 218–230.

Shackley, Simon, and Brian Wynne. 1996. Representing uncertainty in global climate change science and policy: Boundary-ordering devices and authority. *Science, Technology, & Human Values* 21, no. 3: 275–302.

Shackley, Simon, and Brian Wynne. 1997. Global warming potentials: Ambiguity or precision as an aid to policy? *Climate Research* 8, May 8: 89–106.

Shackley, Simon, et al. 1998. Uncertainty, complexity and concepts of good science in climate change modeling: Are GCMs the best tools? *Climatic Change* 38: 159–205.

Shapiro, Martin. 1988. *Who Guards the Guardians? Judicial Control of Administration*. University of Georgia Press.

Simon, Herbert A. 1976. *Administrative Behavior: A Study of Decision-Making Processes in Administrative Organization*, third edition. Free Press.

Simon, Richard. 2007. Senate panel OKs bill to boost fuel efficiency standard. *Los Angeles Times*, May 9.

Singer, Fred. 1995. Global warming remains unproved. *New York Times*, September 19.

SMIC (Study of Man's Impact on Climate). 1971. *Inadvertent Climate Modification*. MIT Press.

Smith, Bruce L. R. 1992. *The Advisers: Scientists in the Policy Process*. Brookings Institution.

Smith, James A. 1991. *The Idea Brokers*. Free Press.

Smith, Robert Angus. 1872. Air and Rain, the beginnings of a Chemical Climatology London: Longmans, Green, & Co.

SSCSB (Senate Select Committee on Small Business). 1980. *Economic Impact of Acid Rain: Hearing before the Senate Select Committee on Small Business and the Senate Committee on Environment and Public Works*. 96th Congress, 2nd Session. Government Printing Office.

Star, Susan Leigh, and James R. Griesemer. 1989. Institutional ecology, "translations" and boundary objects: Amateurs and professionals in Berkeley's Museum of Vertebrate Zoology. *Social Studies of Science* 19: 387–420.

Stern, Paul C., and Harvey V. Fineberg, eds. 1996. *Understanding Risk: Informing Decisions in a Democratic Society*. National Academy Press.

Stevens, William K. 1992. Global warming threatens to undo decades of conservation efforts. *New York Times*, February 25.

Stevens, William K. 1996. U.N. climate report was improperly altered, overplaying human role, critics say. *New York Times*, June 17.

Stone, Deborah A. 1989. Causal stories and the formation of policy agendas. *Political Science Quarterly* 104, 2: 281–300.

Stone, Deborah A. 1997. *Policy Paradox: The Art of Political Decision Making*. Norton.

Stott, Peter, et al. 2000. External control of 20th century temperature by natural and anthropogenic forcings. *Science* 290, December 15: 2133–2137.

Takacs, David. 1996. *The Idea of Biodiversity: Philosophies of Paradise*. Johns Hopkins University Press.

Talbert, Jeffrey C., Bryan D. Jones, and Frank R. Baumgartner. 1995. Non-legislative hearings and policy change in Congress. *American Journal of Political Science* 39: 383–405.

Taylor, Frederick W. 1911. *The Principles of Scientific Management*. Harper.

Taylor, Frederick W. 1947. *Scientific Management*. Harper.

Thompson, James D. 1967. *Organizations in Action*. McGraw-Hill.

Thompson, Michael, Richard Ellis, and Aaron Wildavsky. 1990. *Cultural Theory*. Westview.

Traweek, Sharon. 1988. *Beamtimes and Lifetimes: The World of High Energy Physicists*. Harvard University Press.

Truman, David B. 1951. *The Governmental Process: Political Interests and Public Opinion*. Knopf.

Truman, David B. 1959. *The Congressional Party: A Case Study*. Wiley.

Ungar, Sheldon. 1992. The rise and (relative) decline of global warming as a social problem. *Sociological Quarterly* 33, no. 4: 483–501.

United Press International. 1982. Scientists divided on acid rain issue. *New York Times*, May 27.

USCCSP (United States Climate Change Science Program). 2004. *Our Changing Planet: The U.S. Climate Change Science Program for Fiscal Years 2004 and 2005*.

USDA (United States Department of Agriculture). 1976. *Workshop Report on Acid Precipitation and the Forest Ecosystem*. USDA Forest Service General Technical Report NE-26.

U.S. Department of Health and Human Services, National Institutes of Health, National Institute of Environmental Health Sciences. 1990. Administrative document, National Institute of Environmental Health Sciences.

U.S. EPA (Environmental Protection Agency). 1995. *Human Health Benefits from Sulfate Reduction Under Title IV of the 1990 Clean Air Act Amendments.* Office of Air and Radiation, Acid Rain Division.

U.S. EPA. 1997. *1997 Update to ORD's Strategic Plan.* EPA-600-R-97-015.

U.S. EPA. 1998. *1997 Compliance Report: Acid Rain Program*, EPA-430-R-98-012.

USGCRP. 1996 (United States Global Change Research Program). *Our Changing Planet: The FY 1997 U.S. Global Change Research Program.* National Science and Technology Council.

USGCRP. 1997. *Our Changing Planet: The FY 1998 U.S. Global Change Research Program.* National Science and Technology Council.

USGCRP. 2002. *Our Changing Planet: The FY 2003 U.S. Global Change Research Program and Climate Change Research Initiative.* Climate Change Science Program and Subcommittee on Global Change Research.

VanDeveer, Stacy D. 1998. European Politics with a Scientific Face: Transition Countries, International Environmental Assessment, and Long Range Transboundary Air Pollution. ENRP Discussion Paper E-98-9, John F. Kennedy School of Government, Harvard University.

VanDeveer, Stacy D. 2006. European politics with a scientific face: Framing, asymmetrical participation, and capacity in LRTAP. In *Assessments of Regional and Global Environmental Risks: Designing Processes for the Effective Use of Science in Decision Making*, ed. A. Farrell and J. Jager. Resources for the Future.

Vogel, David. 1986. *National Styles of Regulation: Environmental Policy in Great Britain and the United States.* Cornell University Press.

Von Meier, Alexandra, Jennifer Lynn Miller, and Ann C. Keller. 1998. The disposition of excess weapons plutonium: A comparison of three narrative contexts. *Nonproliferation Review 5*, no. 2: 20–31.

Vozzo, Steven F. 1986. *International Directory of Acid Deposition Researchers, 1985–86 Edition.* Acid Rain Foundation.

Wagner, Wendy E. 1995. The science charade in toxic risk regulation. *Columbia Law Review 95*, no. 7: 1613–1723.

Walker, Jack L. 1991. *Mobilizing Interest Groups in America: Patrons, Professions and Social Movements.* University of Michigan Press.

Wall Street Journal. 1980. Information bank abstracts (editorial). June 30.

Wall Street Journal. 1995. Climate panel is confident of man's link to warming. November 30.

Ward, Stephen C. 1994. In the shadow of deconstructed metanarratives: Baudrillard, Latour, and the end of realist epistemology. *History of the Human Sciences* 7, no. 4: 73–94.

Washington Post. 2007. Pelosi reveals who's who on global warming panel. March 12.

Watson, Robert T., et al., eds. 1997. *The Regional Impacts of Climate Change: An Assessment of Vulnerability, Summary for Policy Makers.* Intergovernmental Panel on Climate Change.

Watson, Robert T., and the Core Writing Team, eds. 2001. *IPCC, 2001: Climate Change 2001: Synthesis Report.* Cambridge University Press.

Weart, Spencer R. 2003. *The Discovery of Global Warming.* Harvard University Press.

Weinberg, Alvin. 1972. Science and trans-science. *Minerva* 10: 209–222.

Weiss, Andrew, and Edward Woodhouse. 1992. Reframing incrementalism: A constructive response to the critics. *Policy Sciences* 25, August: 255–274.

Weiss, Carol H. 1989. Congressional committees as users of analysis. *Journal of Policy Analysis and Management* 8, no. 3: 411–431.

White, W. S., Jr. 1980. What we don't know about acid rain (editorial). *New York Times*, October 29.

Whitney, Craig R. 1990. Science urge rapid action of global warming. *New York Times*, May 25.

Wilson, James Q. 1989. *Bureaucracy: What Government Agencies Do and Why They Do It.* Basic Books.

Yanarella, Ernest J. 1985. The foundations of policy immobilism over acid rain control. In *The Acid Rain Debate: Scientific, Economic, and Political Dimensions*, ed. E. Yanarella and R. Ihara. Westview.

Yearly, Stephen. 1991. *The Green Case: A Sociology of Environmental Issues, Arguments, and Politics.* Routledge.

Zehr, Stephen. 1994a. The centrality of scientists and the translation of interests in the U.S. acid rain controversy. *Canadian Review of Sociology and Anthropology* 31, no. 3: 325–353.

Zehr, Stephen. 1994b. Accounting for the ozone hole: Scientific representations of an anomaly and prior incorrect claims in public settings. *Sociological Quarterly* 35, no. 4: 603–619.

Zehr, Stephen. 2005. Comparative boundary work: US acid rain and global climate change policy deliberations. *Science and Public Policy* 32, December: 445–456.

Index

Academic science, 149–154, 159
Acid Rain Program, 141, 162–164, 171, 172, 177, 179
Albritton, Daniel, 113, 117, 119
Arrhenius, Svante, 23, 60, 61, 112
Assessment/management framework, 144–159, 165, 166

Baumgartner, Frank R., 7, 40, 46–49, 74, 75, 81, 87–96, 106, 174, 175
Bush administration (1989–1992), 70, 101
Bush administration (2001–2008), 21, 136
Byrd, Robert C., 101, 135

Carter administration, 53, 56, 101
Causal story, 34, 35, 55
  for acid rain, 53–55
  for climate change, 64, 108
Central Intelligence Agency, 71, 73
Chafee, John H., 85, 109, 112
Chapin, Steven, 19
Christy, John R., 85
Classification
  scientists and, 16–21, 119
  policy makers and, 16–18, 21
Clean Air Act, 92, 102, 109
  1970 Amendments, 93, 101
  1977 Amendments, 101
  1990 Amendments, 101, 135, 141
Clinton administration, 21, 136
Cobb, Roger W., 7, 45–49, 60, 87–89

Cohen, Richard, 92, 93, 96, 101
Congressional committees, 74, 89, 91, 174
Congressional hearings, 8, 14, 50, 85, 86, 89–96, 172–176, 179, 181
  acid rain, 56, 73, 88–91, 95, 98–102, 110–138
  climate change, 62, 63, 67–70, 73, 102–138
  legislative, 89–91, 94
  non-legislative, 90, 94, 106
  oversight, 89, 90
  scientists in, 96–98, 112–138
Control, story of, 34, 54, 64, 74, 78
Co-production, 42, 43, 49, 50, 178, 179
Cowling, Ellis B., 50–54, 58
Credibility
  in congressional settings, 96, 112, 131, 138, 182
  in implementation settings, 148–156, 161, 166, 167, 178
  policy entrepreneurs and, 35, 96, 138, 182
  scientists and, 11–13, 19, 20, 25, 42, 78, 113, 114, 129, 131, 137, 148, 150, 170, 171, 178

Decision making
  democratic, 22, 27, 33, 37, 173, 177, 183, 184
  incremental, 32
  rationalist, 2, 31–37, 40, 42, 183, 184
  synoptic, 2, 31, 32

Decline, story of, 34, 53, 59, 65, 72, 76, 86
DeGregorio, Christine, 87–90, 93, 96
Department of Agriculture, 56, 58, 147
Diermeier, Daniel, 93, 96
Dingell, John D., 101, 135
Distributive politics, 38, 73, 74, 110, 141, 160, 180
Downsian mobilization, 46, 74, 174

Edwards, Paul A., 2–4, 9, 10, 66
Elder, Charles D., 7, 45–49, 60, 87–89
Enlightenment, 39–41, 145
Environmental Health Perspectives, 152
Environmental Protection Agency, 36, 38, 98, 109, 146, 150, 158
  Office of Research and Development, 150–154, 158–162, 166, 167
  Science Advisory Board, 150, 152
Epstein, Steven, 20
Evelyn, John, 50
Expertise, 2, 4, 10, 12, 16–20, 25, 29, 42, 43, 66, 78, 118, 139, 140, 145, 163, 164, 179
  in congressional settings, 4, 10, 41, 86, 90, 91, 94, 122, 124, 139, 176, 177
  in executive branch, 139, 140, 144
Ezrahi, Yaron, 2, 39–41

Feddersen, Timothy, 93, 96
Federal Advisory Committee Act, 143
Food and Drug Administration, 36, 38, 146, 147
Formalization, 10–14, 138, 140, 143, 144, 161, 166, 181
Formal structure, 141–143, 157, 166
Framing of issues, 8, 46, 87, 90, 93, 106
Freedom of Information Act, 143

General circulation models, 66, 77
Gieryn, Thomas, 2, 27, 37, 38, 42, 46, 80, 81, 112, 142, 146–148, 157, 170, 174, 175
Global Change Research Program, 21, 70, 78, 79, 82, 103, 119, 120, 135, 141, 142, 155–157, 160, 161, 165
Gore, Albert, Jr., 108, 109, 116, 132, 133
Guston, David, 2, 3, 9, 38–41, 63, 147

Hansen, James, 70, 105, 106, 119, 120, 132, 133, 166
Hilgartner, Stephen, 3, 19
House Committee on Energy and Commerce, 98
House Committee on Merchant Marine Fisheries, 70
House Committee on Science, Space, and Technology, 98
Huitt, Ralph K., 10, 27, 87, 90–93

Intergovernmental Panel on Climate Change, 42, 78, 79, 108, 109, 113, 114, 120, 121, 135, 136, 157, 161, 165
International Geophysical Year, 21, 61, 62, 110

Jasanoff, Sheila, 2–5, 9, 16, 27, 36–43, 49, 147, 148, 154, 173, 177, 178, 181–183
Jones, Bryan D, 7, 40, 46–49, 74, 75, 81, 87–90, 93–96, 106, 174, 175
Journals, 23, 50, 114, 119, 151, 152, 158, 159
Journalism, 130, 133

Keeling, Charles, 61
Kingdon, John, 6, 7, 10, 23, 48, 89, 91, 132, 169, 180
Knowledge brokers, 17, 91
Krehbiel, Keith, 92, 93, 96
Kyoto Protocol, 82, 109
Kyoto Treaty, 21, 82, 108, 136

Lasswell, Harold, 6
Latour, Bruno, 49, 178
Lieberman, Joseph, 109, 136
Likens, Gene E., 52, 58, 113
Lindblom, Charles, 2, 31–35
Lindzen, Richard, 106, 114
Litfin, Karen, 3, 4, 17, 48, 49, 83, 91
Lowi, Theodore, 38, 73, 74, 110, 141

Mahlman, Jerry D., 116, 119
McCain, John, 109, 114, 136
Media
 and acid rain, 50, 54, 58, 73, 100
 and agenda setting and, 47, 130–133
 and climate change, 21, 67–73, 109, 132, 133, 136
Miller, Clark N., 2–4, 9, 10, 42, 66, 71, 72, 178
Molina, Mario, 23
Montreal Protocol, 3, 4, 78, 117
Muskie, Edmund, 92, 93

National Academy of Sciences, 19, 53, 54, 62, 103, 113, 116, 157
National Acid Precipitation Assessment Program, 53–60, 76, 77, 81, 89, 113, 116–120, 134, 135, 141, 142, 155, 156, 160–167
National Climate Program Act of 1976, 110
National Institute for Environmental Health Sciences, 149–154, 158–160, 166
National Institutes of Health, 38, 41, 141, 146, 158
National Oceanic and Atmospheric Agency, 117
National Research Council, 19, 20, 54, 58, 62, 65, 66, 72, 73, 145–147
Neutral competence, 29
Neutrality, scientific, 15, 25, 43, 81, 85, 86, 97, 130, 132, 168, 169, 176

New York Times, 69
Nixon administration, 101

Objectivity, 16, 20
 boundary work and, 13, 46, 84, 137
 and policy making, 21, 28, 39, 75, 112, 132, 137–139, 144, 145, 149, 150, 167, 169, 176
 scientific, 39, 43, 46, 75, 88, 112, 139, 144, 145, 169
 scientists and, 13, 20, 113, 115, 128, 150
Oden, Svante, 1, 7, 51–53, 56, 58, 76
Organization theory, 142, 143

Peer review, 113, 114, 119, 121, 137, 151, 152, 156–159, 182, 183
Plass, Gilbert, 60
Policy agendas
 formal, 45–48, 56, 58, 60, 69, 70, 81, 83, 87, 88, 102, 110, 130
 systemic, 47–50, 56, 70, 87–90
Policy narratives, 34–36, 48, 49, 53, 59, 75, 81–83, 86, 142, 157, 161–166, 174
Policy venues, 3, 4, 46, 56, 60, 72, 74, 82, 83, 106
Politicization of science, 12, 27, 120
Porter, Theodore, 19, 20
Price, Don, 16, 17, 147, 148
Progressive Era, 29
Public face of science, 15, 172, 173

Reagan administration, 82, 101, 120, 134
Regulatory politics, 38, 73, 74, 110, 141, 160, 180
Regulatory science, 149, 153, 154, 159
Relativism, 33
Revelle, Roger, 33, 61–66, 69
Risk analysis, 12, 144–147, 150, 159, 160
Role expectations, 11–13, 87, 130
Rowland, F. Sherwood, 23
Rule making, 8, 36, 143, 137

Science advisory groups, 36, 37, 41,
    148, 177
Science and Technology Studies, 3,
    43
Science narratives, 11, 26, 49, 50, 76,
    78, 83, 91, 176
  for acid rain, 24, 26, 46, 50, 53–60,
    73–77, 80–82, 110, 129, 133–135,
    161–165, 177
  for climate change, 24, 26, 46, 50,
    64–67, 70–83, 110, 129, 133–135,
    141, 165
Science/policy boundary, 2, 11–14,
    25, 30, 37, 38, 44, 46, 73, 75, 80,
    86, 117–119, 129–133, 137–144,
    147, 148, 154–157, 166, 169, 173,
    176, 180, 181
Senate Committee on Energy and
    Natural Resources, 98, 103, 106
Senate Committee on Environment
    and Public Works, 69, 98, 106,
    134
Smith, Robert Angus, 23, 50, 51
Social contract for science, 41, 63
Stone, Deborah, 7, 33–38, 43, 47–49,
    53, 78, 174

Talbert, Jeffrey C., 87–90, 93–96,
    106
Technocracy, 12, 27–30, 36, 145
Trans-science, 31, 33

Views of science,
    rationalist, 28–37, 40–44, 142, 184
    relativist, 39
    positivist, 29–33

Weinberg, Alvin, 3, 9, 31, 33, 149,
    153